THE NOBLE ART OF POLITICS

Political Cartoons 1994-96

IRISH MEDIA AWARDS
COMMENTATOR OF THE YEAR
1995

Martyn Turner

THE NOBLE ART OF POLITICS

Political Cartoons 1994–96

In association with
Irish Times Books

THE
BLACKSTAFF
PRESS

BELFAST

For Dick Walsh
and for Noel and Margaret

Almost all the cartoons in this book first appeared in
the *Irish Times* except for a few that were commissioned by
the *Sunday Express* and one, by some quirk, that made it to
the *Belfast Telegraph* three days before getting to its
rightful home in the *Irish Times*.
Agents for the cartoons herein are
The Cartoonists' & Writers' Syndicate,
67 Riverside Drive, New York City
(who ain't half as grand as they sound).

First published in 1996 by
The Blackstaff Press Limited
3 Galway Park, Dundonald, Belfast BT16 0AN, Northern Ireland
in association with
Irish Times Books

© Text and cartoons, Martyn Turner, 1996
All rights reserved

Printed in Northern Ireland by
W. & G. Baird Limited

A CIP catalogue record for this book
is available from the British Library

ISBN 0-85640-583-3

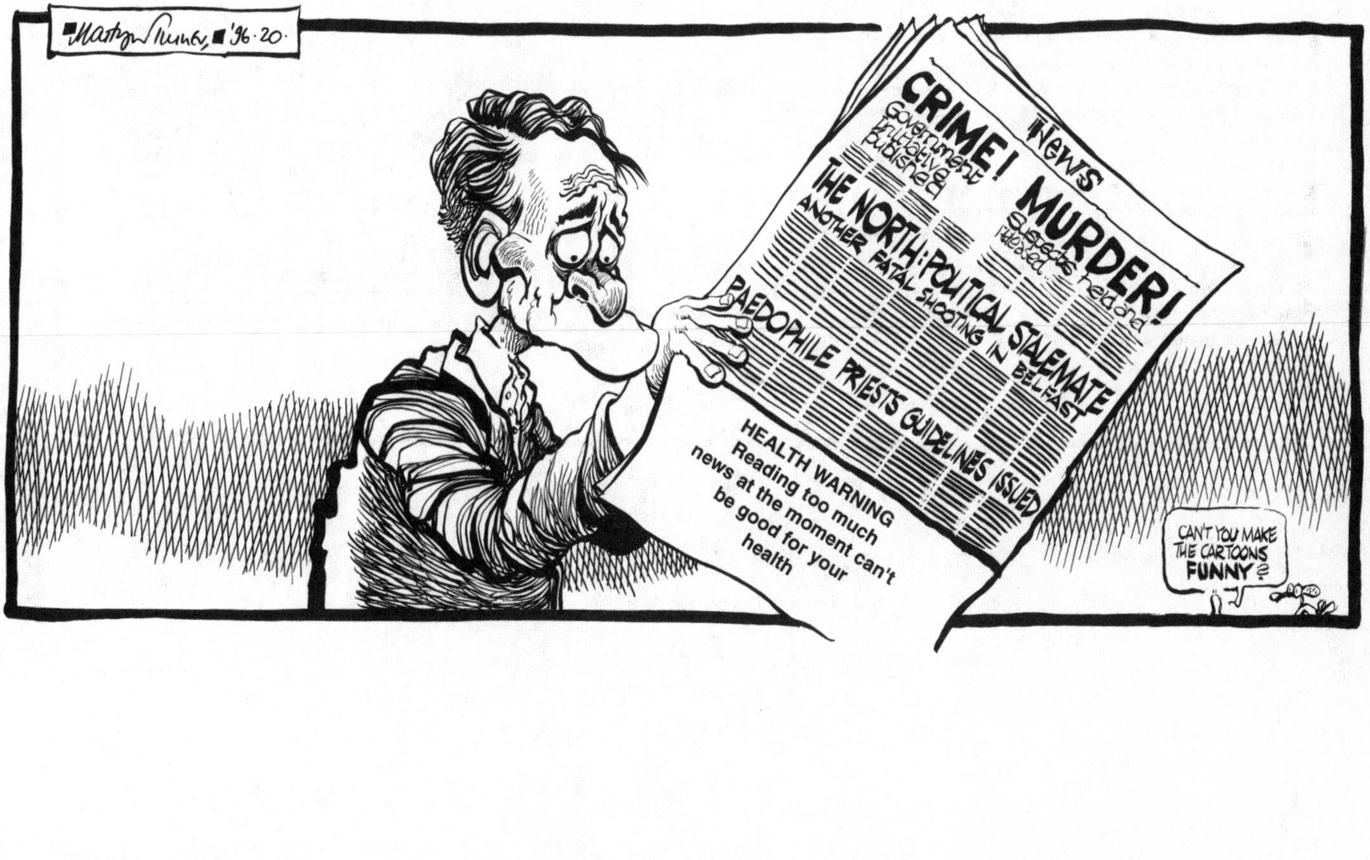
Martyn Turner '96·20·
News
CRIME!
Government initiative published
MURDER!
Suspects held and released
THE NORTH: POLITICAL STALEMATE
ANOTHER FATAL SHOOTING IN BELFAST
PAEDOPHILE PRIESTS GUIDELINES ISSUED
HEALTH WARNING
Reading too much news at the moment can't be good for your health
CAN'T YOU MAKE THE CARTOONS FUNNY?

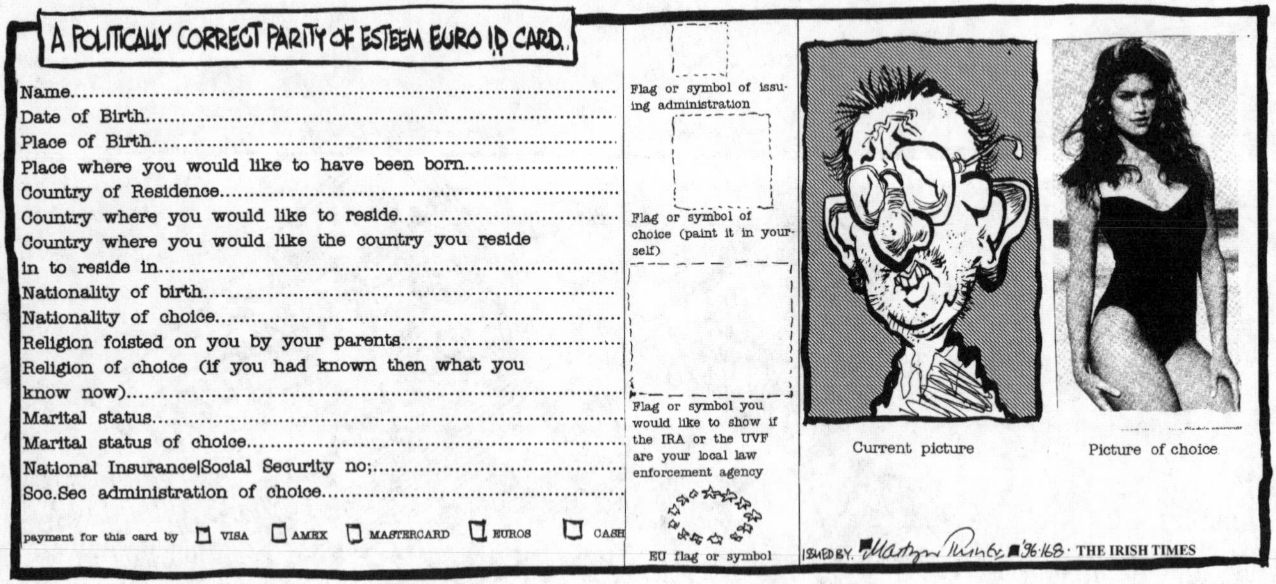
A POLITICALLY CORRECT PARITY OF ESTEEM EURO I.D CARD.
Name......
Date of Birth......
Place of Birth......
Place where you would like to have been born......
Country of Residence......
Country where you would like to reside......
Country where you would like the country you reside in to reside in......
Nationality of birth......
Nationality of choice......
Religion foisted on you by your parents......
Religion of choice (if you had known then what you know now)......
Marital status......
Marital status of choice......
National Insurance|Social Security no;......
Soc.Sec administration of choice......
payment for this card by VISA AMEX MASTERCARD EUROS CASH
Flag or symbol of issuing administration
Flag or symbol of choice (paint it in yourself)
Flag or symbol you would like to show if the IRA or the UVF are your local law enforcement agency
EU flag or symbol
Current picture
Picture of choice
ISSUED BY.
'96·168 · THE IRISH TIMES

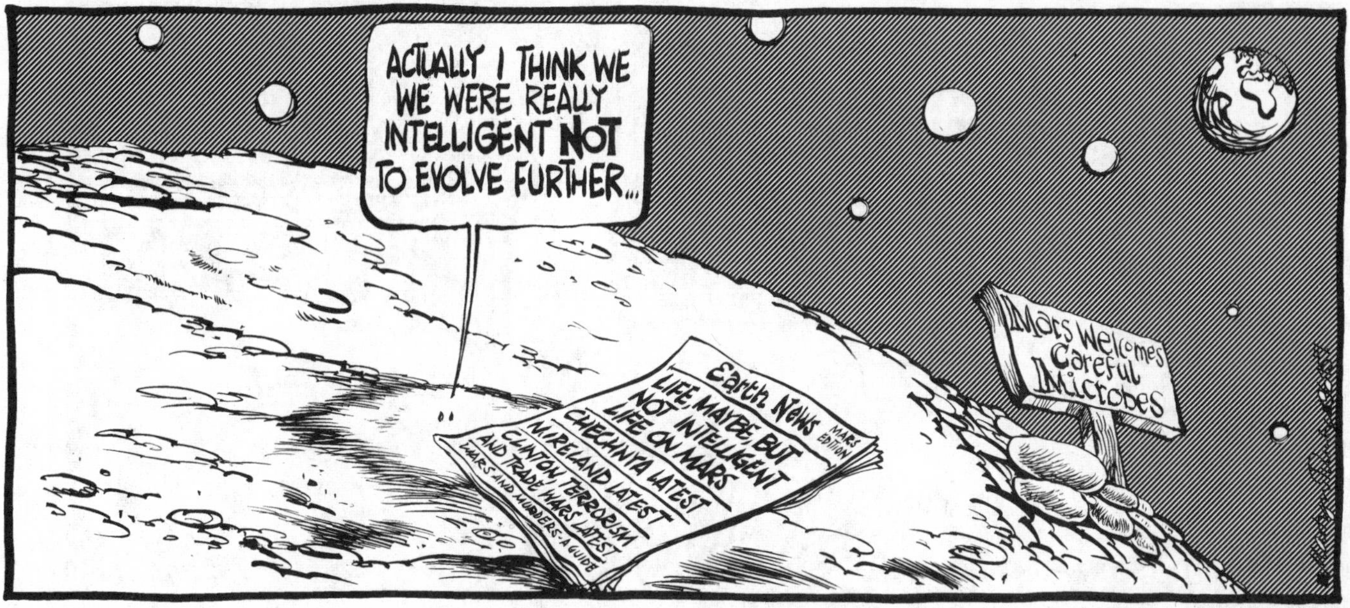
ACTUALLY I THINK WE
WE WERE REALLY
INTELLIGENT NOT
TO EVOLVE FURTHER...
Earth News
MARS EDITION
LIFE MAYBE BUT
NOT INTELLIGENT
LIFE ON MARS
CHECHNYA LATEST
N IRELAND LATEST
CLINTON, TERRORISM
AND TRADE WARS LATEST
WARS AND MURDERS - A GUIDE
Mars Welcomes
Careful
Microbes

INTRODUCTION

A friend, a fellow cartoonist, wrote to me a few years back about how desperate the state of the world looked: wars, greed, corruption, political shenanigans, terrorism, infighting and intrigue. Should be a great year for us, he said. Sempé, the great French cartoonist, once drew a cartoon where you could see not only the theatre audience but also, behind the fallen curtain, the actors. The audience, having just seen a tragedy, were leaving the theatre in tears; the cast, having performed the play so well that the audience had been moved to tears, were celebrating wildly. The cartoonist's function is the

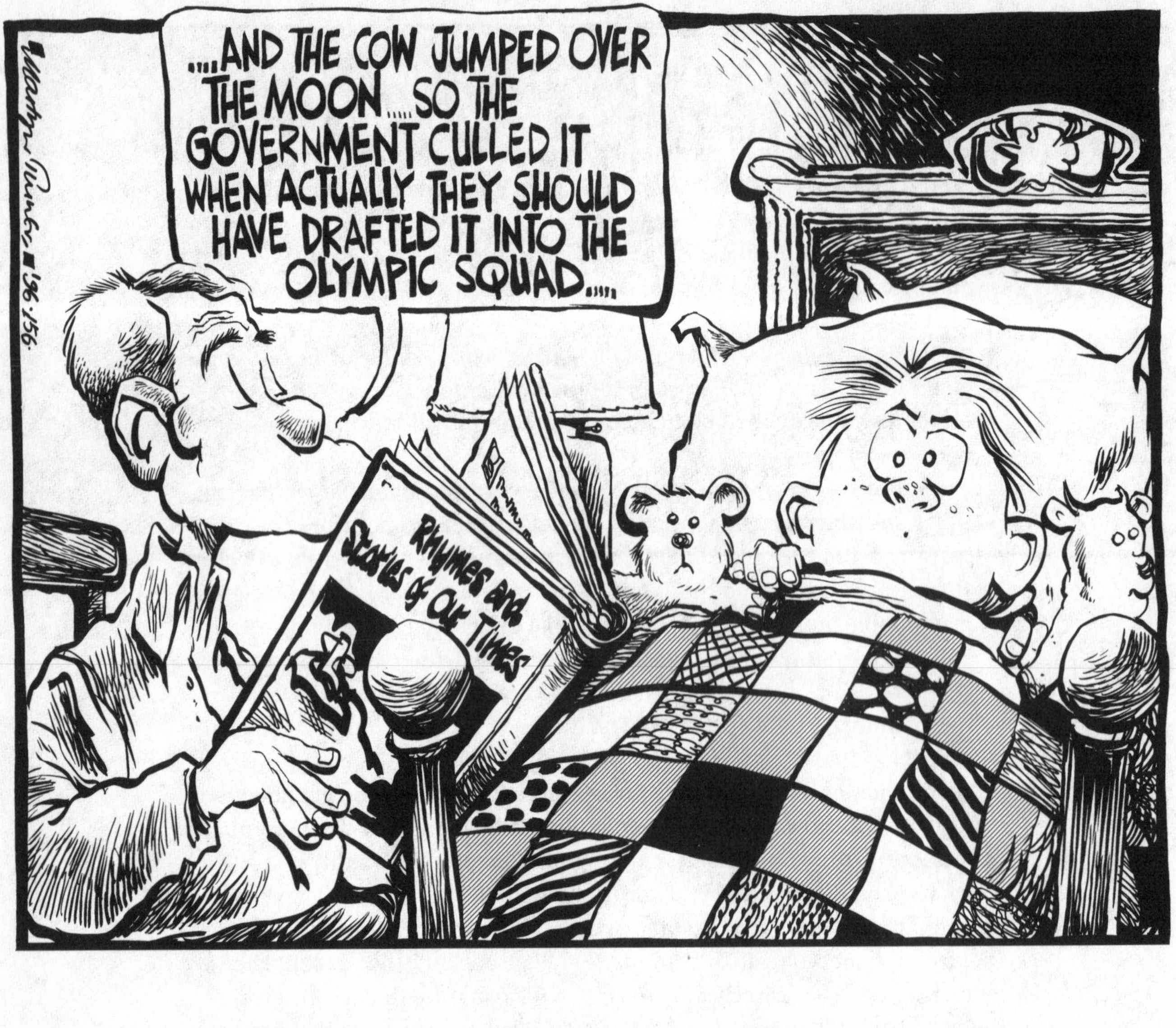
....AND THE COW JUMPED OVER THE MOON.....SO THE GOVERNMENT CULLED IT WHEN ACTUALLY THEY SHOULD HAVE DRAFTED IT INTO THE OLYMPIC SQUAD.....
Rhymes and Stories of Our Times

reverse of the tragedian's; we try to extract something from the misery out there that will keep the audience smiling – if not actual laughter, then at least a grunt of agreement or a laugh of desperation.

So why *The NOble Art of Politics*? Well, the 'noble art' is boxing, and politics in this country is the next worst thing to boxing. And the NO in 'NOble' is because all our politicians have a proclivity to saying NO, as if compromise was some sort of disease to be avoided at all costs. And then the 'ble' bit is pronounced *bull* and when they are not saying NO, the politicos are usually spouting bull. It's amazing, with all those things going for it, that I hadn't used the title before now. This is, after all, my eleventh book of cartoons (some of the others still available in good bookshops).

The last two years were probably somewhat worse for the world than usual and therefore, theoretically, somewhat better for cartoonists. But there is a limit to everything. The day I write this the two main news stories are the bombing of Grozny and the aftermath of the Belgian paedophilia murder cases. There are some things that are just uncartoonable. At home we have had the aftermath of the ending of the IRA ceasefire. It has been equally hard to be creative and imaginative when, for example, we enjoy the utterings of creative and imaginative politicians who can blame an IRA bomb in London on the British government or who can call Drumcree a triumph for democracy and tolerance. Follow that. Well, I tried to, and in these 120 pages you can see how . . .

MARTYN TURNER
AUGUST 1996

1994

No sooner had I published a collection of cartoons, in October 1994, with a cover featuring Dick Spring and Albert Reynolds skipping the light fantastic, than the odd couple started treading on one another's toes, getting completely out of step with each other and eventually finished up jiving solo in different rooms. The end of 1994 was taken up with pure politicking as Fianna Fáil dumped Albert, took on Bertie, who got dumped by Dick, who took on John (and Proinsias). I remember it as a time when the news broke so fast, when rumours were as rife as rife could be, that some days I had to draw three cartoons just to keep up with events. I still haven't caught up on the lost sleep.

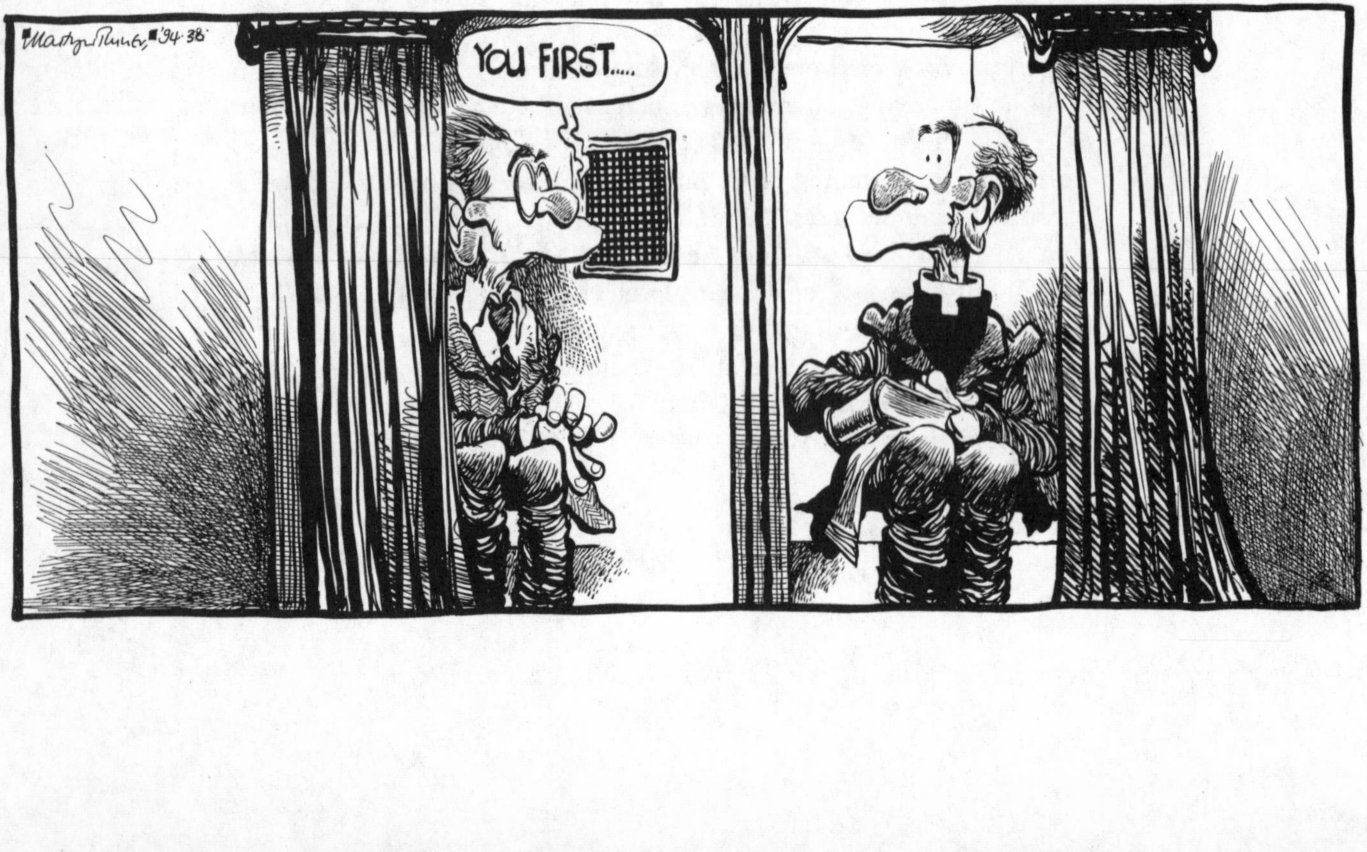
YOU FIRST.....

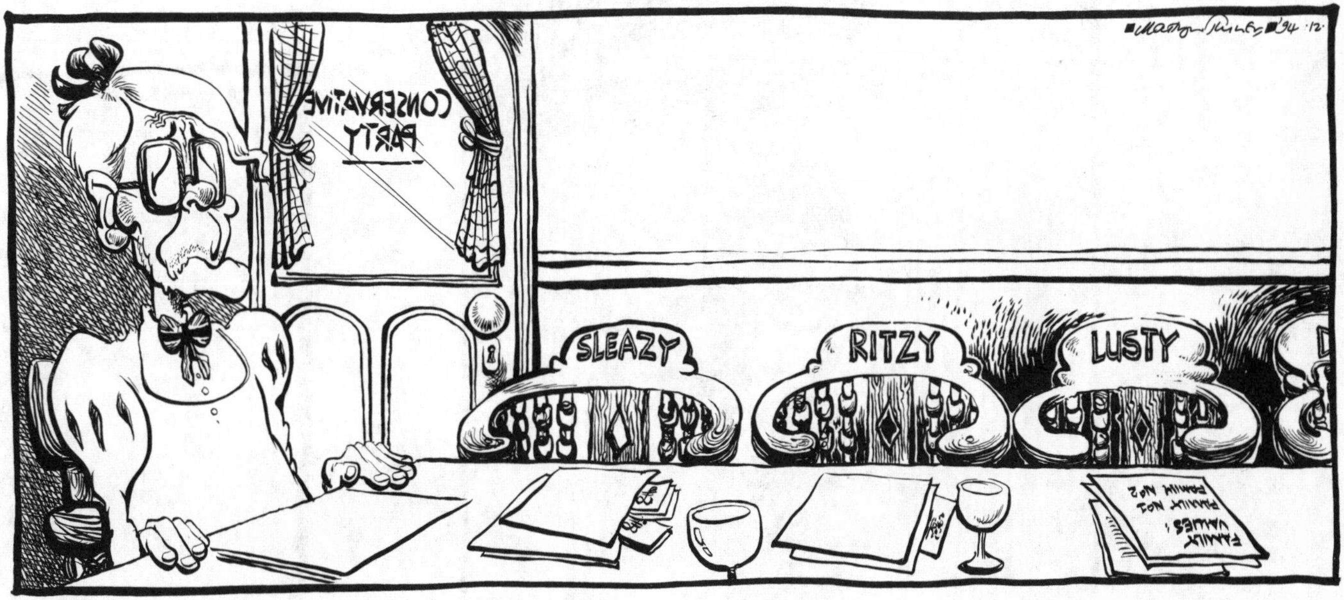
CONSERVATIVE PARTY
SLEAZY
RITZY
LUSTY
FAMILY VALUES:
FAMILY No1
FAMILY No2

Tuesday's Statement
Martyn Turner '94·23

Martyn Turner '94·27

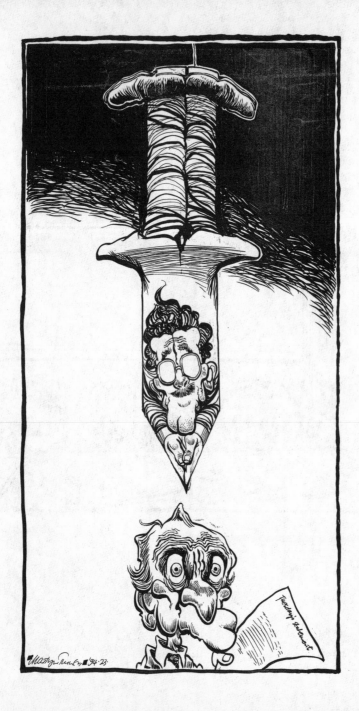

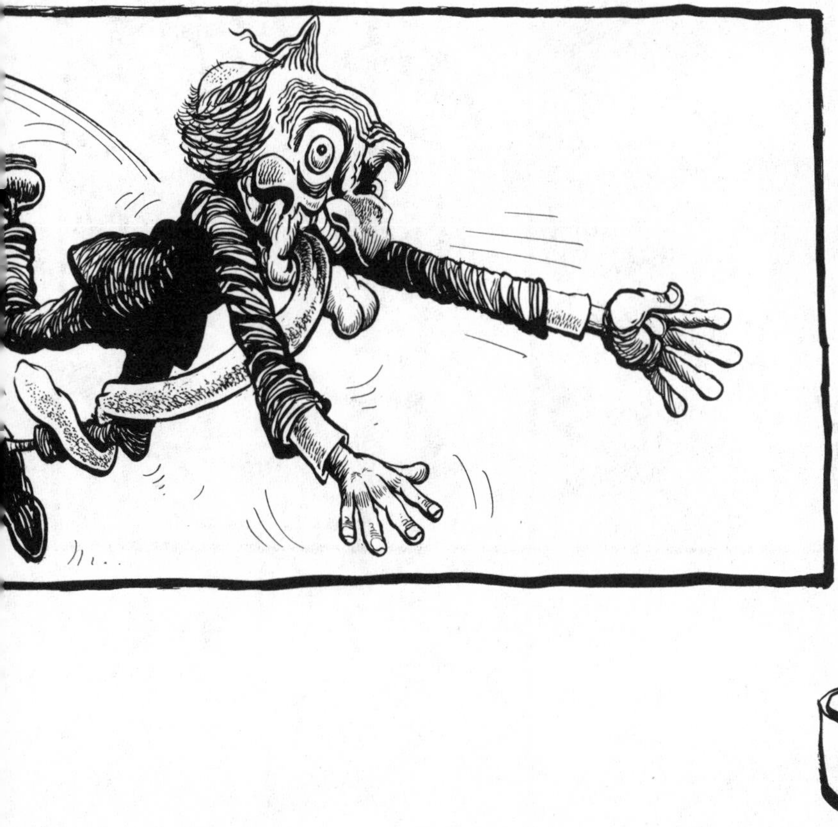

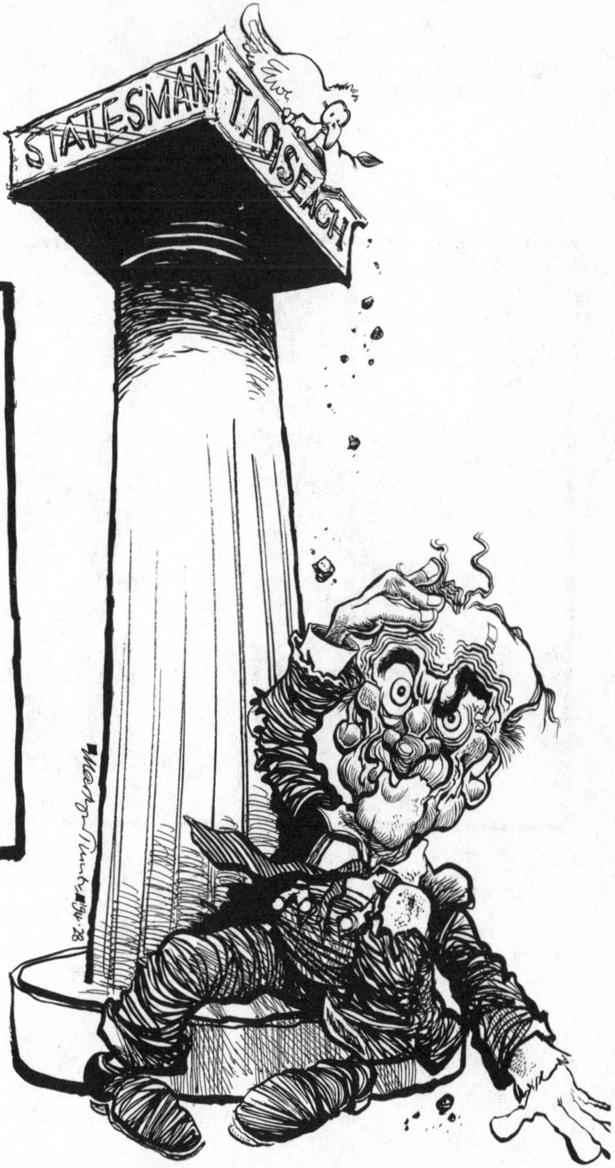
STATESMAN
TAOISEACH

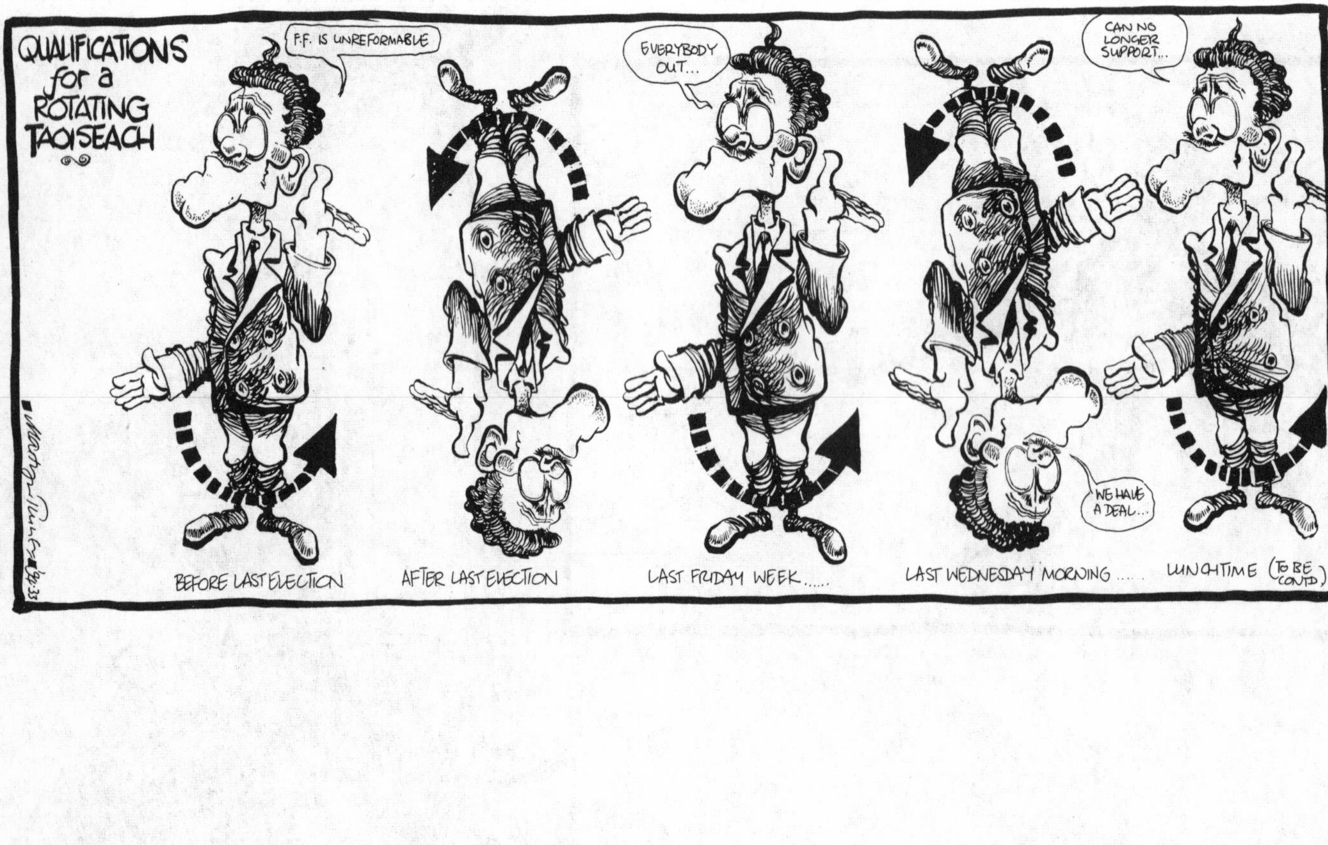
QUALIFICATIONS for a ROTATING TAOISEACH
F.F. IS UNREFORMABLE
EVERYBODY OUT...
CAN NO LONGER SUPPORT...
WE HAVE A DEAL...
BEFORE LAST ELECTION
AFTER LAST ELECTION
LAST FRIDAY WEEK.....
LAST WEDNESDAY MORNING .....
LUNCHTIME (TO BE CONTD)

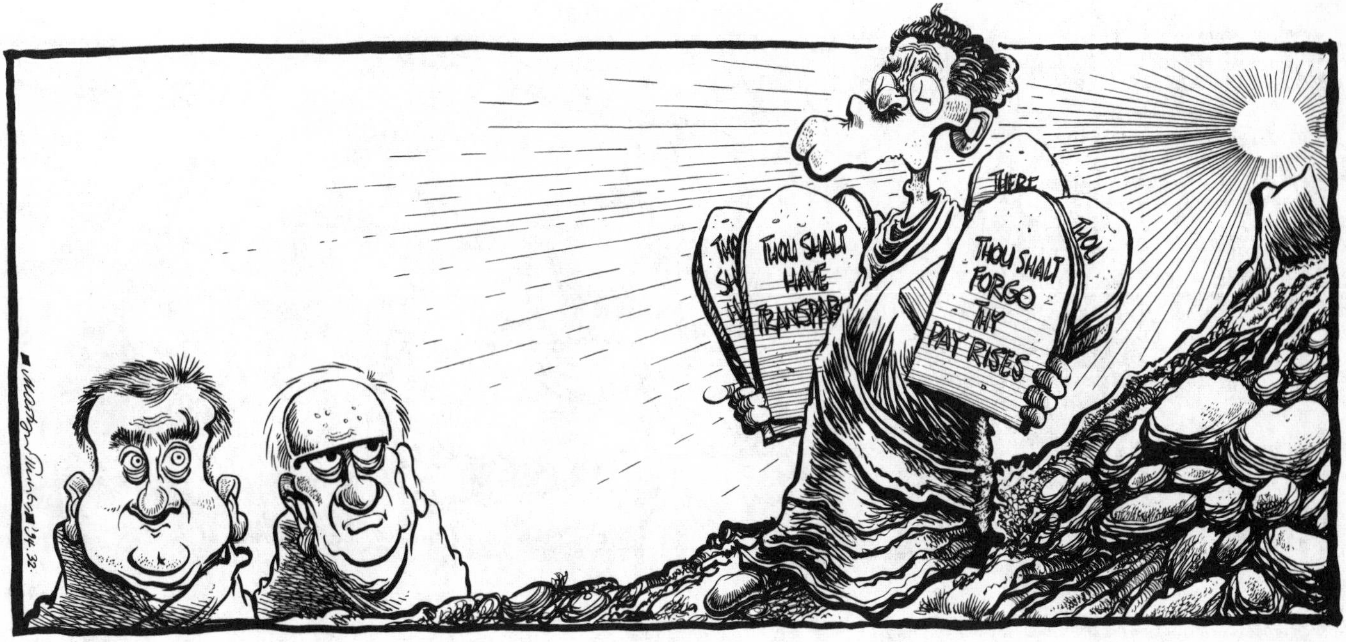
THERE
THOU
THOU SHALT HAVE
THOU SHALT FORGO THY PAY RISES

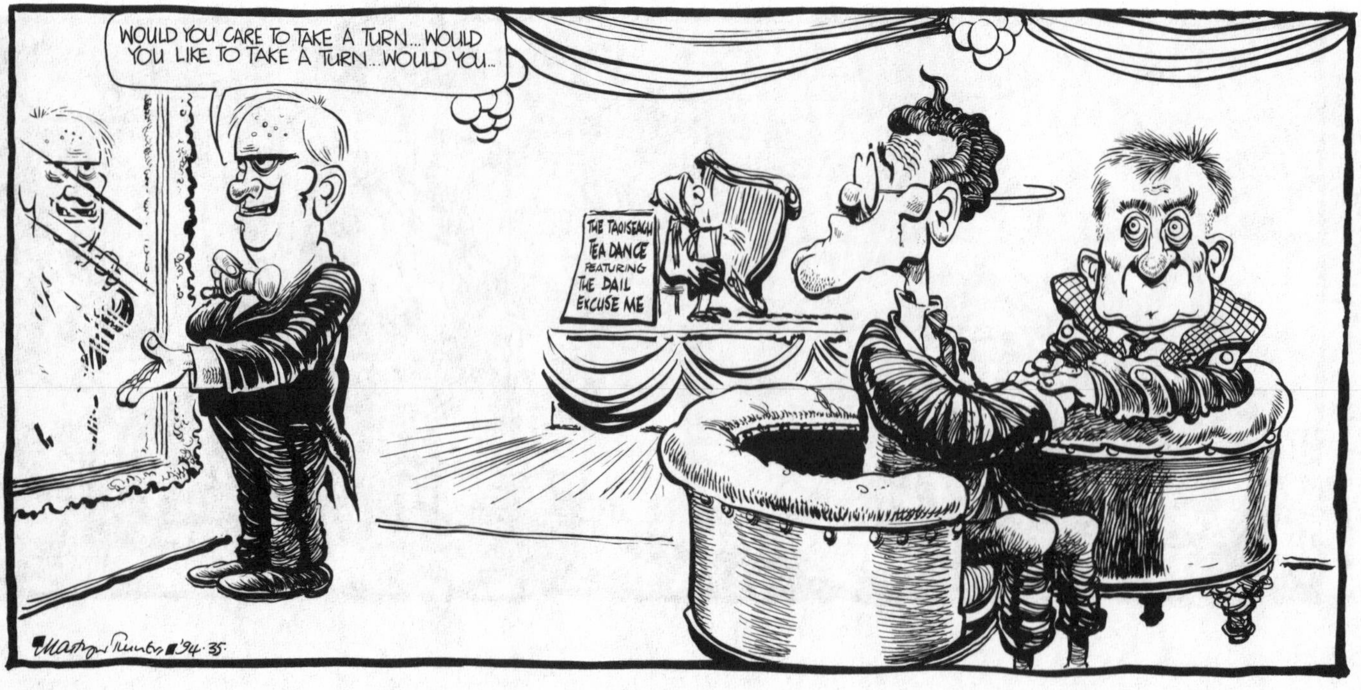
WOULD YOU CARE TO TAKE A TURN... WOULD YOU LIKE TO TAKE A TURN... WOULD YOU...
THE TAOISEACH TEA DANCE FEATURING THE DAIL EXCUSE ME

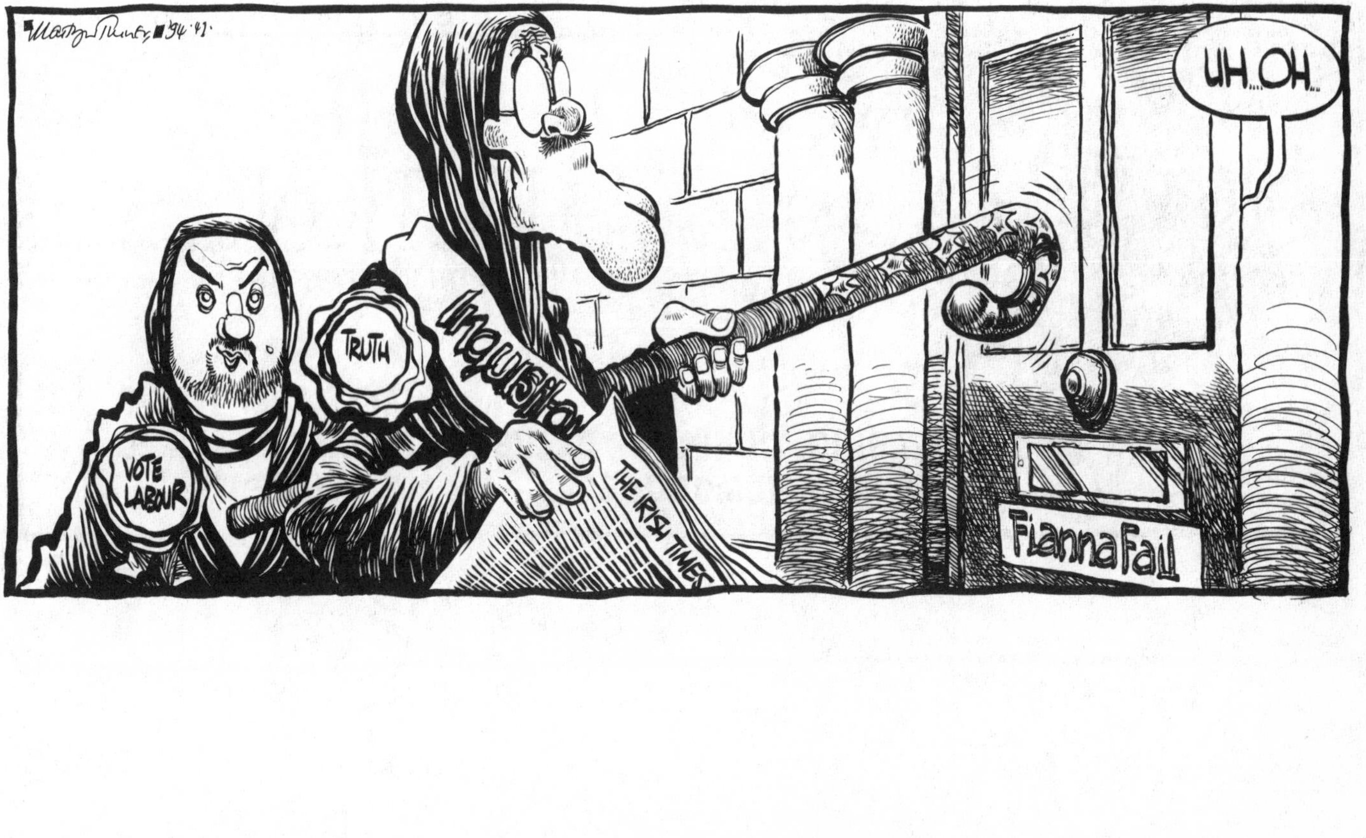
UH...OH...
Inquisition
TRUTH
VOTE LABOUR
THE IRISH TIMES
Fianna Fail

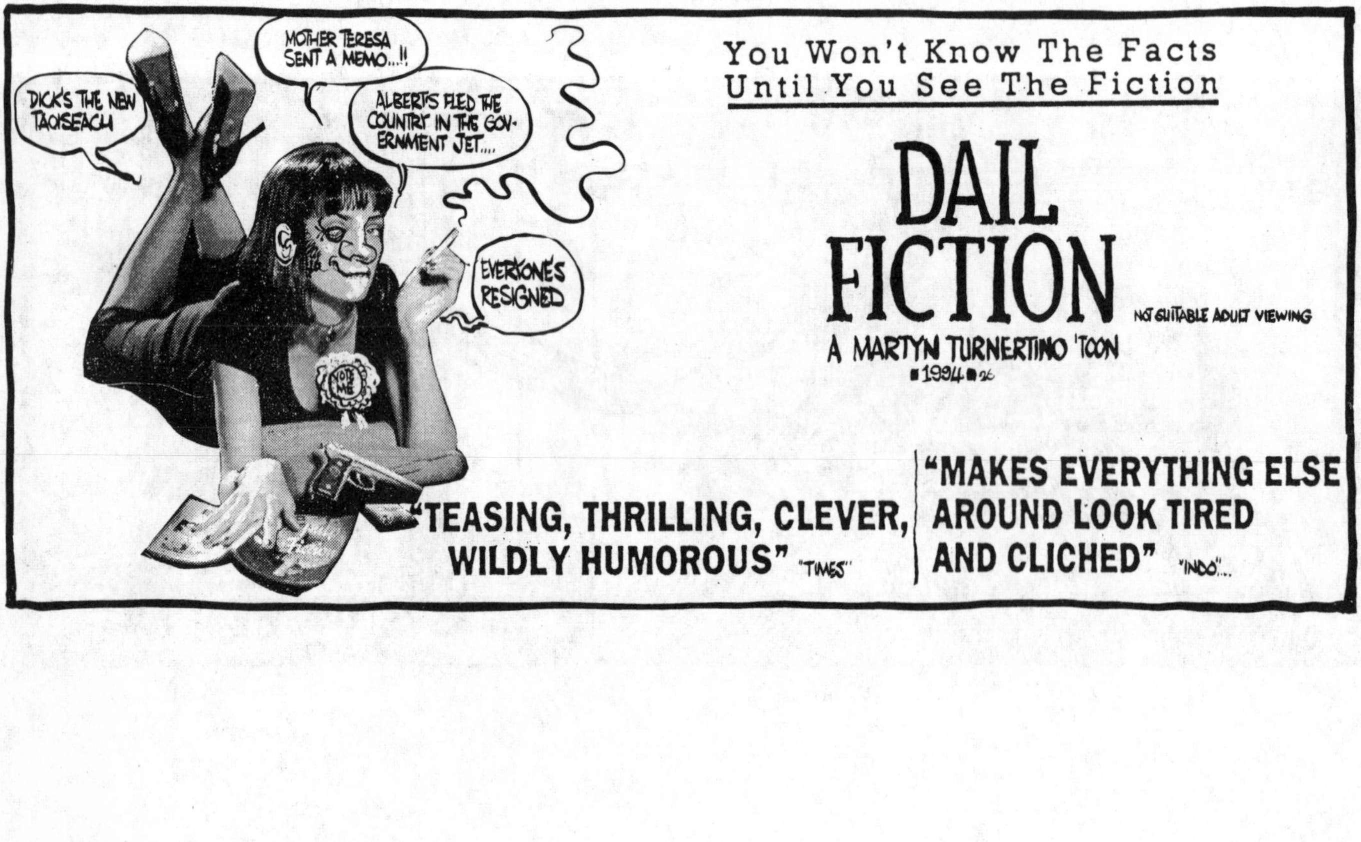
DICK'S THE NEW TAOISEACH
MOTHER TERESA SENT A MEMO...!!
ALBERT'S FLED THE COUNTRY IN THE GOV-ERNMENT JET....
EVERYONE'S RESIGNED
VOTE ME
You Won't Know The Facts Until You See The Fiction
DAIL FICTION
NOT SUITABLE ADULT VIEWING
A MARTYN TURNERTINO 'TOON
1994 26
"TEASING, THRILLING, CLEVER, WILDLY HUMOROUS" "TIMES"
"MAKES EVERYTHING ELSE AROUND LOOK TIRED AND CLICHED" "INDO"...

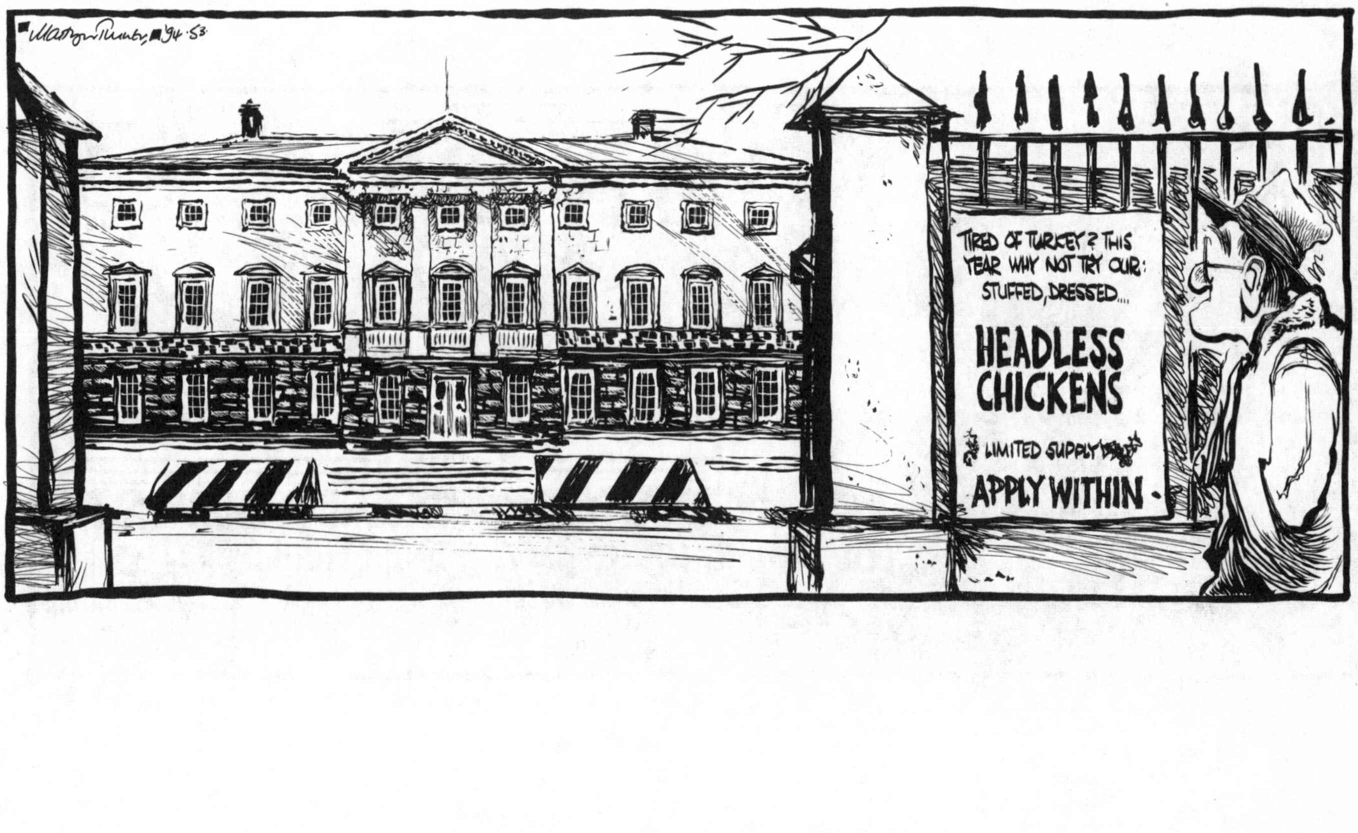
TIRED OF TURKEY? THIS YEAR WHY NOT TRY OUR:
STUFFED, DRESSED....
HEADLESS CHICKENS
LIMITED SUPPLY
APPLY WITHIN

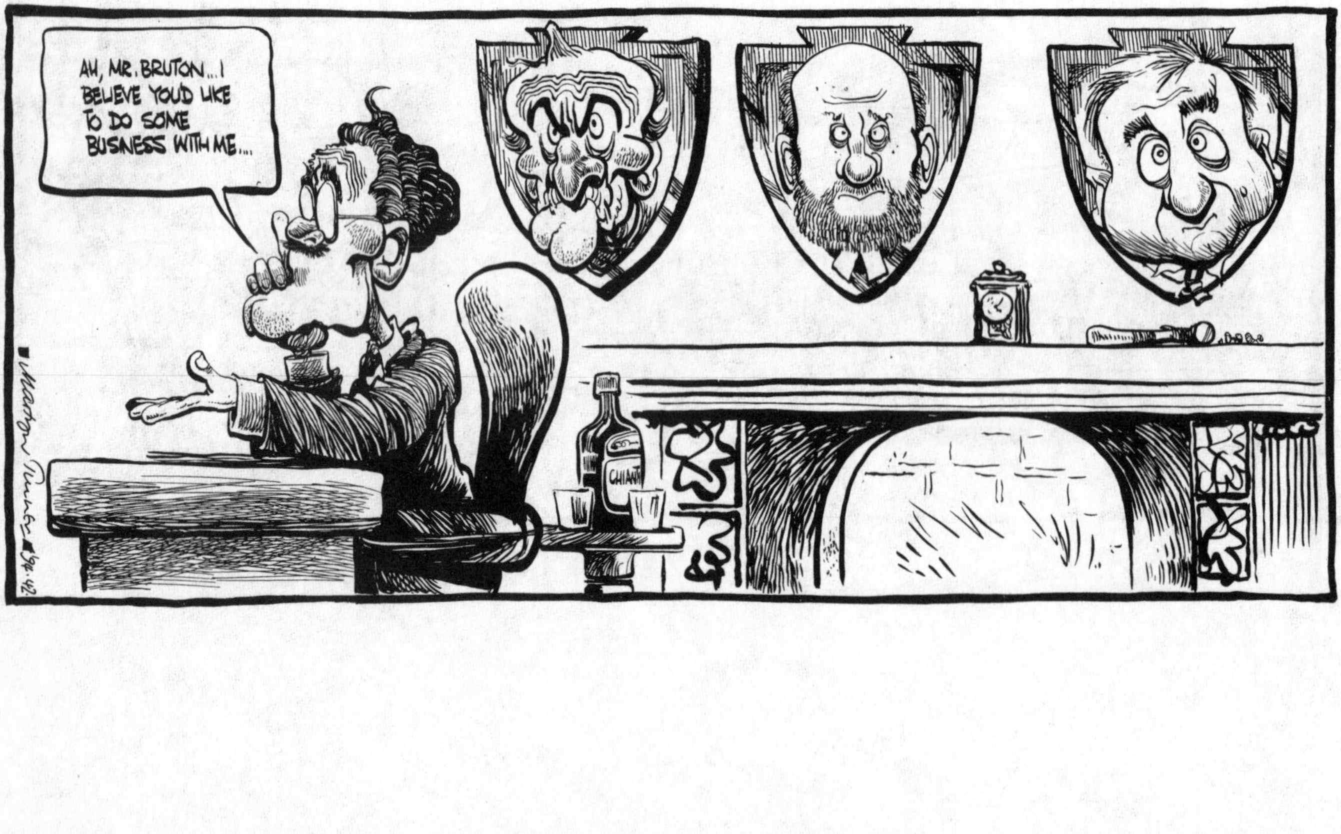
AH, MR. BRUTON... I BELIEVE YOU'D LIKE TO DO SOME BUSINESS WITH ME...
CHIANTI

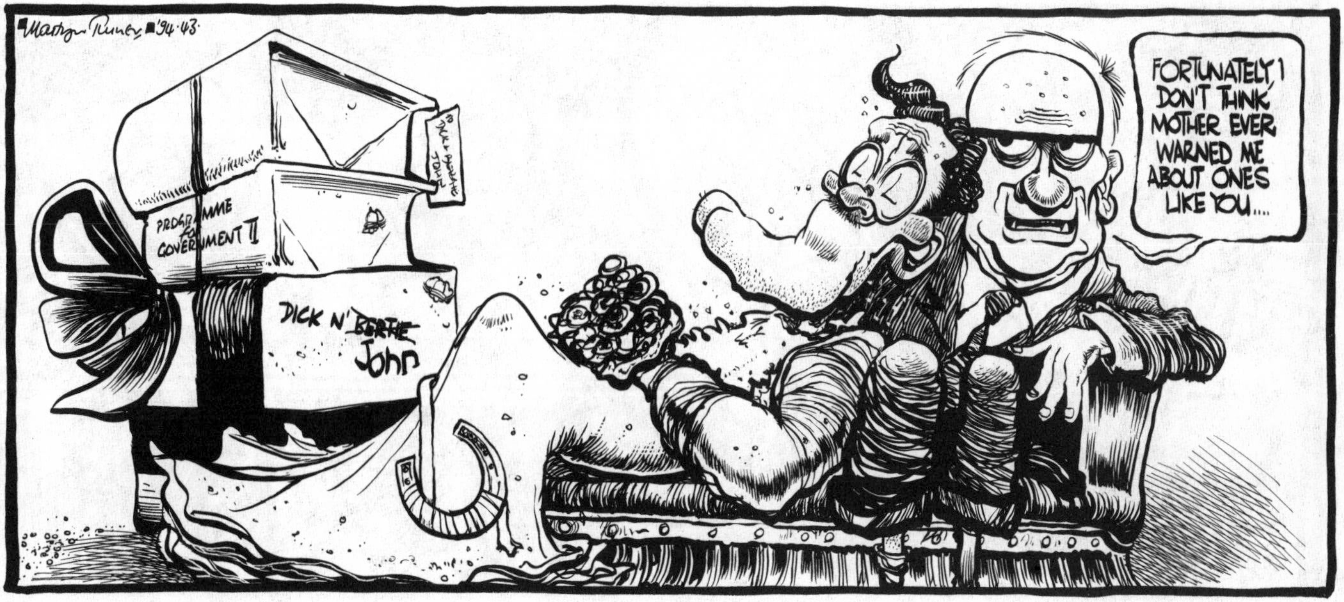
PROGRAMME FOR GOVERNMENT II
DICK N' ~~BERTIE~~ John
FORTUNATELY, I DON'T THINK MOTHER EVER WARNED ME ABOUT ONES LIKE YOU....

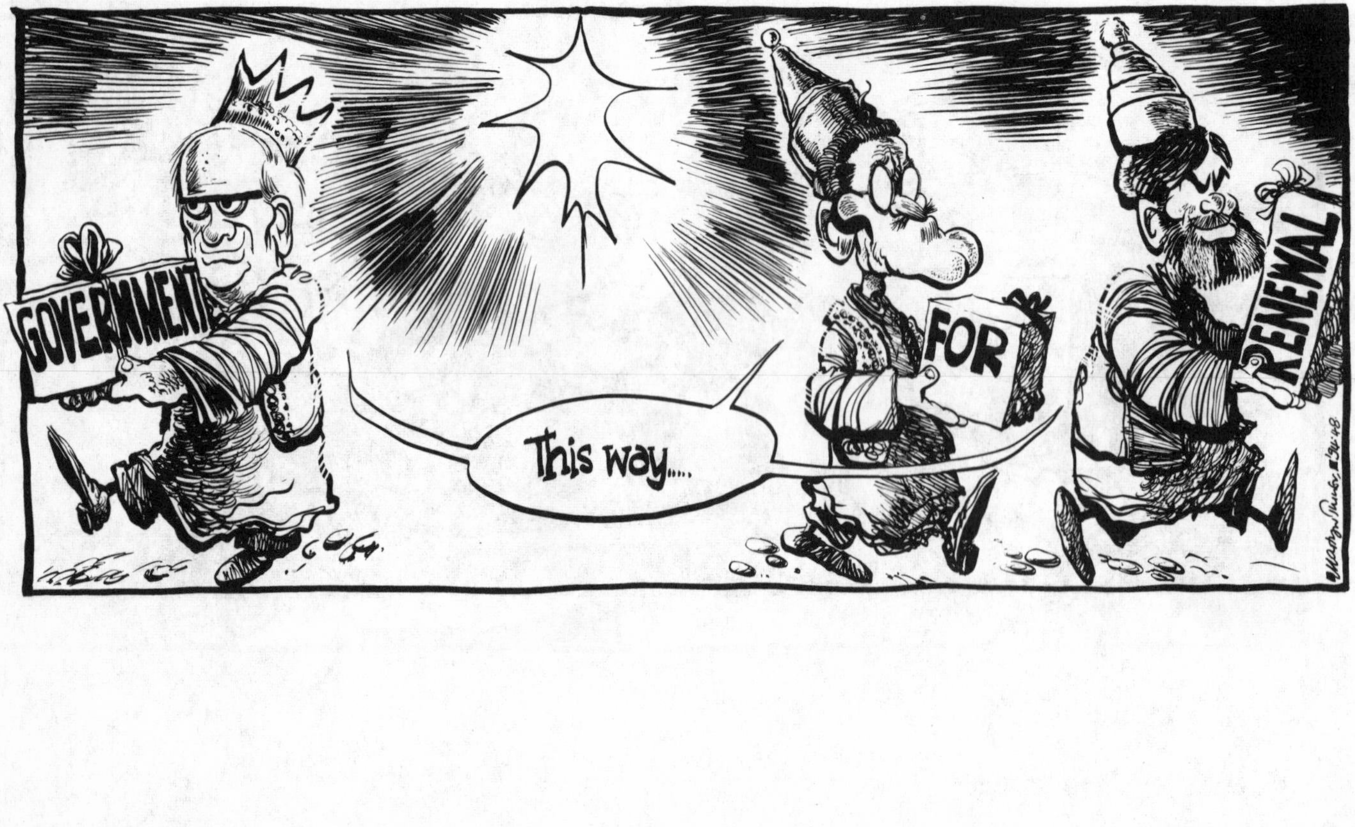
GOVERNMENT
FOR
RENEWAL
This way....

1995

The year started much as the last one ended; daftness in the Dáil and an exciting change of government in Dublin that introduced brand-new economic policies that were identical to the last government's. Nick Leeson brought down Barings, a song was written for the new leader of Fianna Fáil, Boris went into battle, or bottle, over Chechnya, wickedness continued apace in Bosnia, and Saddam Hussein had a domestic. The North reliably continued to surprise no one as no one did nothing that was of any use to man nor beast . . . but they said an awful lot and complained if they couldn't say it to the right person in the right place at the right time. In the South we had the diversion of the Divorce Referendum, another victory for tolerance, ecumenism, understanding, pragmatism and the secular state . . . by a handful of votes.

GREAT DAIL ROWS of our TIME
A ....over 1 High Court Judgeship....
B ....over 2 Junior Ministers....
C ....over 300,000 jobless.....

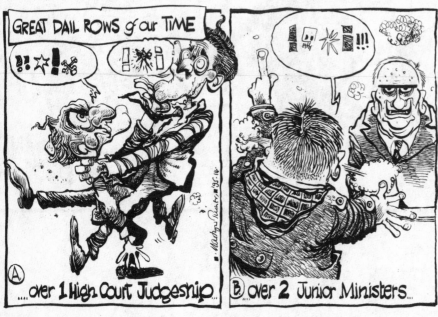

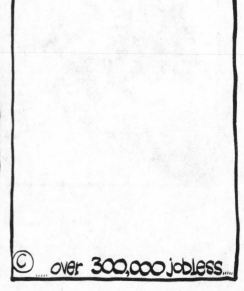

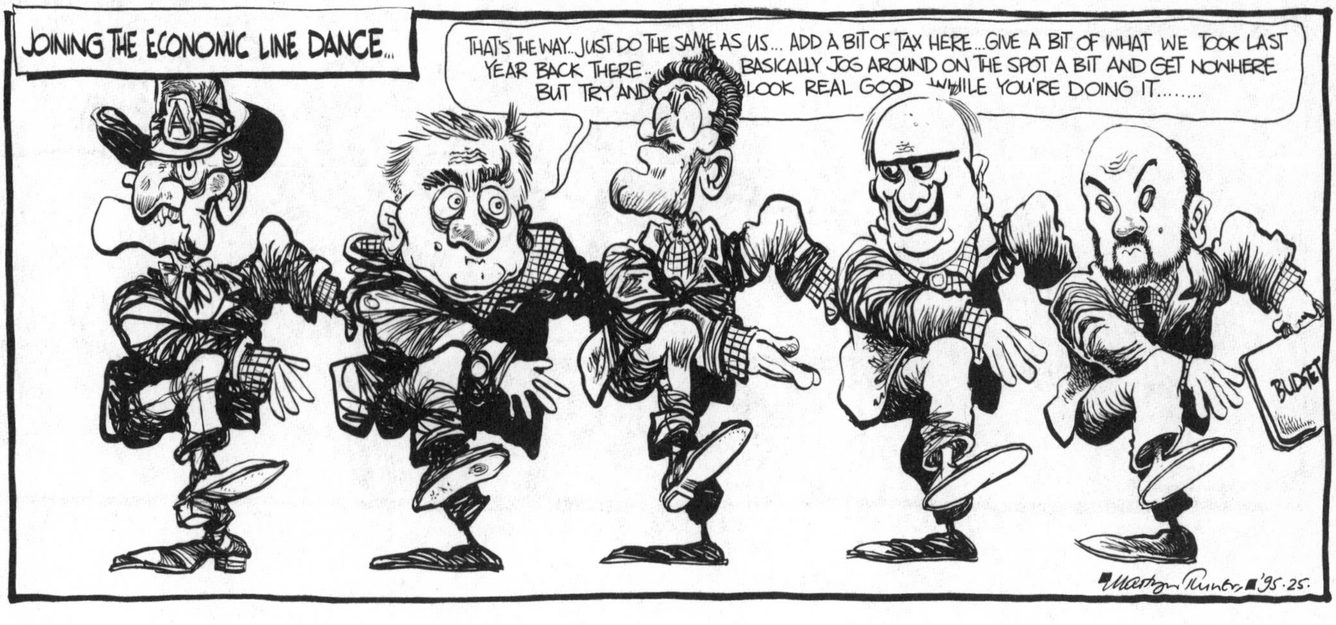
JOINING THE ECONOMIC LINE DANCE...
THAT'S THE WAY...JUST DO THE SAME AS US... ADD A BIT OF TAX HERE...GIVE A BIT OF WHAT WE TOOK LAST YEAR BACK THERE... BASICALLY JOG AROUND ON THE SPOT A BIT AND GET NOWHERE BUT TRY AND LOOK REAL GOOD WHILE YOU'RE DOING IT........
BUDGET
'95.25.

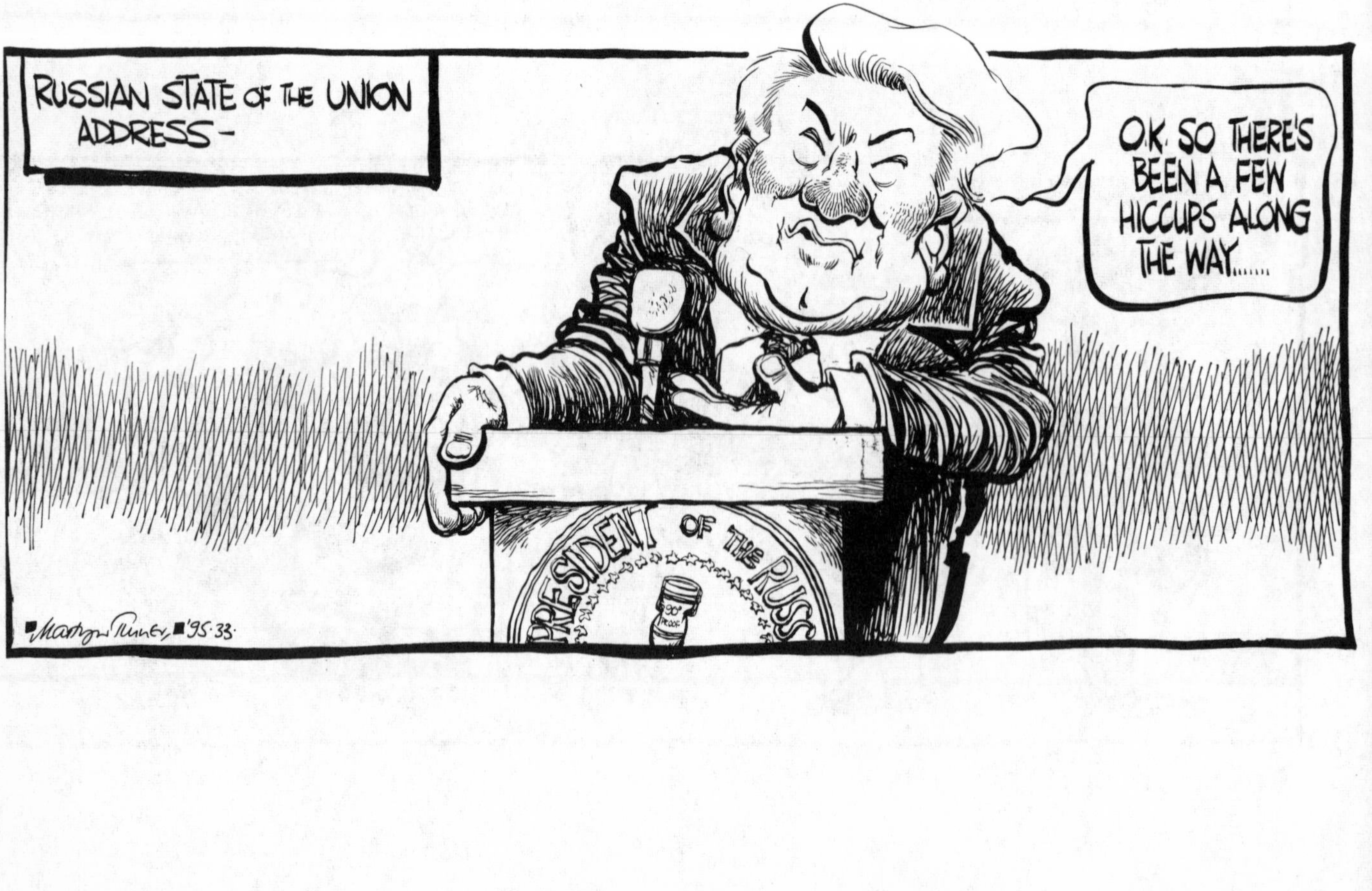
RUSSIAN STATE OF THE UNION ADDRESS -
O.K. SO THERE'S BEEN A FEW HICCUPS ALONG THE WAY.......
PRESIDENT OF THE RUSS

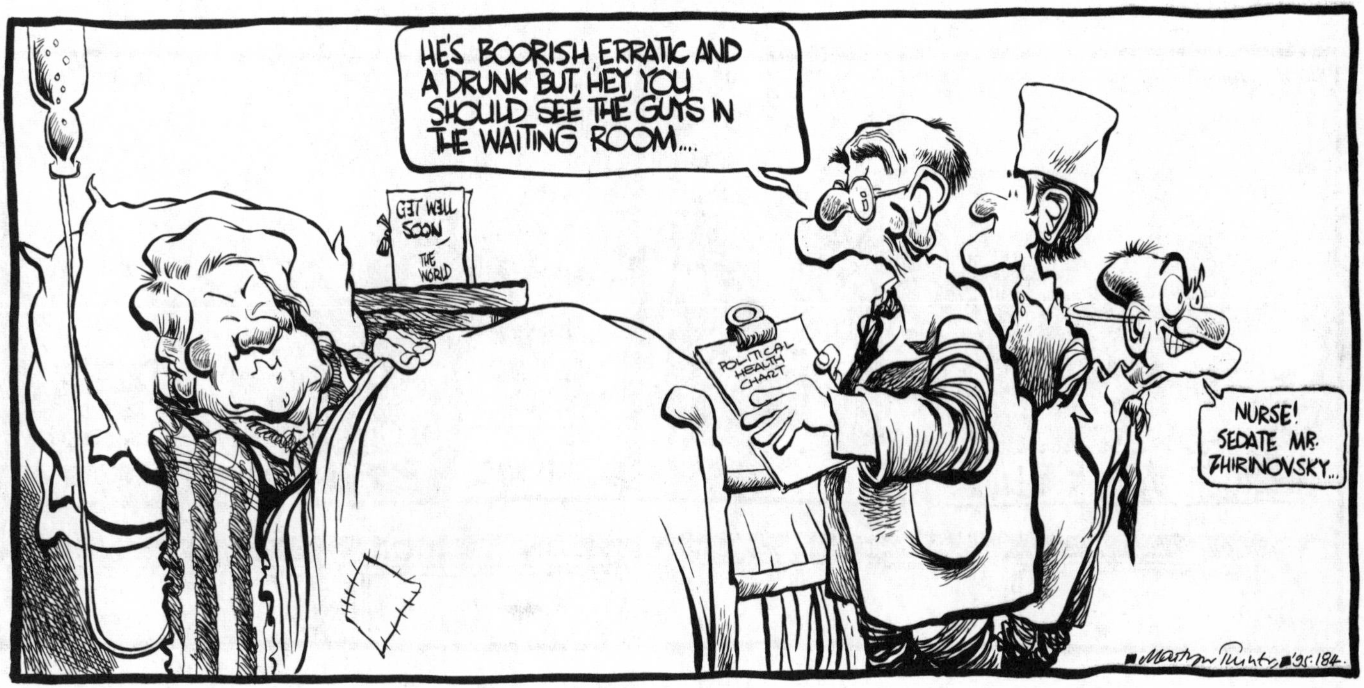
HE'S BOORISH, ERRATIC AND A DRUNK BUT, HEY, YOU SHOULD SEE THE GUYS IN THE WAITING ROOM....
GET WELL SOON — THE WORLD
POLITICAL HEALTH CHART
NURSE! SEDATE MR. ZHIRINOVSKY...

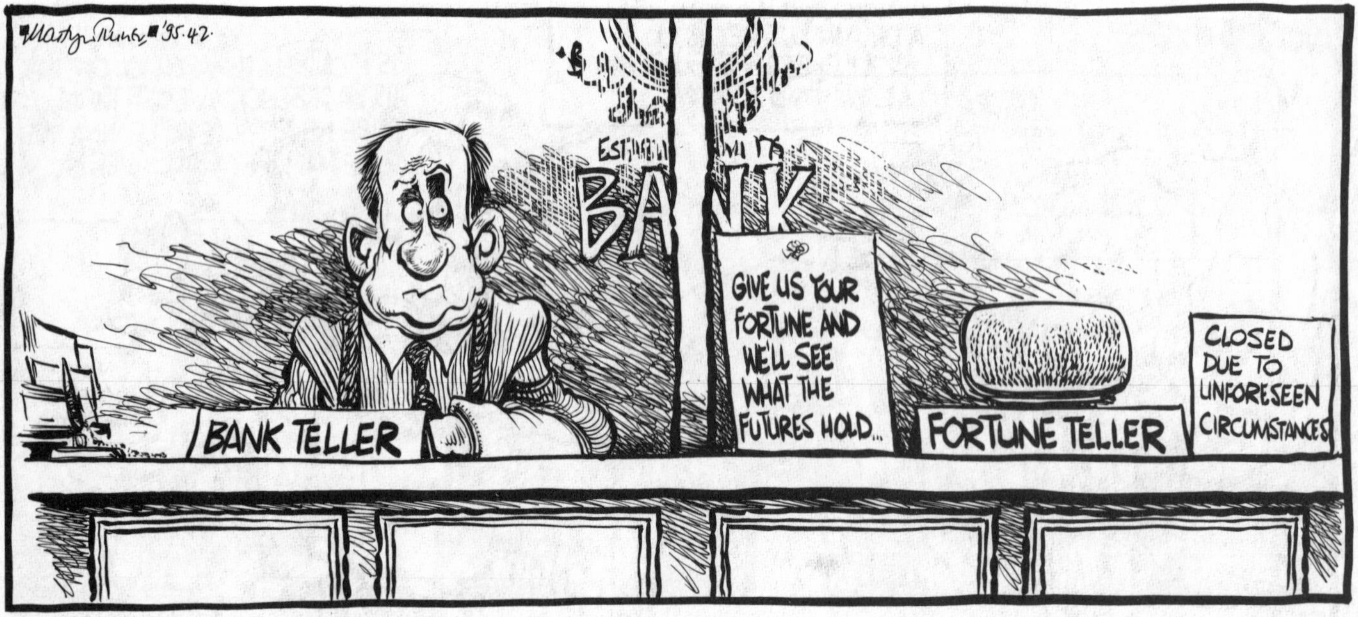
BA
K
GIVE US YOUR FORTUNE AND WE'LL SEE WHAT THE FUTURES HOLD...
BANK TELLER
FORTUNE TELLER
CLOSED DUE TO UNFORESEEN CIRCUMSTANCES

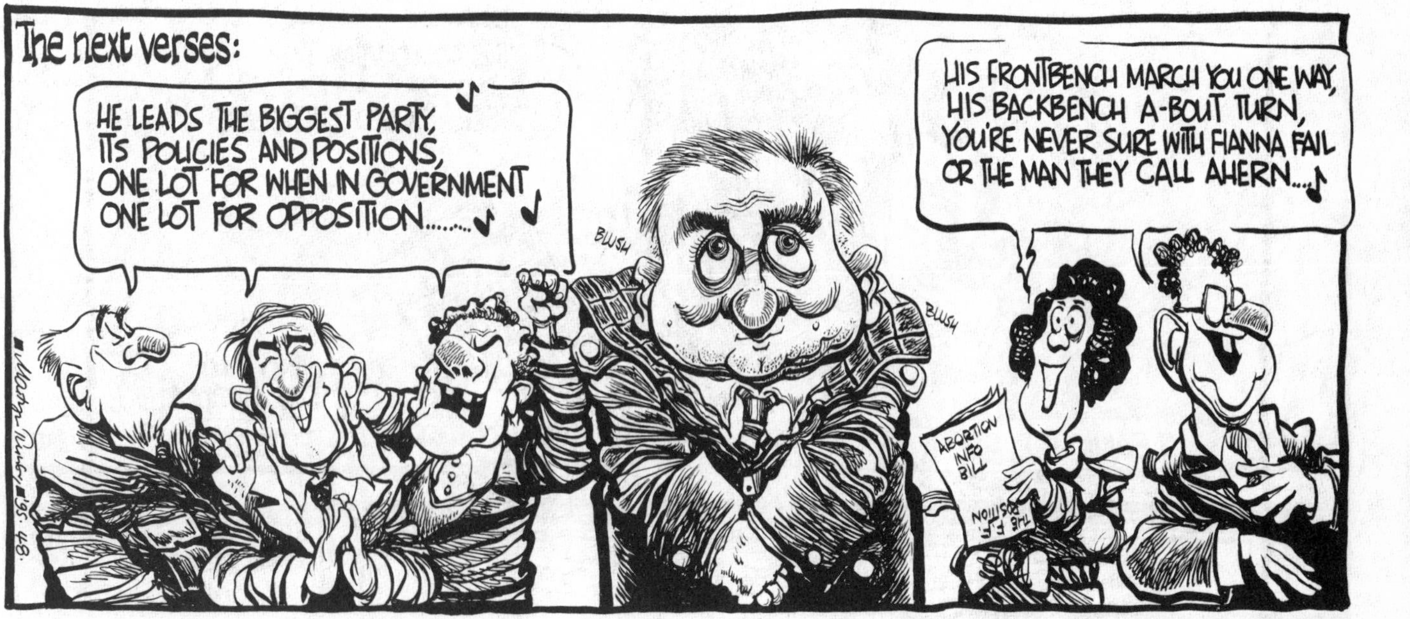
The next verses:
HE LEADS THE BIGGEST PARTY, ITS POLICIES AND POSITIONS, ONE LOT FOR WHEN IN GOVERNMENT ONE LOT FOR OPPOSITION.......
BLUSH
BLUSH
HIS FRONTBENCH MARCH YOU ONE WAY, HIS BACKBENCH A-BOUT TURN, YOU'RE NEVER SURE WITH FIANNA FAIL OR THE MAN THEY CALL AHERN....
ABORTION INFO BILL
THE F.F. POSITION

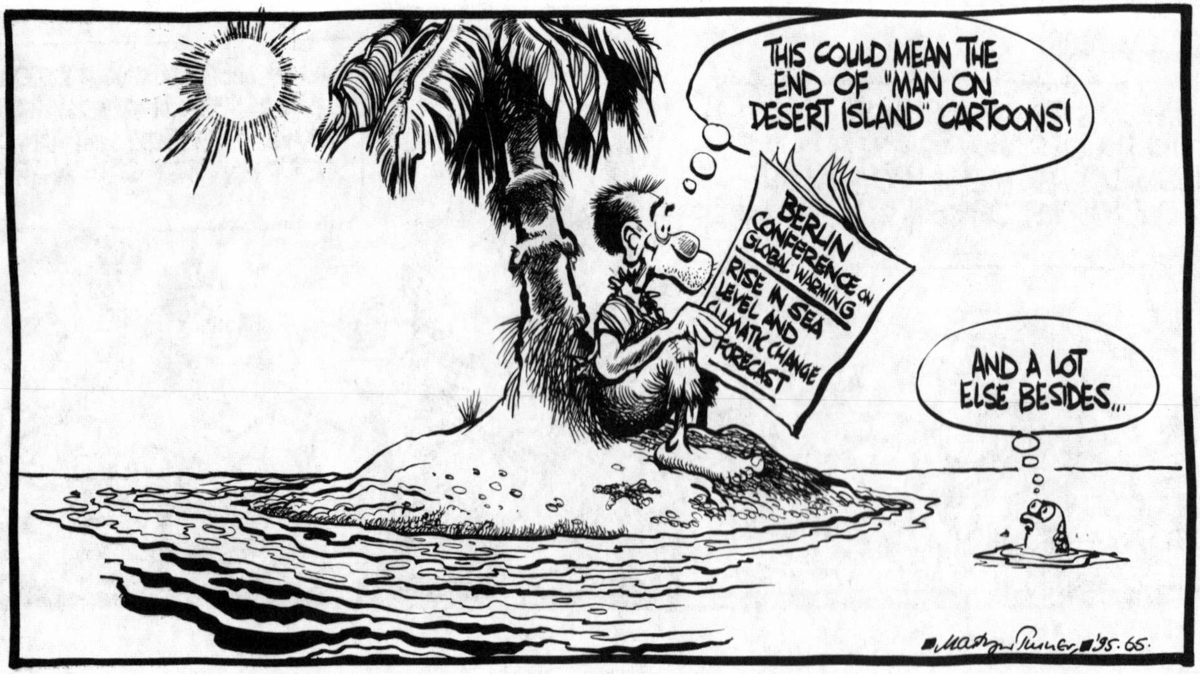
THIS COULD MEAN THE END OF "MAN ON DESERT ISLAND" CARTOONS!
BERLIN CONFERENCE ON GLOBAL WARMING
RISE IN SEA LEVEL AND CLIMATIC CHANGE FORECAST
AND A LOT ELSE BESIDES...
'95.65.

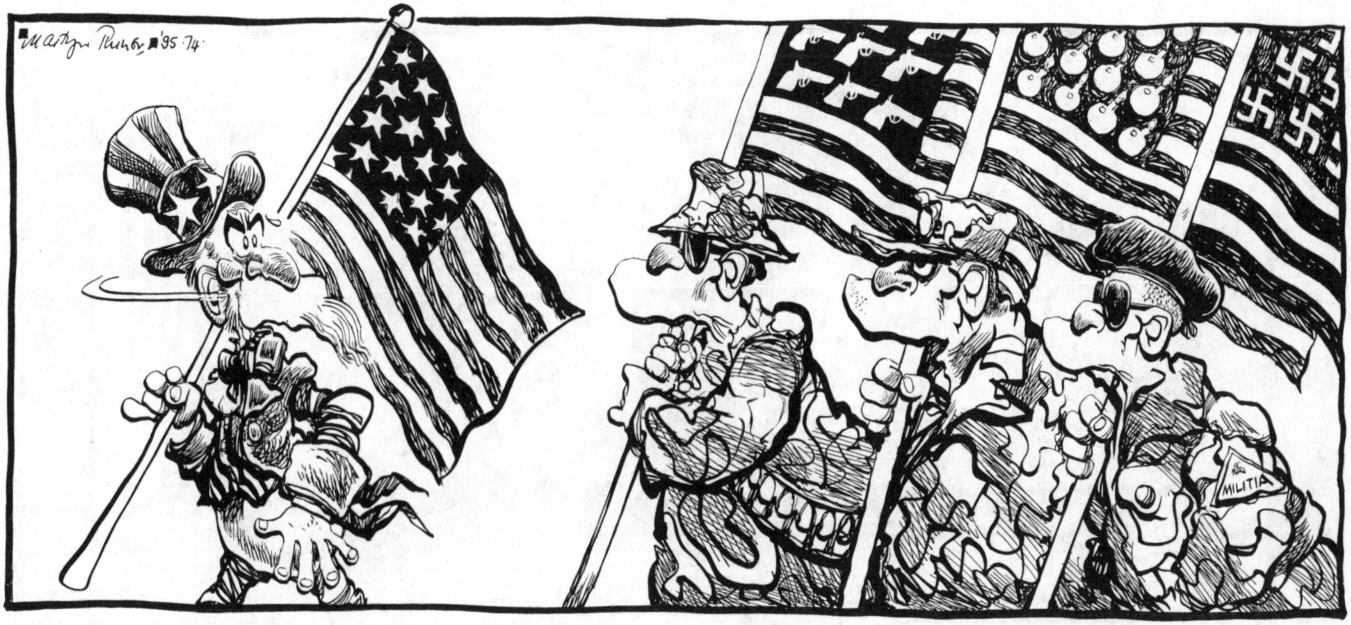
MILITIA

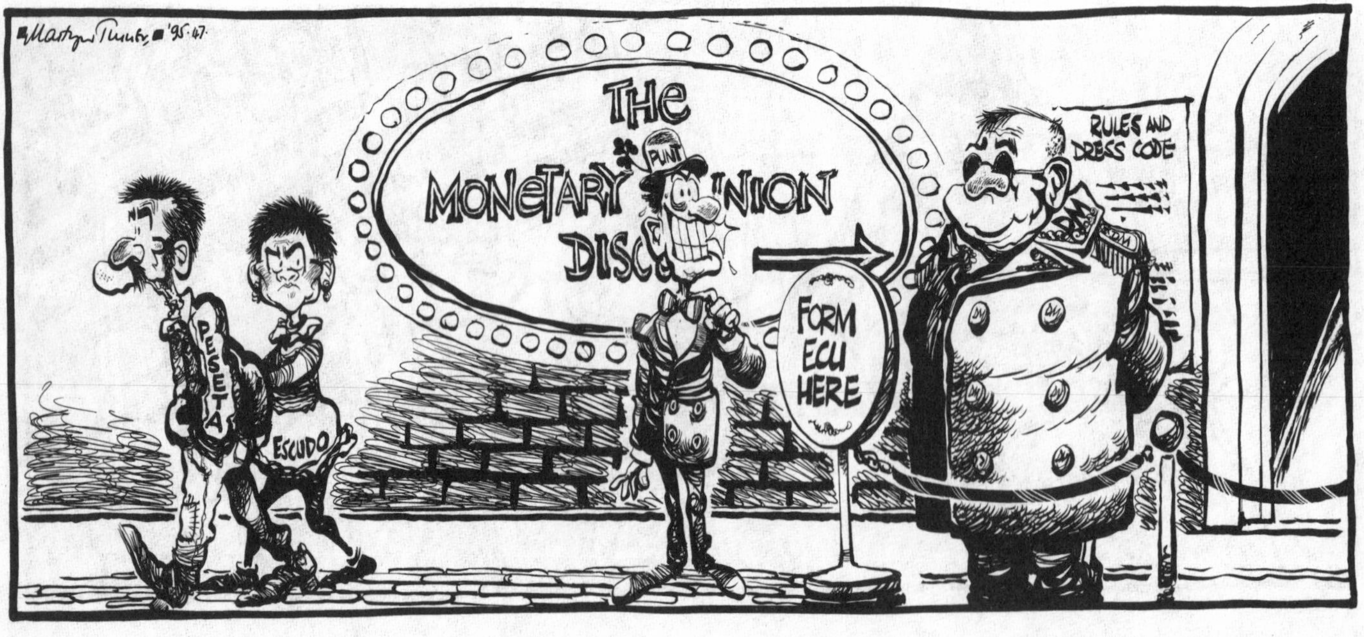
Martyn Turner '95.47.
THE MONETARY UNION DISCO
PUNT
PESETA
ESCUDO
FORM ECU HERE
RULES AND DRESS CODE
DM

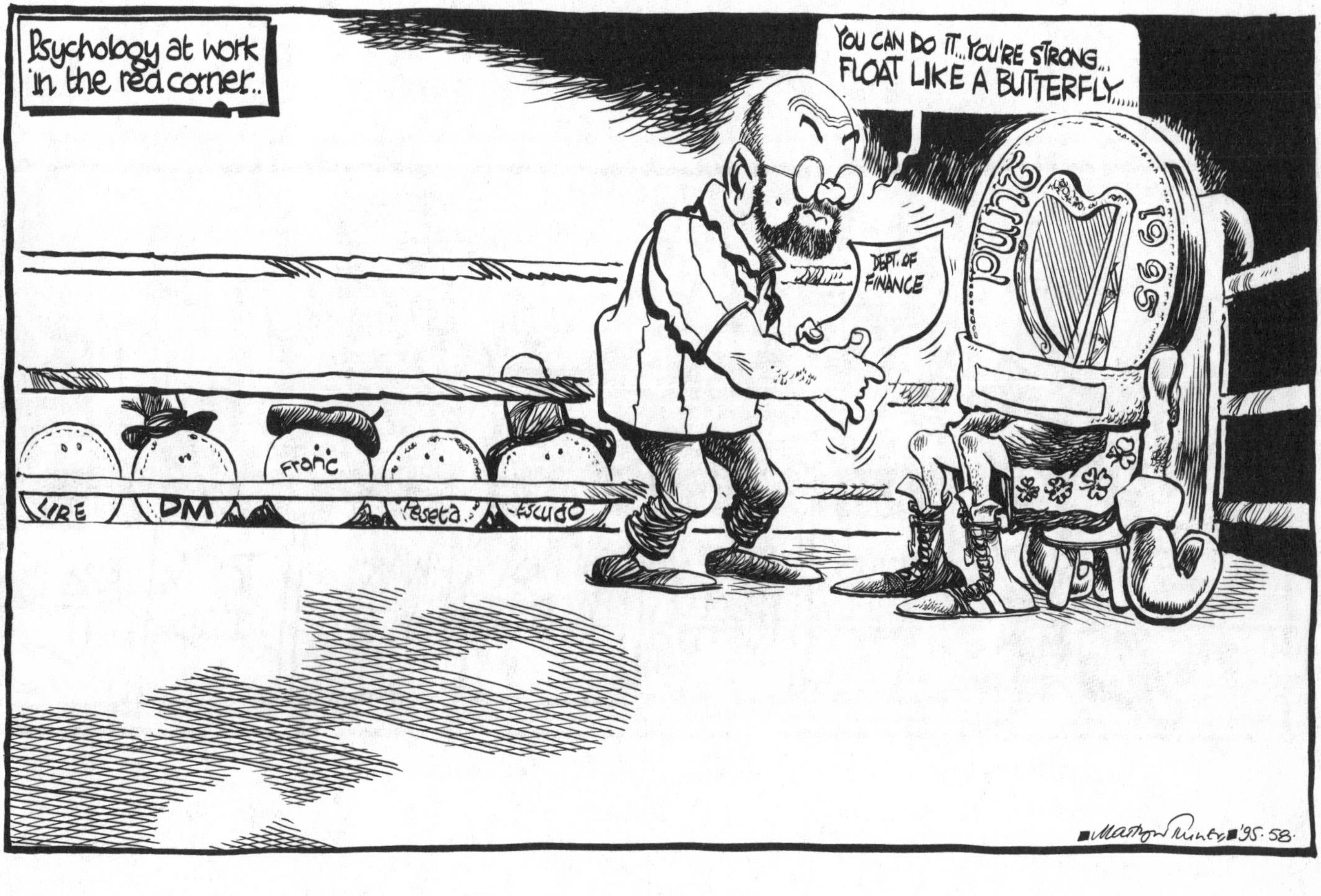
Psychology at work in the red corner..
YOU CAN DO IT...YOU'RE STRONG... FLOAT LIKE A BUTTERFLY...
DEPT. OF FINANCE
Punt 1995
LIRE
DM
Franc
Peseta
Escudo
Martyn Turner '95. 58.

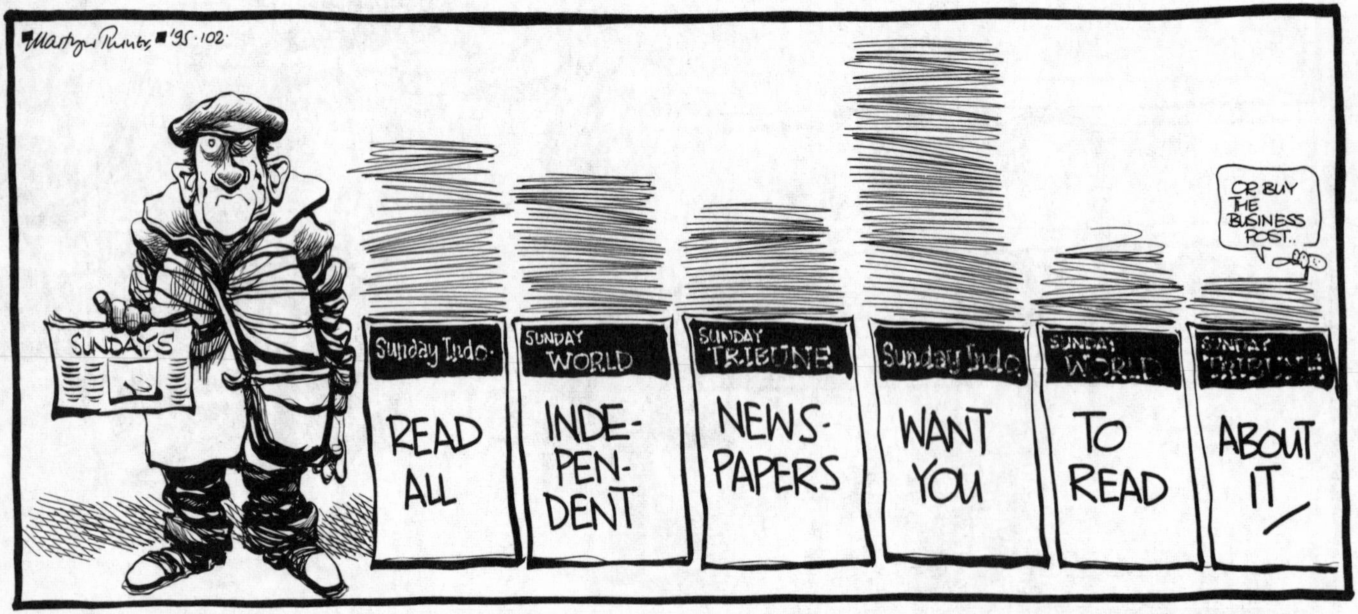
Martyn Turner '95.102.
SUNDAYS
Sunday Indo.
READ ALL
SUNDAY WORLD
INDE-PEN-DENT
SUNDAY TRIBUNE
NEWS-PAPERS
Sunday Indo.
WANT YOU
SUNDAY WORLD
TO READ
SUNDAY TRIBUNE
ABOUT IT
OR BUY THE BUSINESS POST..

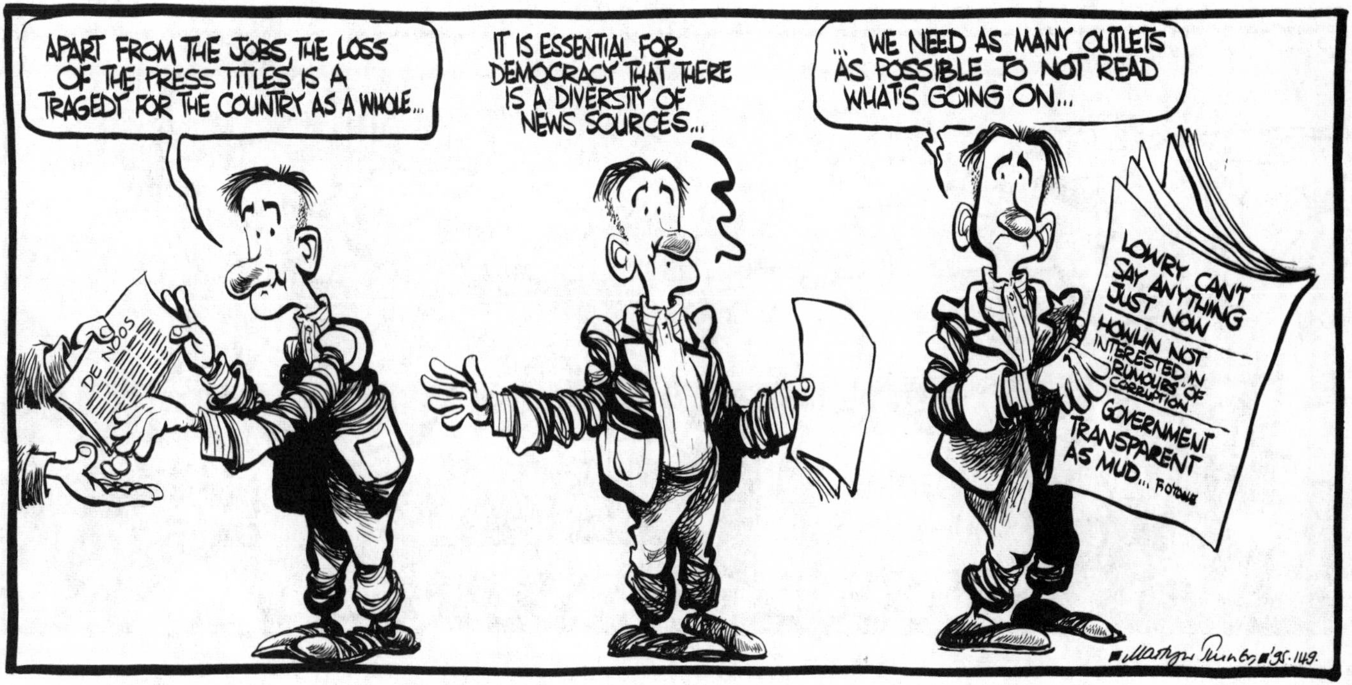
APART FROM THE JOBS, THE LOSS OF THE PRESS TITLES IS A TRAGEDY FOR THE COUNTRY AS A WHOLE...
DE NOOS
IT IS ESSENTIAL FOR DEMOCRACY THAT THERE IS A DIVERSITY OF NEWS SOURCES...
... WE NEED AS MANY OUTLETS AS POSSIBLE TO NOT READ WHAT'S GOING ON...
LOWRY CAN'T SAY ANYTHING JUST NOW
HOWLIN NOT INTERESTED IN "RUMOURS" OF CORRUPTION
GOVERNMENT TRANSPARENT AS MUD...

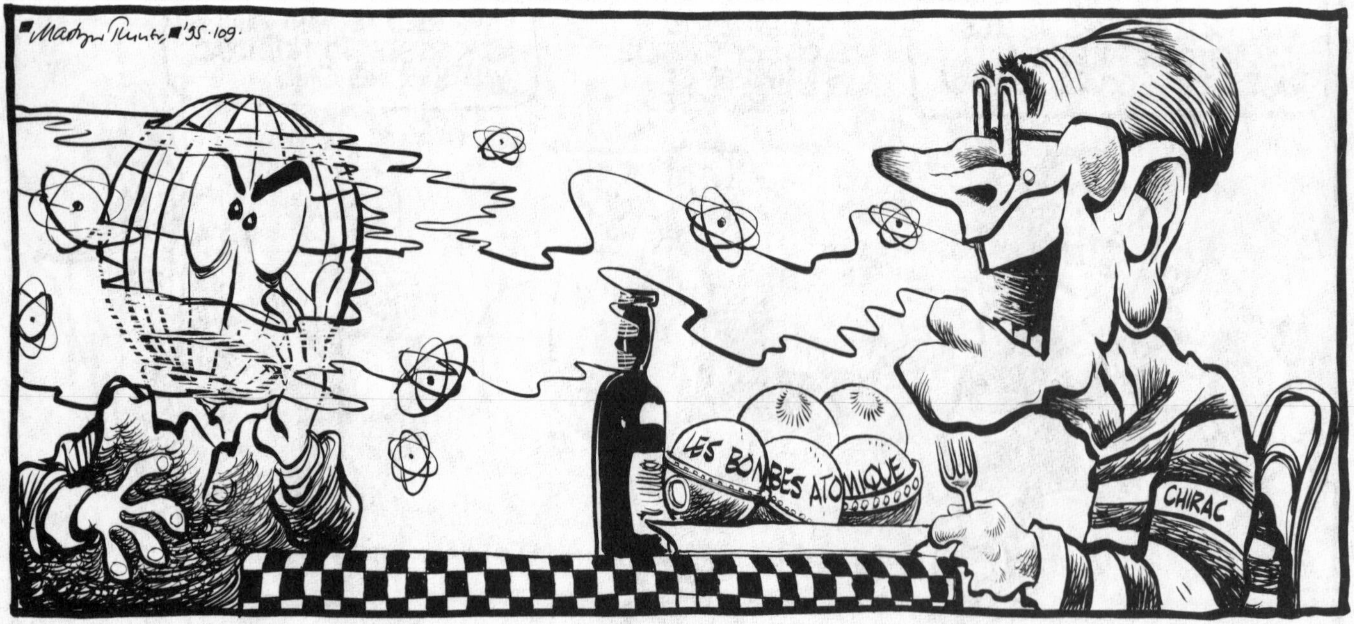
LES BOMBES ATOMIQUE
CHIRAC

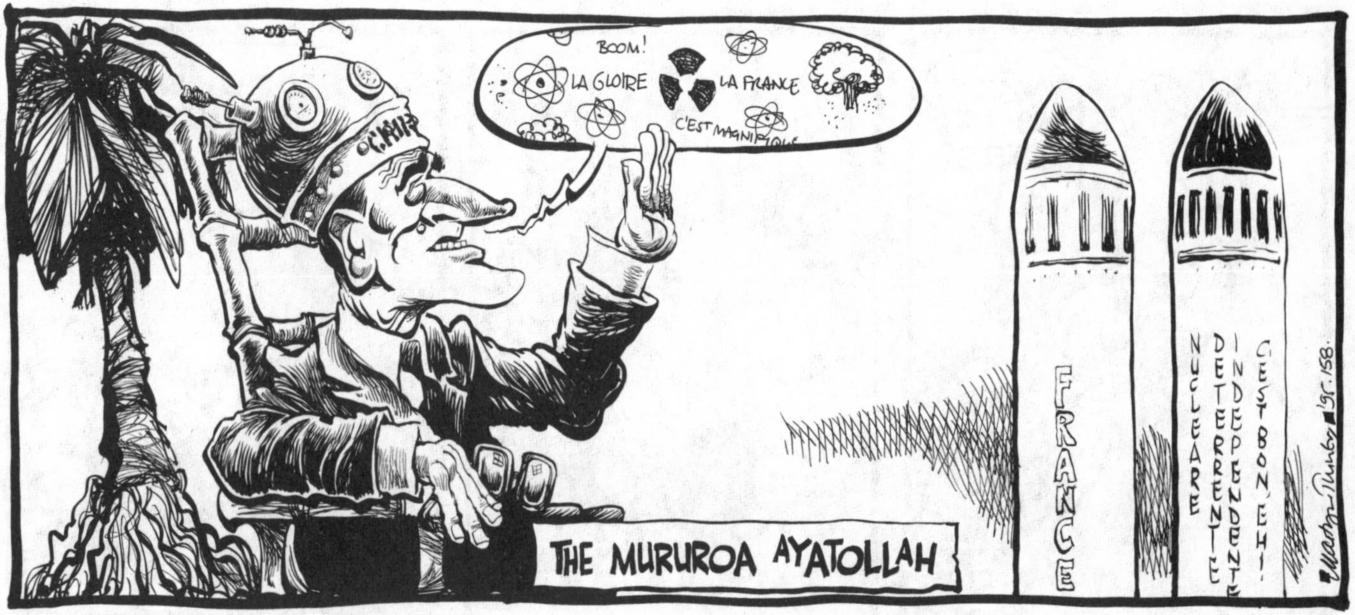
BOOM!
LA GLOIRE
LA FRANCE
C'EST MAGNIFI
THE MURUROA AYATOLLAH
FRANCE
NUCLEARE
DETERRENTE
INDEPENDENTE
C'EST BON, EH!

UN
WHO'S THE KING OF THE JUNGLE?
DON'T GET MAD JUST 'COS YOU DON'T KNOW THE ANSWER....
UN
BOSNIAN SERBS

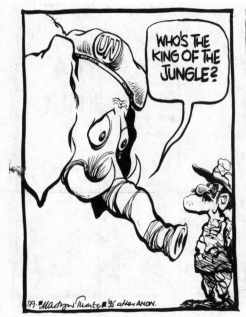

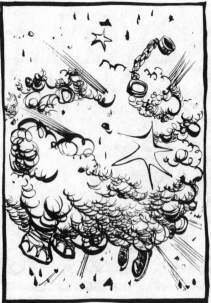

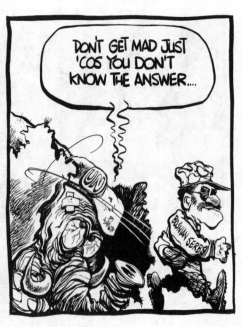

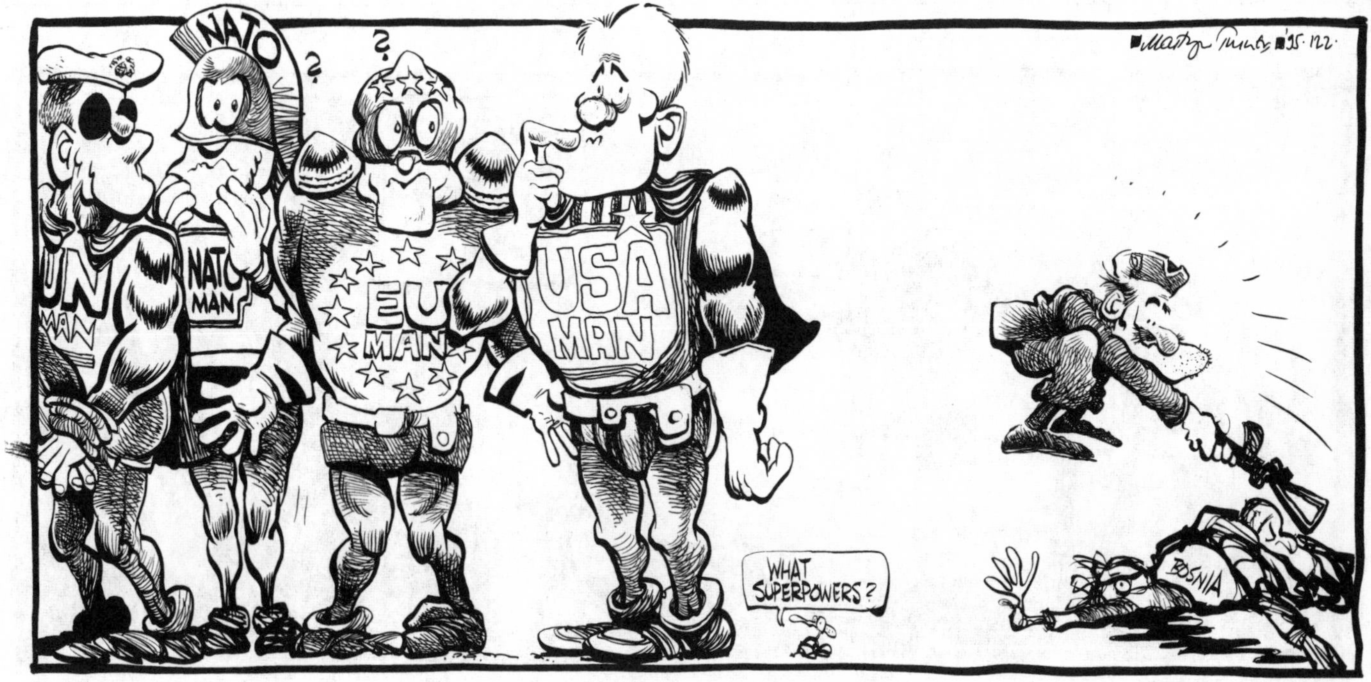
NATO
UN MAN
NATO MAN
EU MAN
USA MAN
WHAT SUPERPOWERS?
BOSNIA

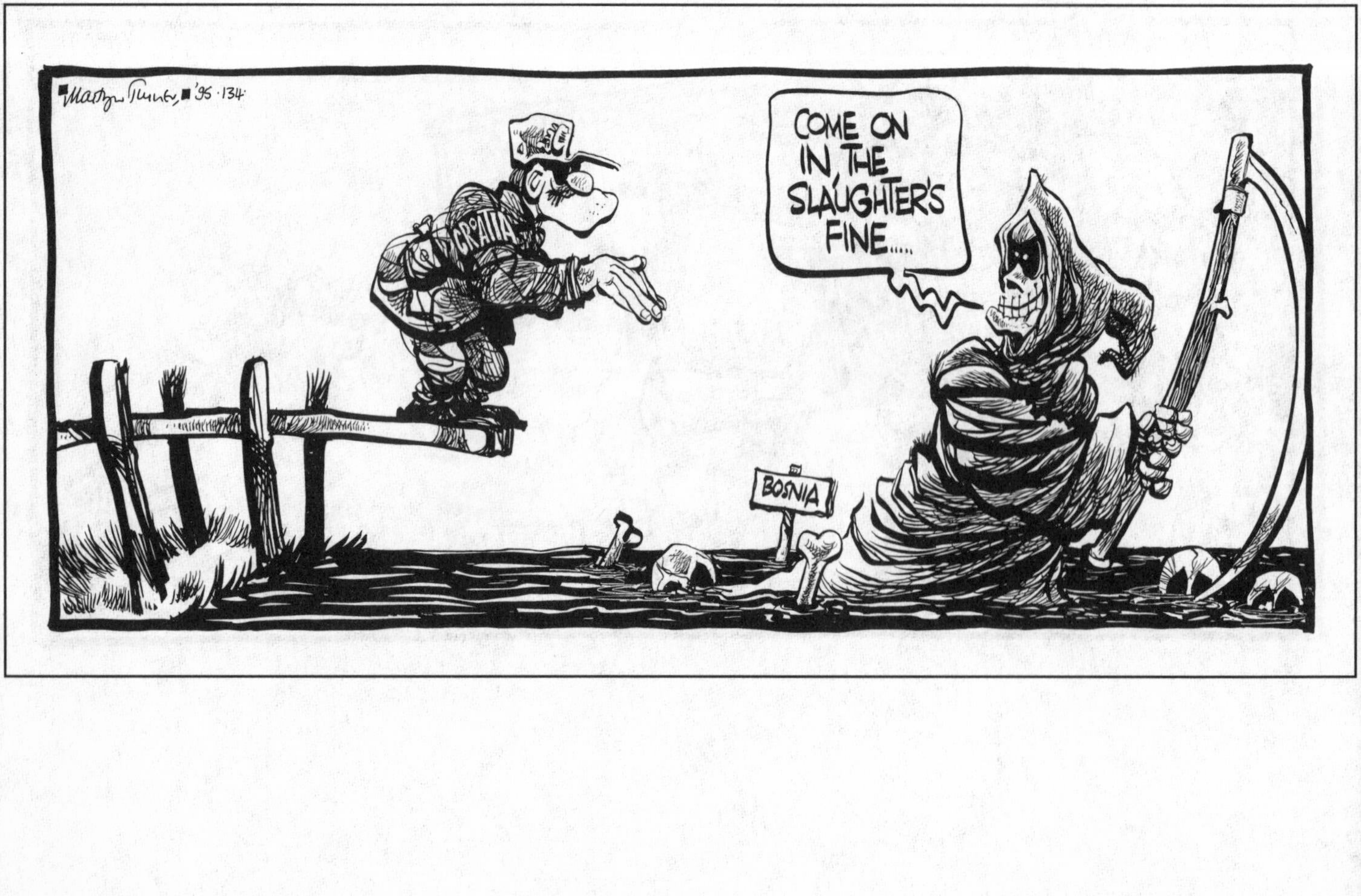
Martyn Turner '95 ·134·
COME ON IN THE SLAUGHTER'S FINE.....
CROATIA
BOSNIA

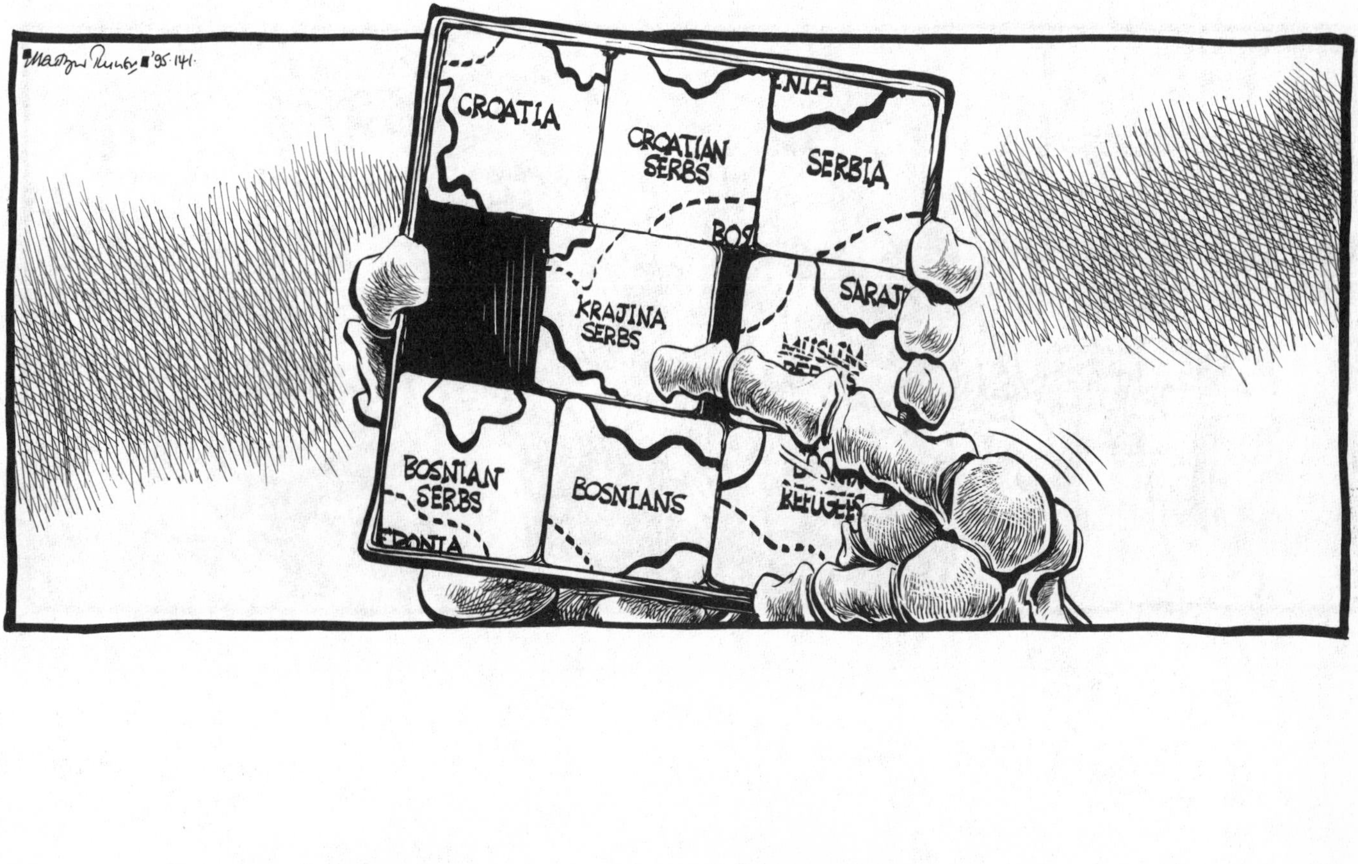
CROATIA
CROATIAN SERBS
SERBIA
KRAJINA SERBS
BOSNIAN SERBS
BOSNIANS

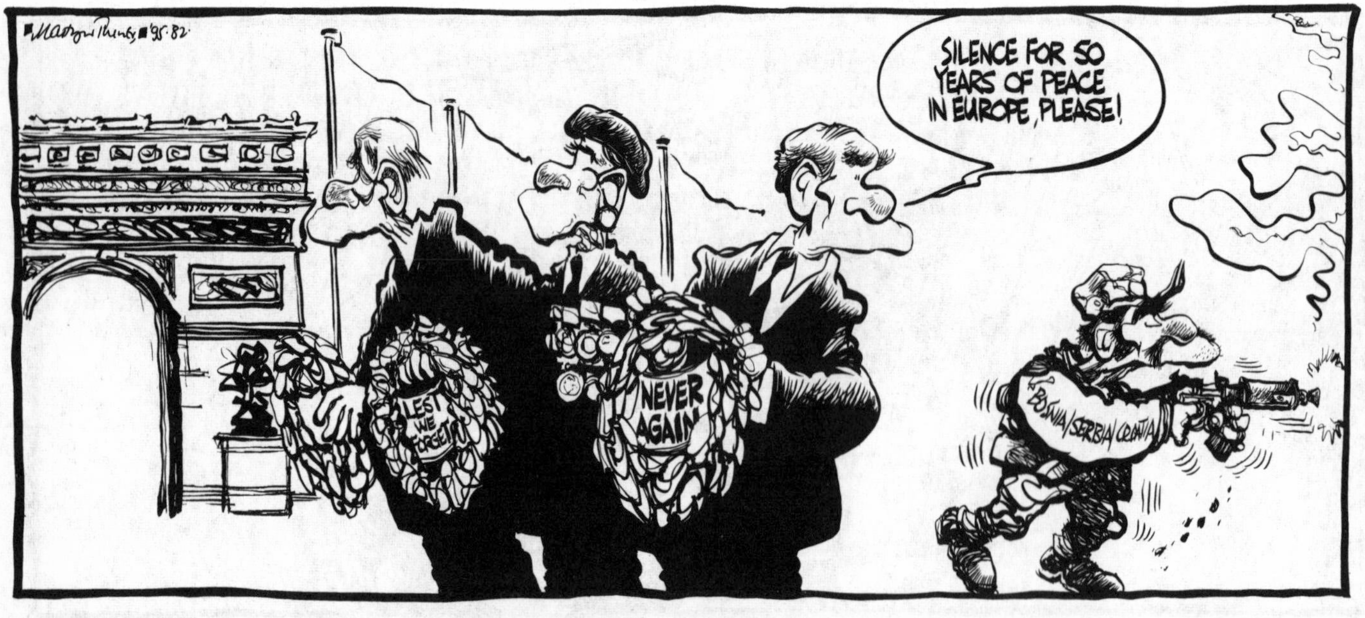
Mahood Punch '95 82
SILENCE FOR 50 YEARS OF PEACE IN EUROPE, PLEASE!
LEST WE FORGET
NEVER AGAIN
BOSNIA/SERBIA/CROATIA

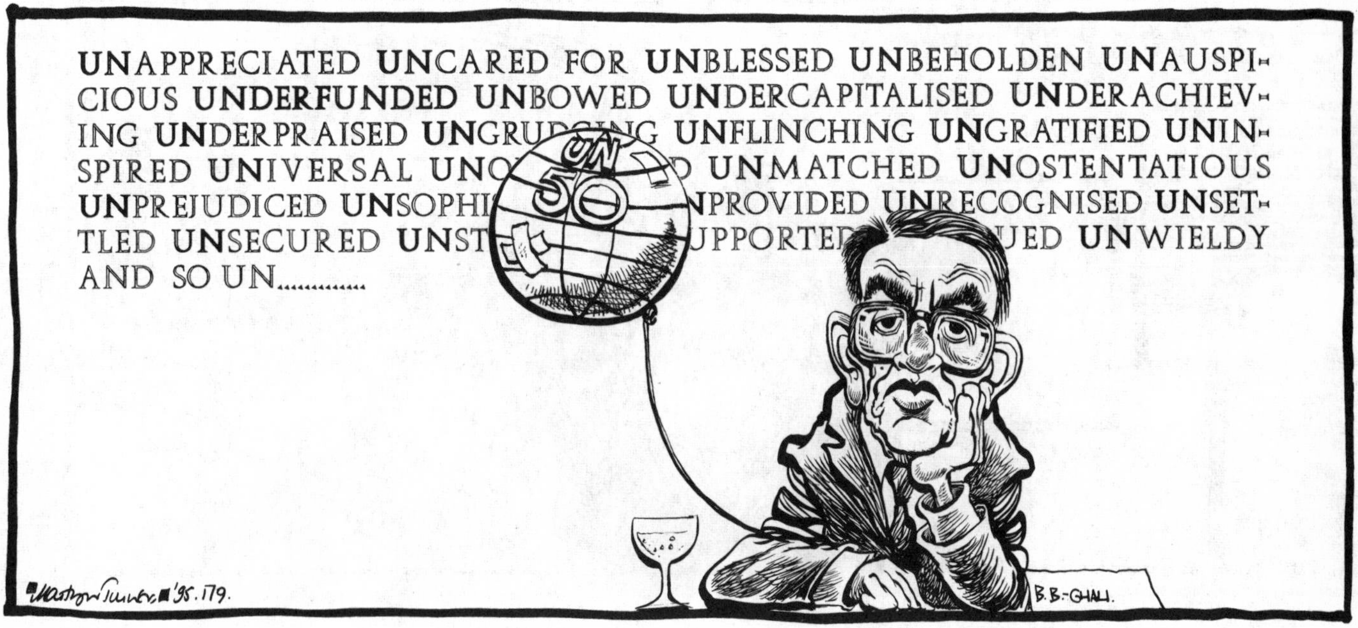
UNAPPRECIATED UNCARED FOR UNBLESSED UNBEHOLDEN UNAUSPI-
CIOUS UNDERFUNDED UNBOWED UNDERCAPITALISED UNDERACHIEV-
ING UNDERPRAISED UNGRU G UNFLINCHING UNGRATIFIED UNIN-
SPIRED UNIVERSAL UNO D UNMATCHED UNOSTENTATIOUS
UNPREJUDICED UNSOPHI NPROVIDED UNRECOGNISED UNSET-
TLED UNSECURED UNST UPPORTED UED UNWIELDY
AND SO UN.............
UN 50
B.B.-GHALI.

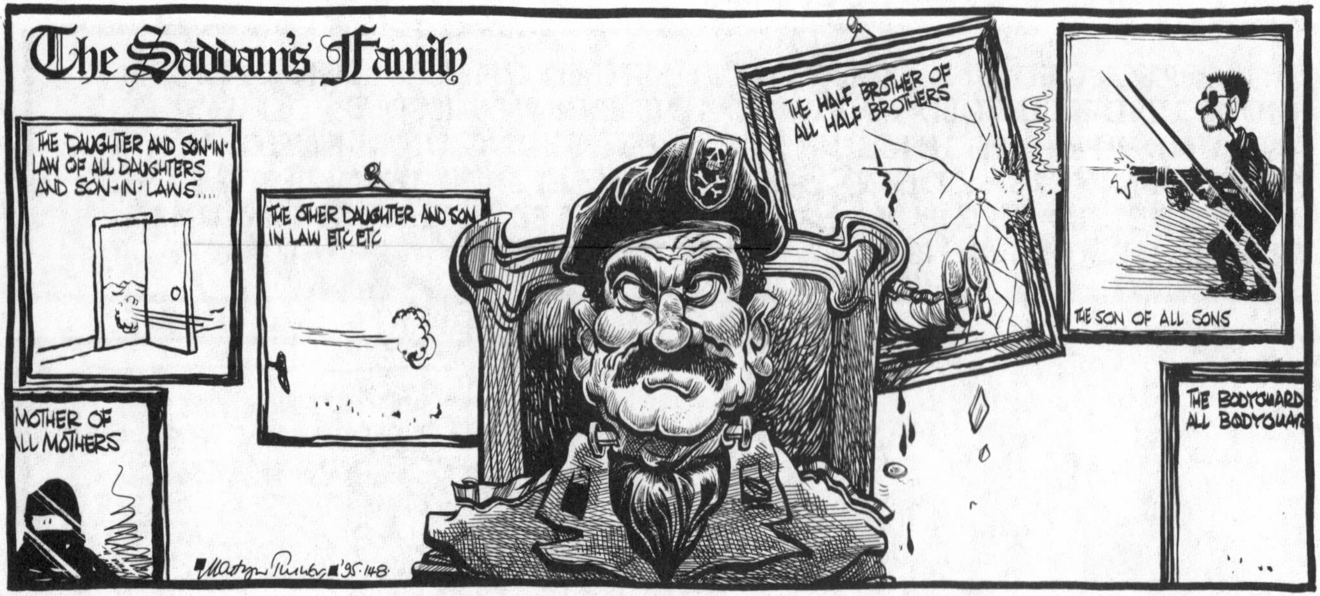
The Saddam's Family
THE DAUGHTER AND SON-IN-LAW OF ALL DAUGHTERS AND SON-IN-LAWS....
THE OTHER DAUGHTER AND SON IN LAW ETC ETC
THE HALF BROTHER OF ALL HALF BROTHERS
THE SON OF ALL SONS
MOTHER OF ALL MOTHERS
THE BODYGUARD ALL BODYGUAR
'95·148·

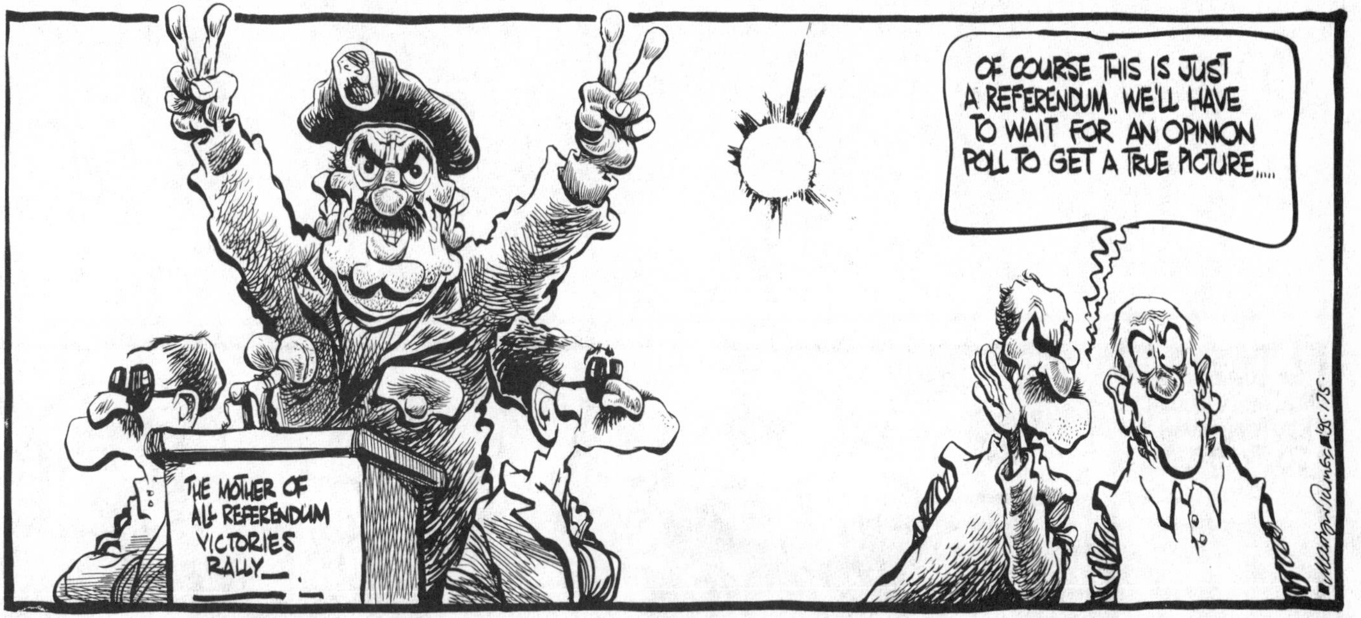

THE MOTHER OF ALL REFERENDUM VICTORIES RALLY___
OF COURSE THIS IS JUST A REFERENDUM.. WE'LL HAVE TO WAIT FOR AN OPINION POLL TO GET A TRUE PICTURE.....

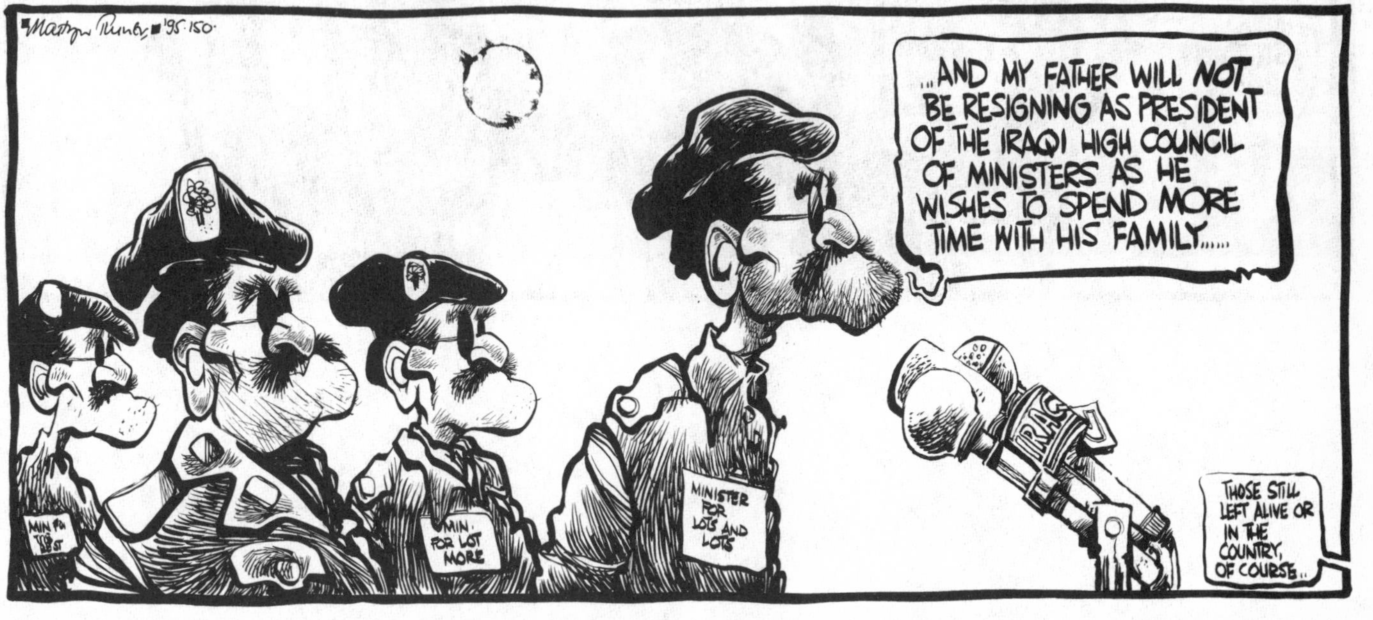

..AND MY FATHER WILL NOT BE RESIGNING AS PRESIDENT OF THE IRAQI HIGH COUNCIL OF MINISTERS AS HE WISHES TO SPEND MORE TIME WITH HIS FAMILY.....
MIN. FOR LOT MORE
MINISTER FOR LOTS AND LOTS
THOSE STILL LEFT ALIVE OR IN THE COUNTRY, OF COURSE..

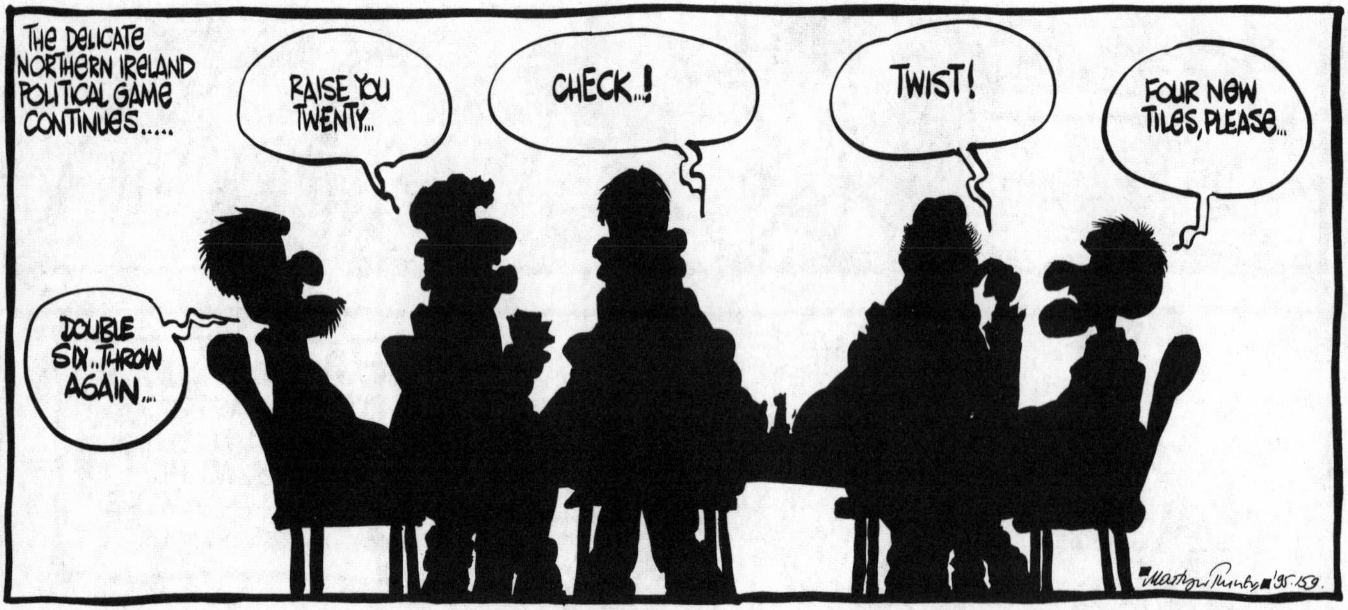
THE DELICATE NORTHERN IRELAND POLITICAL GAME CONTINUES.....
DOUBLE SIX..THROW AGAIN...
RAISE YOU TWENTY...
CHECK..!
TWIST!
FOUR NEW TILES, PLEASE...
'95.159.

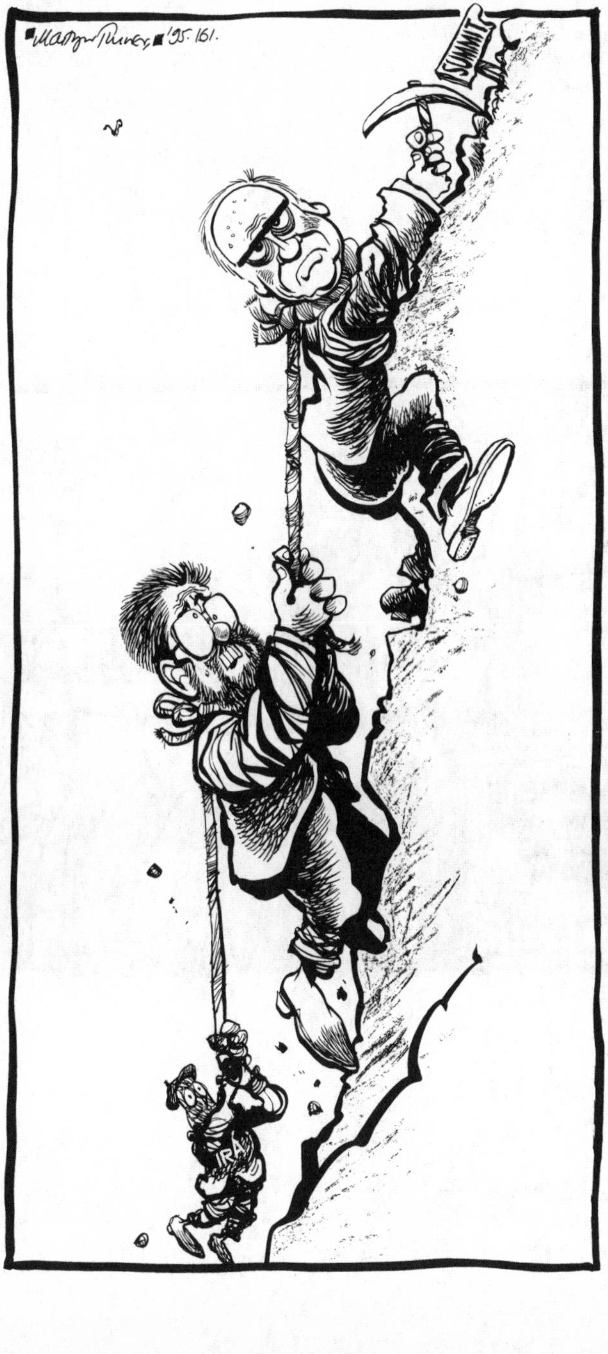
SUMMIT
IRA

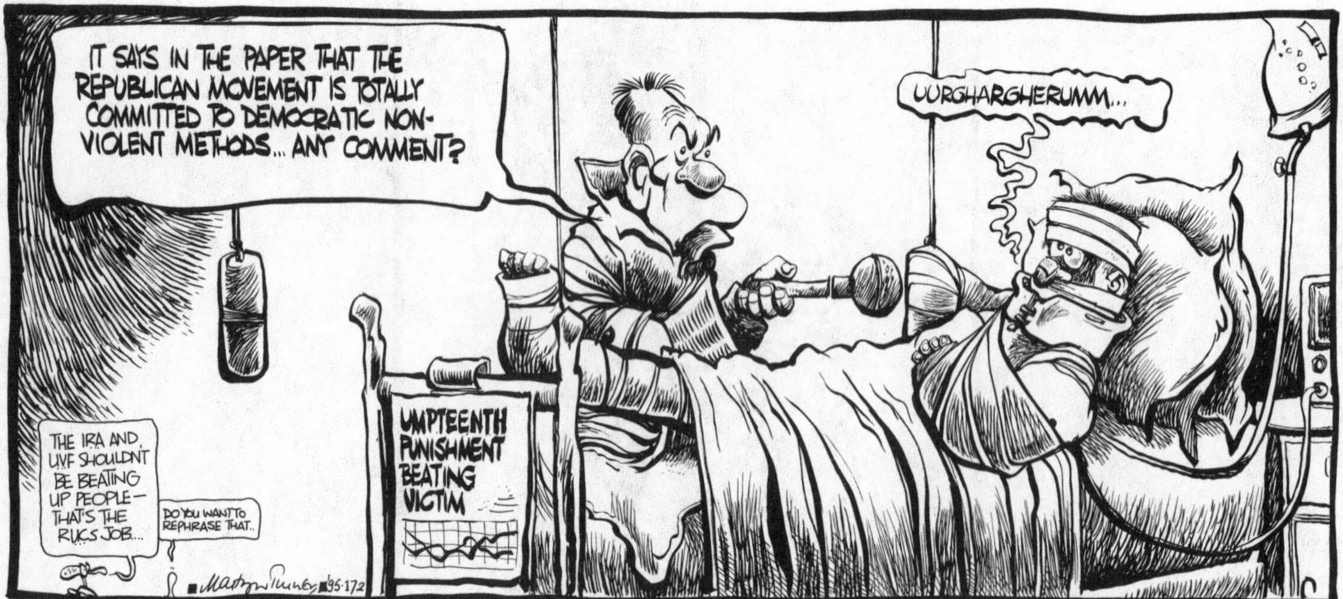
IT SAYS IN THE PAPER THAT THE REPUBLICAN MOVEMENT IS TOTALLY COMMITTED TO DEMOCRATIC NON-VIOLENT METHODS... ANY COMMENT?
UURGHARGHERUMM...
UMPTEENTH PUNISHMENT BEATING VICTIM
THE IRA AND UVF SHOULDN'T BE BEATING UP PEOPLE— THAT'S THE RUCS JOB....
DO YOU WANT TO REPHRASE THAT..
Martyn Turner '95·172

AFTER 25 YEARS OF SENSELESS VIOLENCE IT'S TIME TO REFLECT UPON THE VICTIMS......
VICTIMS OF IRA VIOLENCE
RIP
VICTIMS OF STATE VIOLENCE
RIP
VICTIMS OF LOYALIST VIOLENCE
RIP
.... AND SEE HOW WE CAN USE THEM TO CONTINUE ANTAGONISING EACH OTHER.....
NO TALKS WITH MURDERERS!
VICTIMS OF IRA VIOLENCE
VICTIMS OF STATE VIOLENCE
RIP
GIBRALTAR! LOUGHALL!

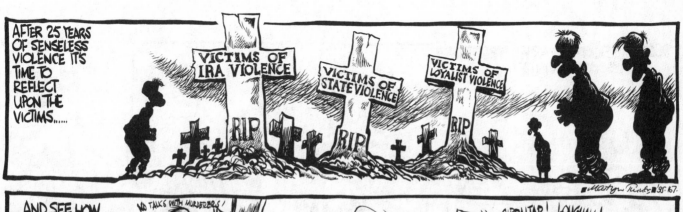

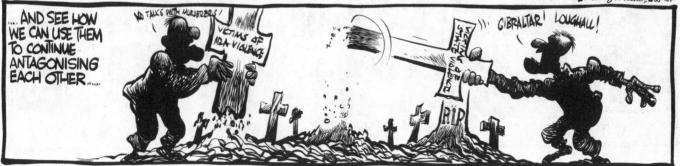

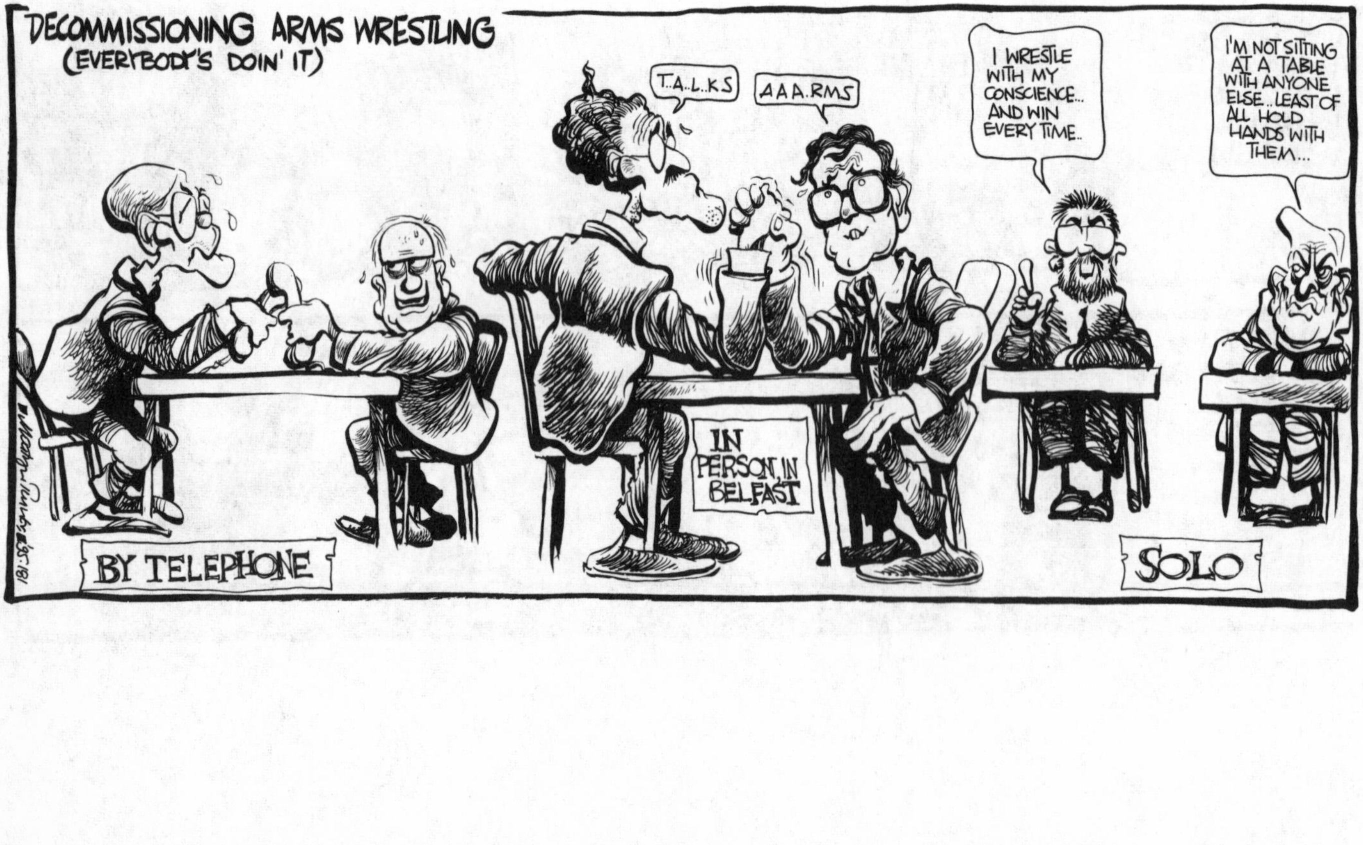
DECOMMISSIONING ARMS WRESTLING
(EVERYBODY'S DOIN' IT)
T..A..L..K.S
AAA.RMS
I WRESTLE WITH MY CONSCIENCE... AND WIN EVERY TIME..
I'M NOT SITTING AT A TABLE WITH ANYONE ELSE.. LEAST OF ALL HOLD HANDS WITH THEM...
IN PERSON, IN BELFAST
BY TELEPHONE
SOLO

THAT 15 TONS OF CANNABIS-COULD IT BE DESTROYED BY BURNING IT IN BELFAST, PLEASE...
..RELAX...... COOL.. .PEACE... LOVE.... WOW... MAN... AMAZING... TOGETHER... WHATEVER YOU SAY...... ...TAKE IT EASY, HANG LOOSE, LIVE AND LET LIVE......
FAR OUT... YOU KNOW... LET'S REALLY LIVE TOGETHER... ISN'T IT GREAT HERE..... LIKE .... LOVE YA ALL..
WHO NEEDS WEAPONS... LET'S GROW FLOWERS
BOMBER? BUMMER!

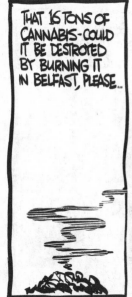

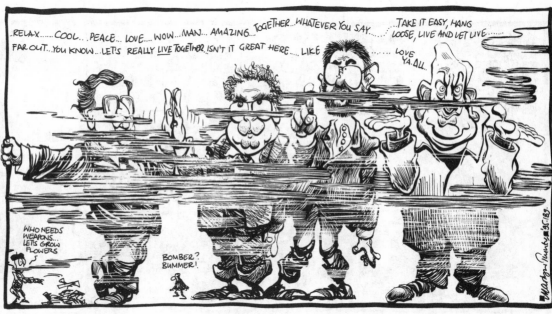

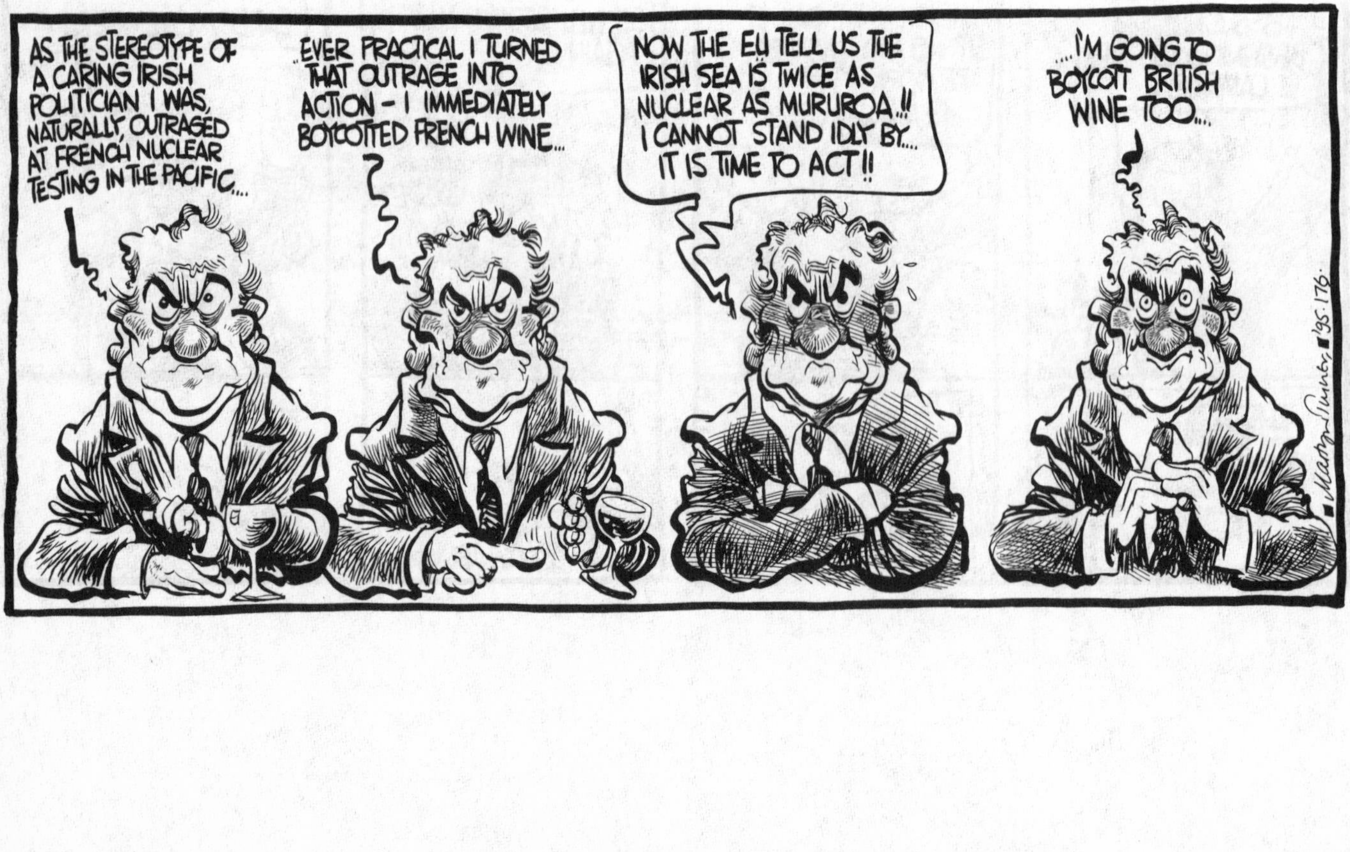
AS THE STEREOTYPE OF A CARING IRISH POLITICIAN I WAS, NATURALLY, OUTRAGED AT FRENCH NUCLEAR TESTING IN THE PACIFIC....
..EVER PRACTICAL I TURNED THAT OUTRAGE INTO ACTION - I IMMEDIATELY BOYCOTTED FRENCH WINE...
NOW THE EU TELL US THE IRISH SEA IS TWICE AS NUCLEAR AS MURUROA.!! I CANNOT STAND IDLY BY... IT IS TIME TO ACT!!
....I'M GOING TO BOYCOTT BRITISH WINE TOO....
'95.176.

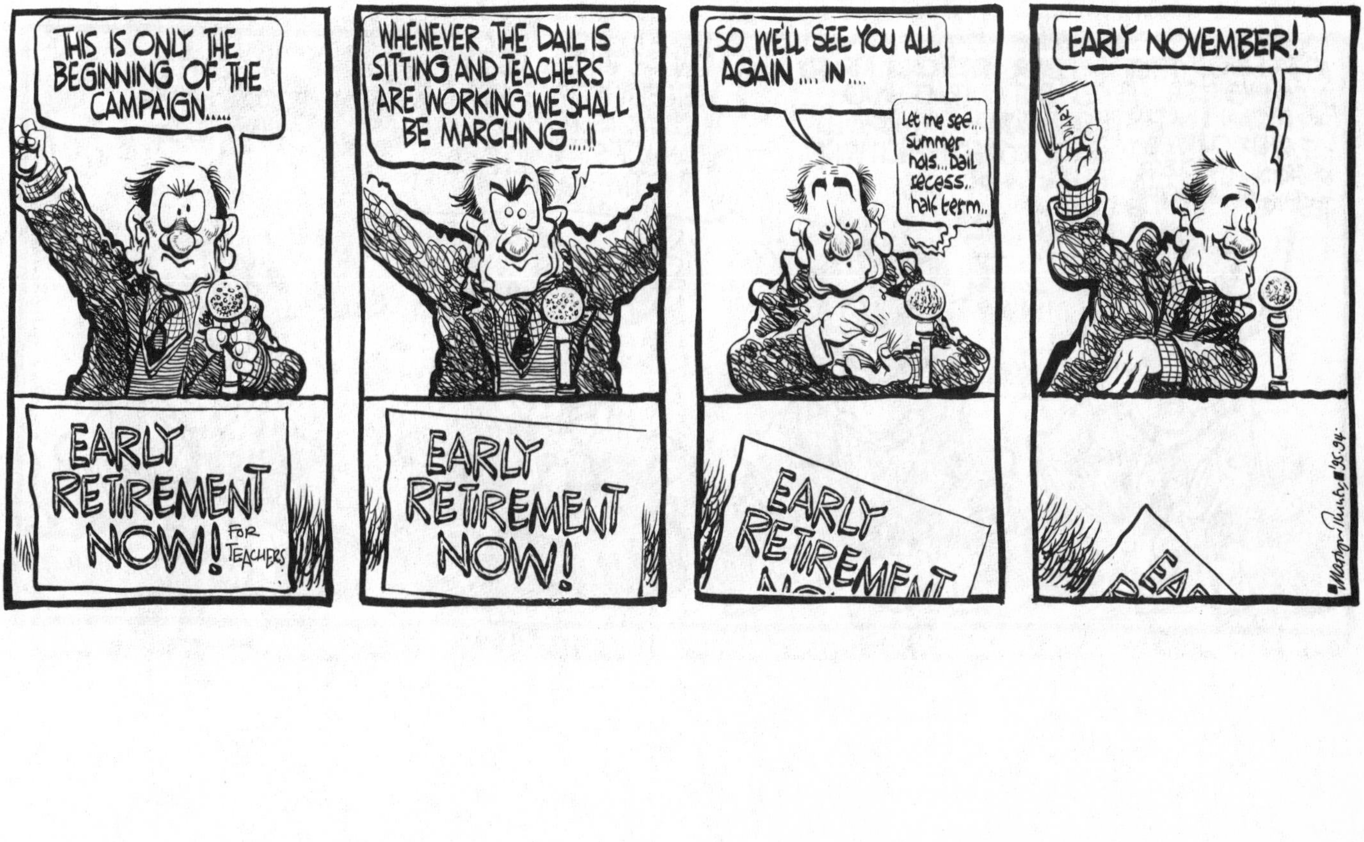
THIS IS ONLY THE BEGINNING OF THE CAMPAIGN.....
EARLY RETIREMENT NOW! FOR TEACHERS
WHENEVER THE DAIL IS SITTING AND TEACHERS ARE WORKING WE SHALL BE MARCHING...!!
EARLY RETIREMENT NOW!
SO WE'LL SEE YOU ALL AGAIN.... IN....
Let me see... Summer hols... Dail recess.. half term..
EARLY RETIREMENT
EARLY NOVEMBER!
DIARY
Martyn Turner '95.94

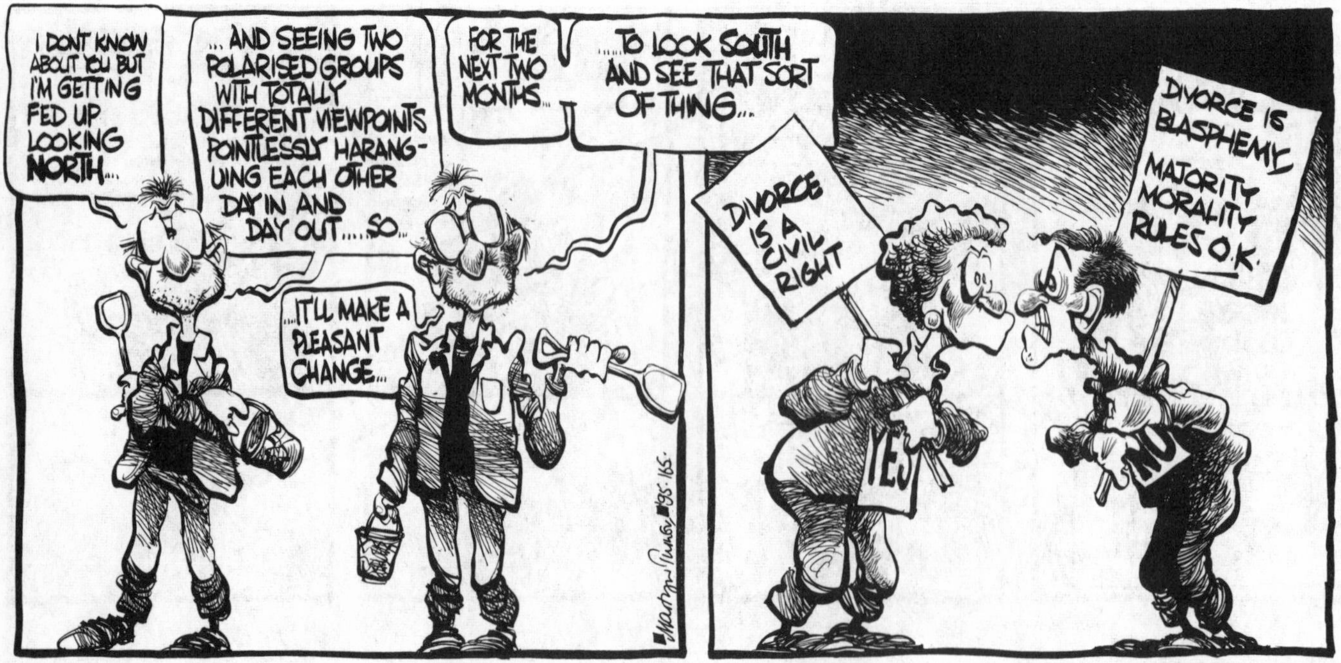

I DONT KNOW ABOUT YOU BUT I'M GETTING FED UP LOOKING NORTH...
... AND SEEING TWO POLARISED GROUPS WITH TOTALLY DIFFERENT VIEWPOINTS POINTLESSLY HARANGUING EACH OTHER DAY IN AND DAY OUT.... SO...
...IT'LL MAKE A PLEASANT CHANGE...
FOR THE NEXT TWO MONTHS...
.....TO LOOK SOUTH AND SEE THAT SORT OF THING...
DIVORCE IS A CIVIL RIGHT
DIVORCE IS BLASPHEMY
MAJORITY MORALITY RULES O.K.
YES
NO

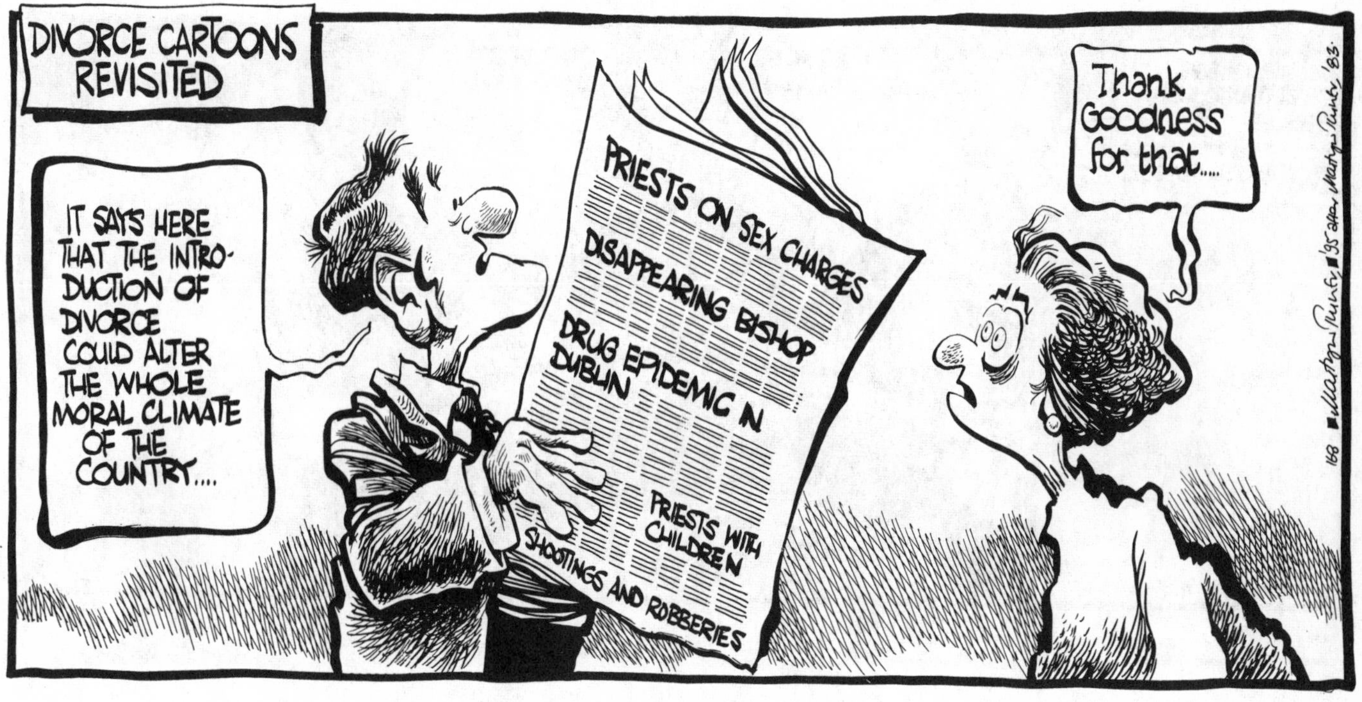
DIVORCE CARTOONS REVISITED
IT SAYS HERE THAT THE INTRODUCTION OF DIVORCE COULD ALTER THE WHOLE MORAL CLIMATE OF THE COUNTRY....
PRIESTS ON SEX CHARGES
DISAPPEARING BISHOP
DRUG EPIDEMIC IN DUBLIN
PRIESTS WITH CHILDREN
SHOOTINGS AND ROBBERIES
Thank Goodness for that.....

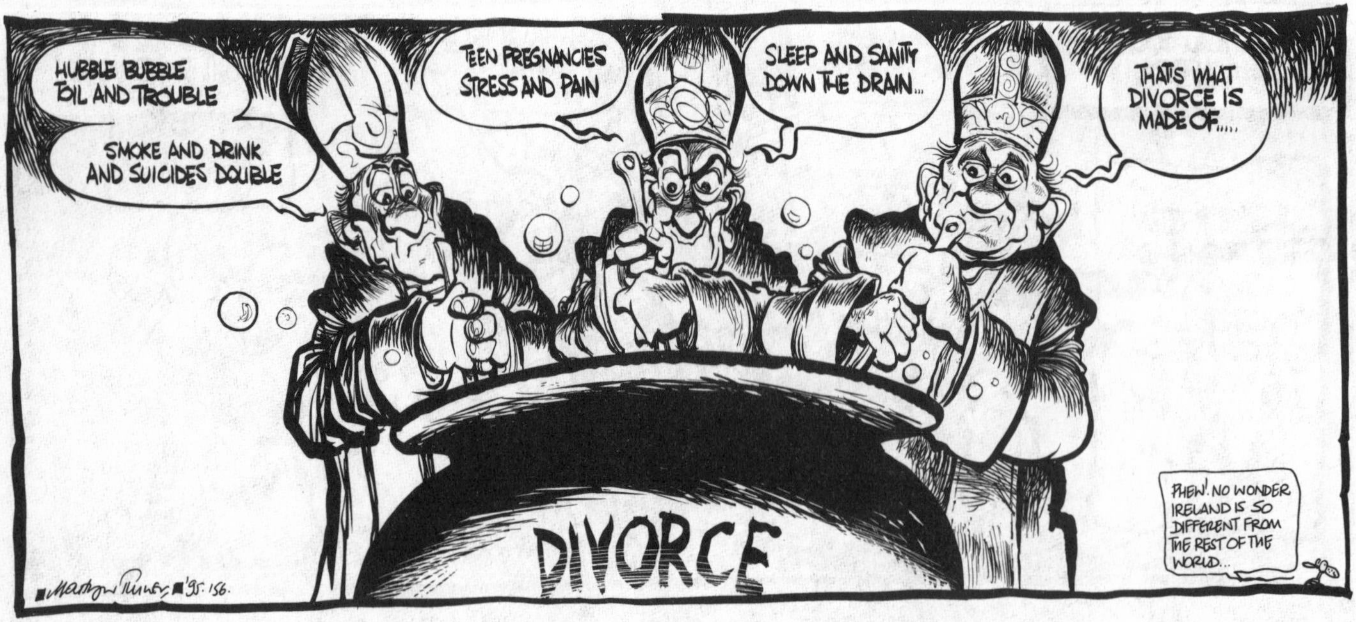
HUBBLE BUBBLE TOIL AND TROUBLE
SMOKE AND DRINK AND SUICIDES DOUBLE
TEEN PREGNANCIES STRESS AND PAIN
SLEEP AND SANITY DOWN THE DRAIN...
THAT'S WHAT DIVORCE IS MADE OF.....
DIVORCE
PHEW! NO WONDER IRELAND IS SO DIFFERENT FROM THE REST OF THE WORLD...
'95. 156.

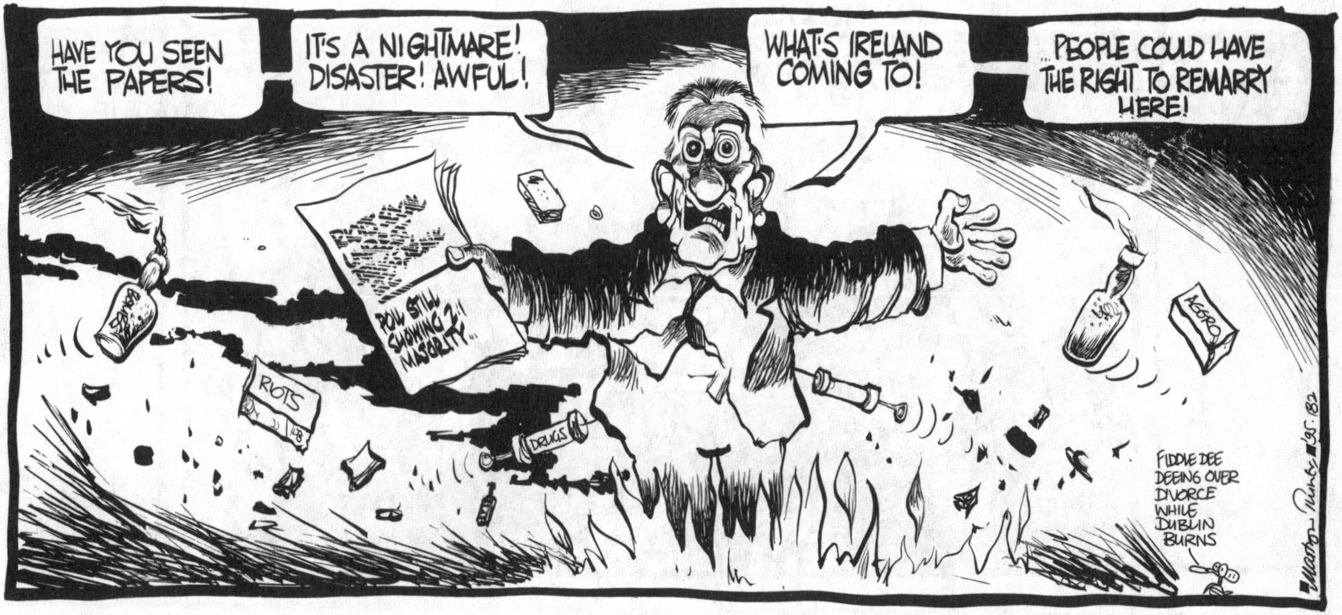
HAVE YOU SEEN THE PAPERS!
IT'S A NIGHTMARE! DISASTER! AWFUL!
WHAT'S IRELAND COMING TO!
...PEOPLE COULD HAVE THE RIGHT TO REMARRY HERE!
POLL STILL SHOWING 2:1 MAJORITY...
RIOTS
DRUGS
AGGRO
FIDDLE DEE DEEING OVER DIVORCE WHILE DUBLIN BURNS

SINCE THE LAST OPINION POLL SUPPORT FOR THE RIGHT TO REMARRY HAS DROPPED......
SINCE THE LAST OPINION POLL ALL THE DAIL PARTIES HAVE BEGUN TO CAMPAIGN IN FAVOUR OF THE RIGHT TO REMARRY.........
FF YES
DL YES
FG YES
LAB YES
PD YES
GREEN YES
...DRAW YOUR OWN CONCLUSIONS...
C'MON PEOPLE.. JUST 'COS THEY'RE POLITICIANS IT DOESN'T AUTOMATICALLY MEAN THEY'RE WRONG

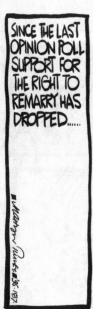

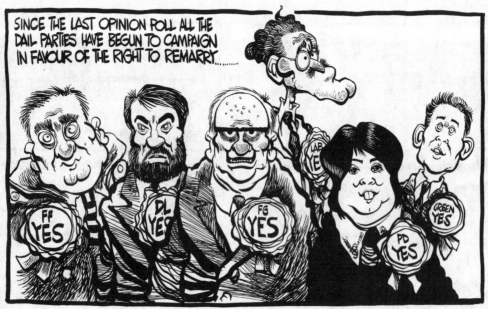

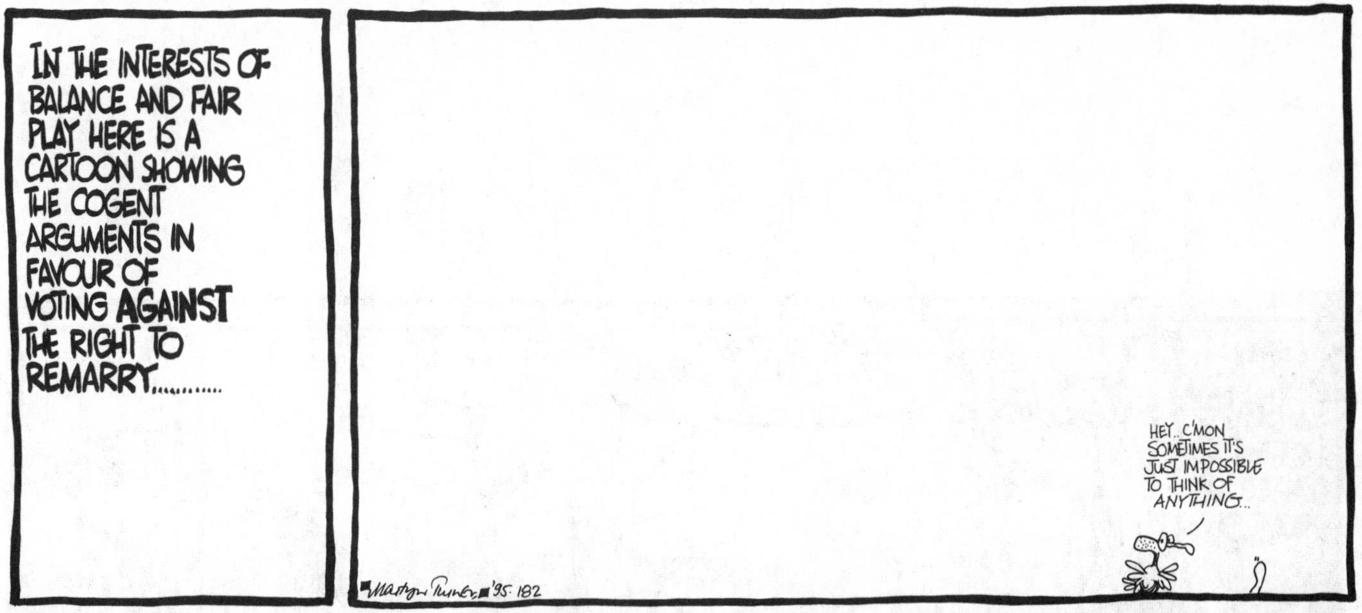
IN THE INTERESTS OF BALANCE AND FAIR PLAY HERE IS A CARTOON SHOWING THE COGENT ARGUMENTS IN FAVOUR OF VOTING AGAINST THE RIGHT TO REMARRY.........
HEY.. C'MON SOMETIMES IT'S JUST IMPOSSIBLE TO THINK OF ANYTHING..

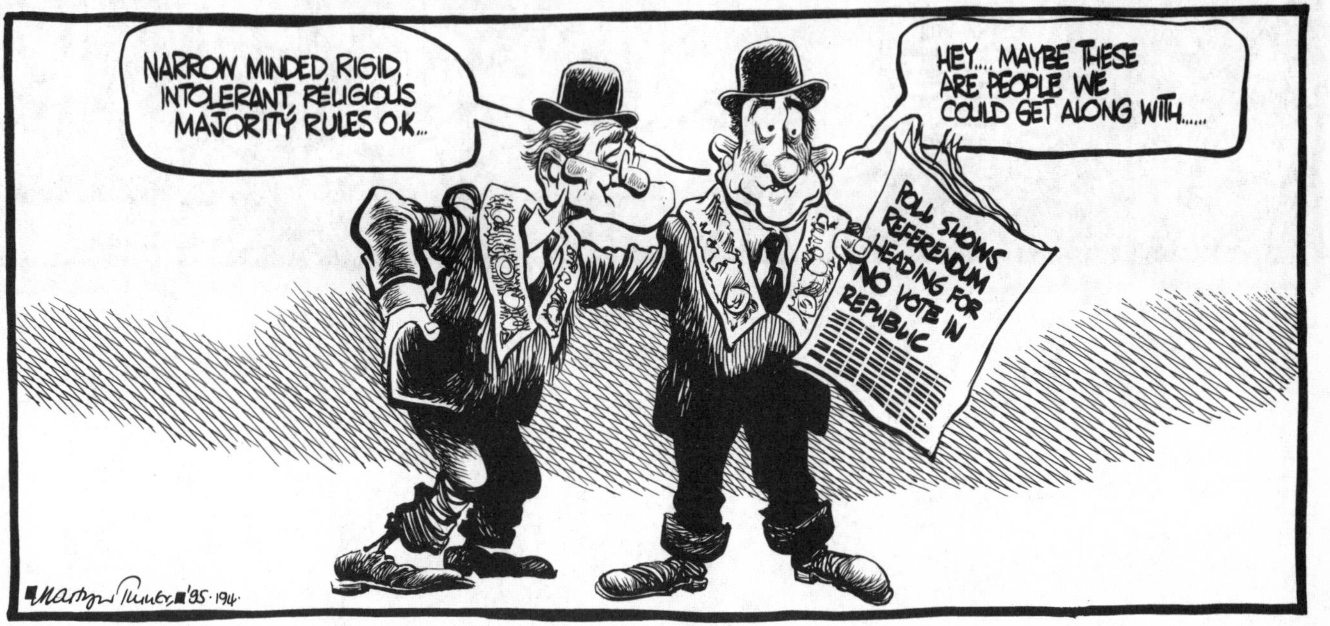
NARROW MINDED, RIGID, INTOLERANT, RELIGIOUS MAJORITY RULES O.K...
HEY.... MAYBE THESE ARE PEOPLE WE COULD GET ALONG WITH......
POLL SHOWS REFERENDUM HEADING FOR NO VOTE IN REPUBLIC

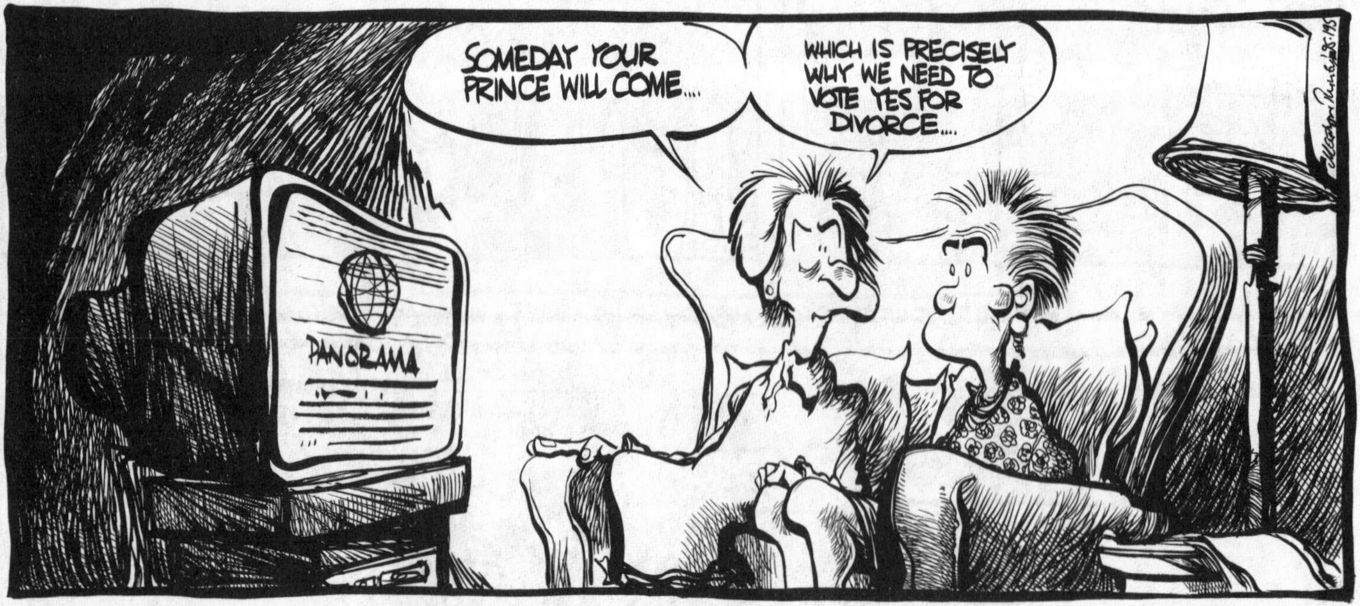
SOMEDAY YOUR PRINCE WILL COME....
WHICH IS PRECISELY WHY WE NEED TO VOTE YES FOR DIVORCE....
PANORAMA

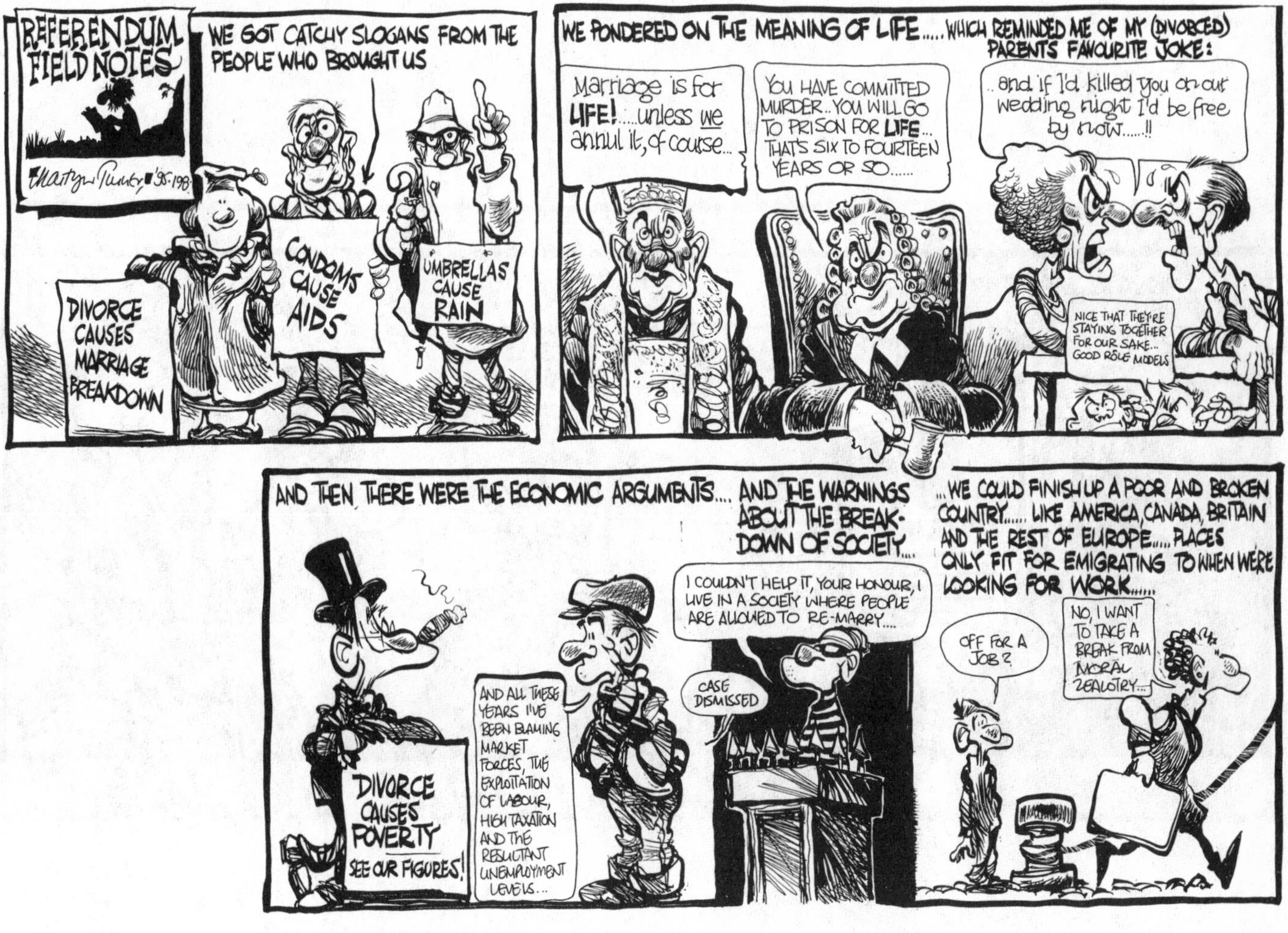
REFERENDUM FIELD NOTES
WE GOT CATCHY SLOGANS FROM THE PEOPLE WHO BROUGHT US
DIVORCE CAUSES MARRIAGE BREAKDOWN
CONDOMS CAUSE AIDS
UMBRELLAS CAUSE RAIN
WE PONDERED ON THE MEANING OF LIFE..... WHICH REMINDED ME OF MY (DIVORCED) PARENTS' FAVOURITE JOKE:
Marriage is for LIFE!.....unless we annul it, of course...
YOU HAVE COMMITTED MURDER.. YOU WILL GO TO PRISON FOR LIFE... THAT'S SIX TO FOURTEEN YEARS OR SO......
..and if I'd killed you on our wedding night I'd be free by now......!!
NICE THAT THEY'RE STAYING TOGETHER FOR OUR SAKE... GOOD RÔLE MODELS
AND THEN, THERE WERE THE ECONOMIC ARGUMENTS....
DIVORCE CAUSES POVERTY
SEE OUR FIGURES!
AND ALL THESE YEARS I'VE BEEN BLAMING MARKET FORCES, THE EXPLOITATION OF LABOUR, HIGH TAXATION AND THE RESULTANT UNEMPLOYMENT LEVELS...
AND THE WARNINGS ABOUT THE BREAK-DOWN OF SOCIETY....
I COULDN'T HELP IT, YOUR HONOUR, I LIVE IN A SOCIETY WHERE PEOPLE ARE ALLOWED TO RE-MARRY....
CASE DISMISSED
...WE COULD FINISH UP A POOR AND BROKEN COUNTRY...... LIKE AMERICA, CANADA, BRITAIN AND THE REST OF EUROPE..... PLACES ONLY FIT FOR EMIGRATING TO WHEN WE'RE LOOKING FOR WORK......
OFF FOR A JOB?
NO, I WANT TO TAKE A BREAK FROM MORAL ZEALOTRY...

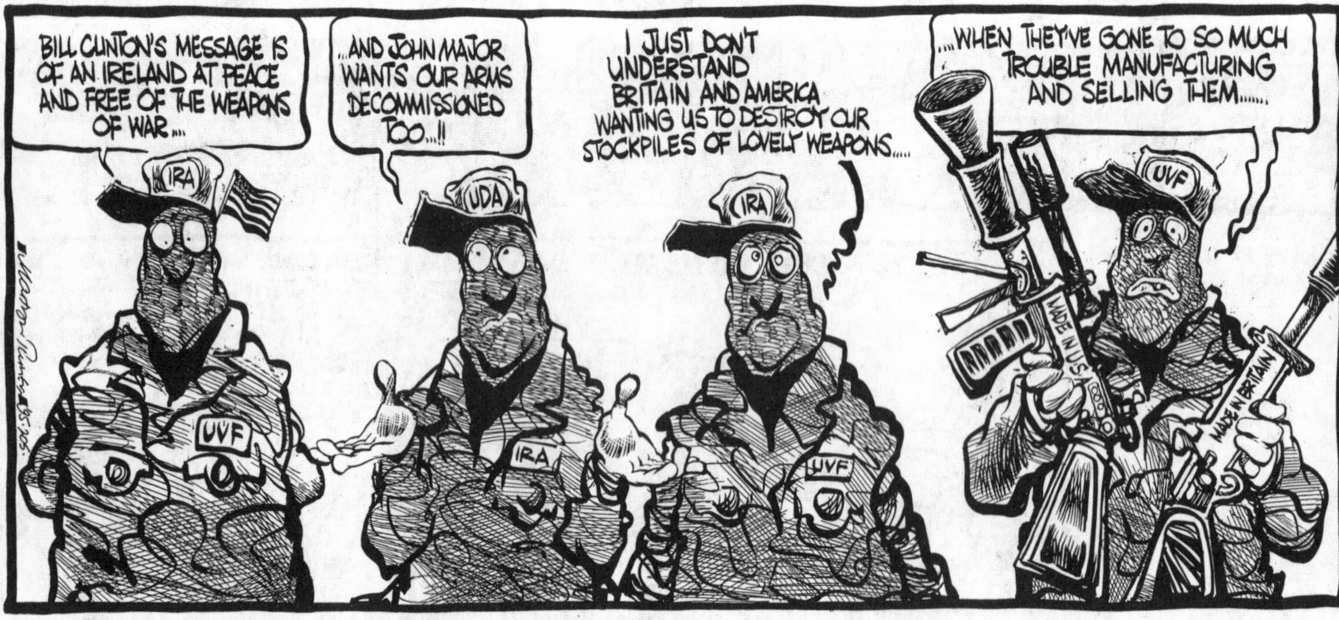
BILL CLINTON'S MESSAGE IS OF AN IRELAND AT PEACE AND FREE OF THE WEAPONS OF WAR...
...AND JOHN MAJOR WANTS OUR ARMS DECOMMISSIONED TOO...!!
I JUST DON'T UNDERSTAND BRITAIN AND AMERICA WANTING US TO DESTROY OUR STOCKPILES OF LOVELY WEAPONS....
...WHEN THEY'VE GONE TO SO MUCH TROUBLE MANUFACTURING AND SELLING THEM......
IRA
UVF
UDA
IRA
IRA
UVF
UVF
MADE IN USA
MADE IN BRITAIN

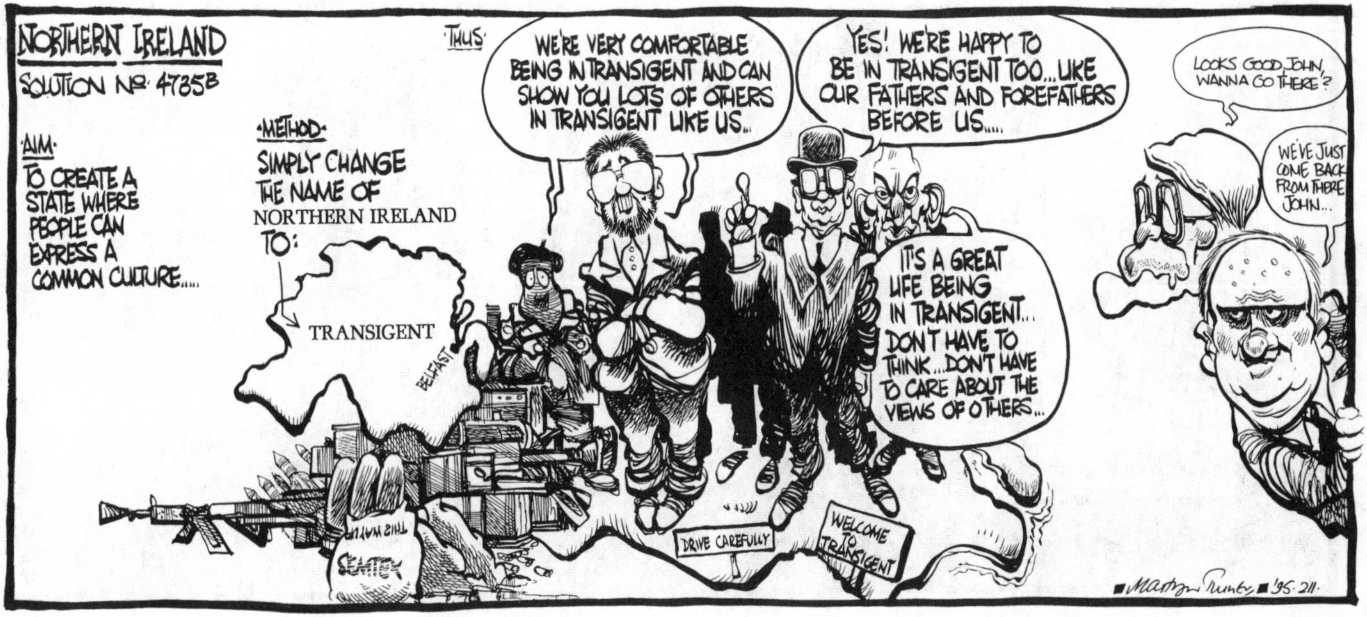
NORTHERN IRELAND
SOLUTION No. 4785B
·AIM·
TO CREATE A STATE WHERE PEOPLE CAN EXPRESS A COMMON CULTURE.....
·METHOD·
SIMPLY CHANGE THE NAME OF NORTHERN IRELAND TO:
TRANSIGENT
BELFAST
·THUS·
WE'RE VERY COMFORTABLE BEING IN TRANSIGENT AND CAN SHOW YOU LOTS OF OTHERS IN TRANSIGENT LIKE US...
YES! WE'RE HAPPY TO BE IN TRANSIGENT TOO...LIKE OUR FATHERS AND FOREFATHERS BEFORE US.....
IT'S A GREAT LIFE BEING IN TRANSIGENT... DON'T HAVE TO THINK...DON'T HAVE TO CARE ABOUT THE VIEWS OF OTHERS...
LOOKS GOOD JOHN, WANNA GO THERE?
WE'VE JUST COME BACK FROM THERE JOHN...
SEMTEX
THIS WAY UP
DRIVE CAREFULLY
WELCOME TO TRANSIGENT
Martyn Turner '95 211

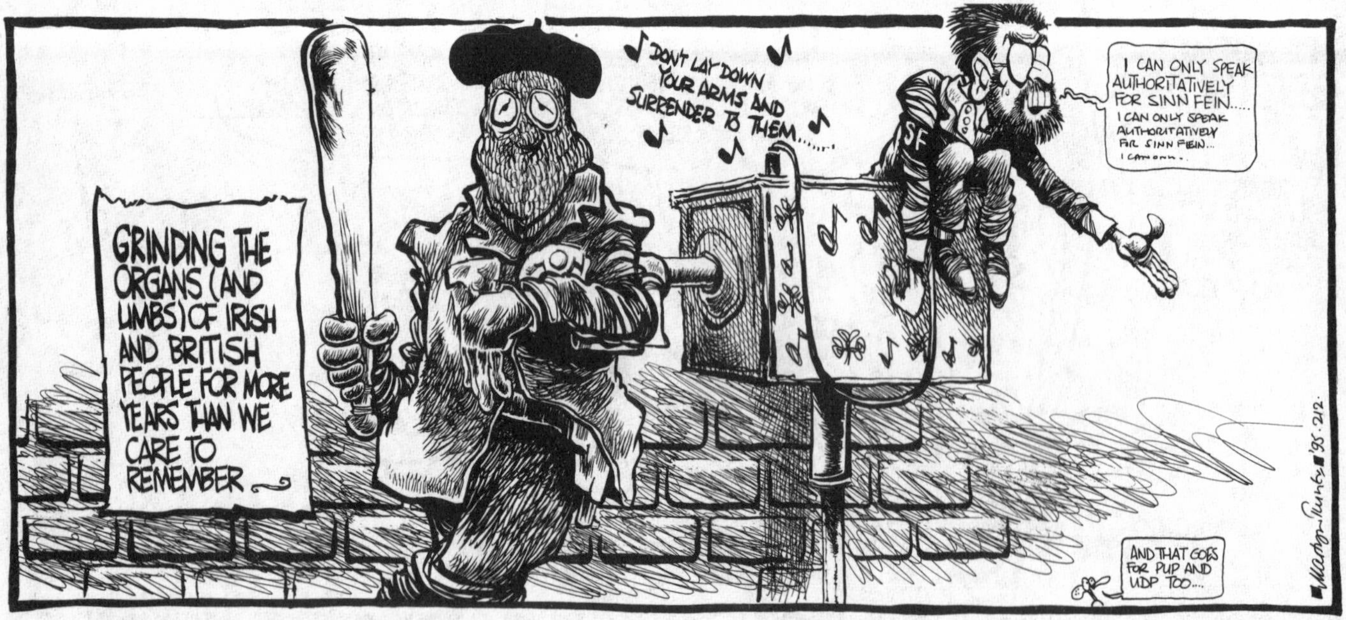
GRINDING THE ORGANS (AND LIMBS) OF IRISH AND BRITISH PEOPLE FOR MORE YEARS THAN WE CARE TO REMEMBER
DON'T LAY DOWN YOUR ARMS AND SURRENDER TO THEM.....
SF
I CAN ONLY SPEAK AUTHORITATIVELY FOR SINN FEIN..... I CAN ONLY SPEAK AUTHORITATIVELY FOR SINN FEIN...
AND THAT GOES FOR PUP AND UDP TOO...

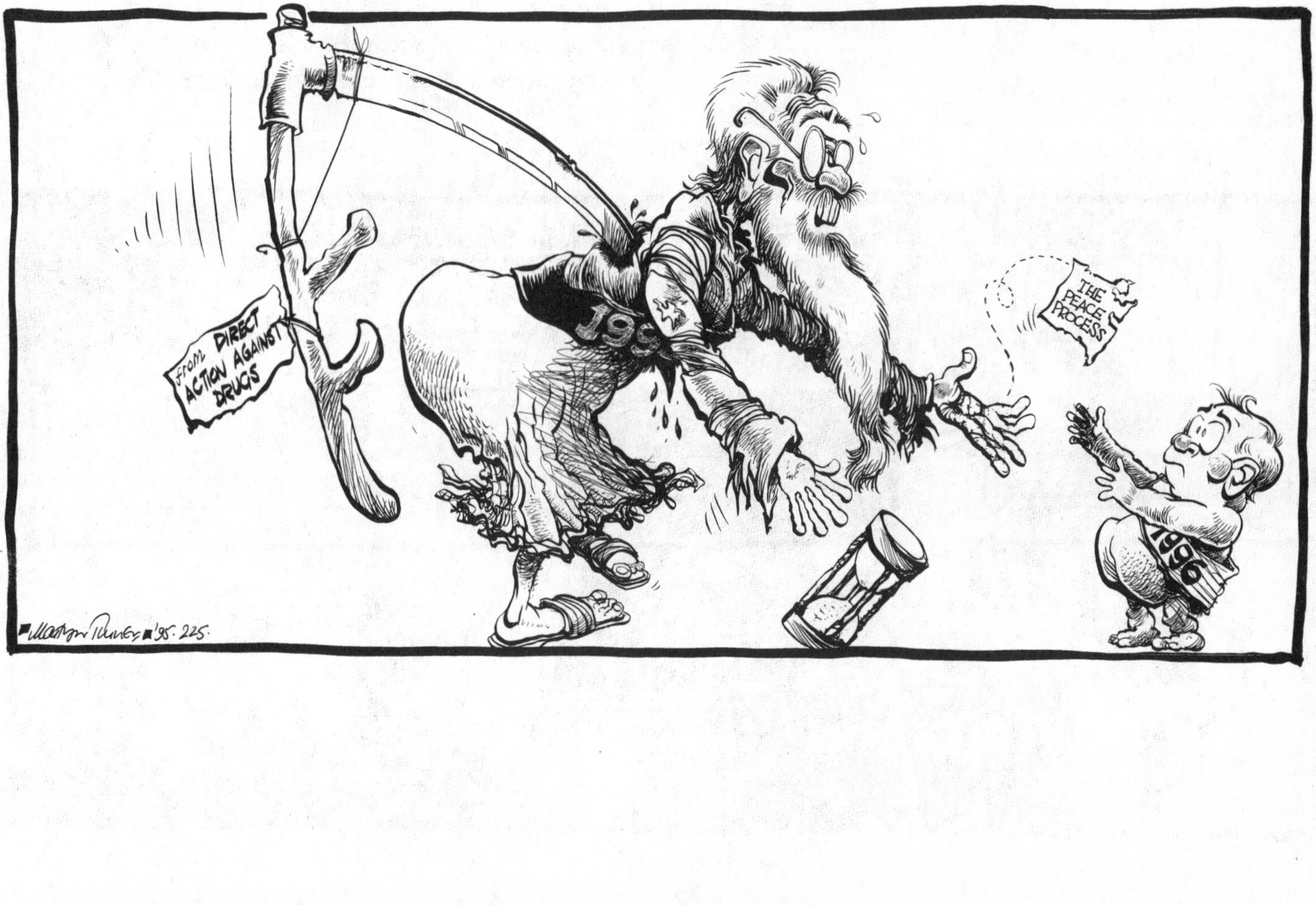
from DIRECT ACTION AGAINST DRUGS
1995
THE PEACE PROCESS
1996
Martyn Turner '95. 225.

1996

The British government's response to the Mitchell Report and the threat of elections, negotiations and compromise, so horrified the republican movement that they retreated back to what they know best – bombs, violence and sermons on 'peace and the way forward'. Later in the year, following Drumcree, we all, north and south, east and west, retreated back to what we know best – tribalism and sectarianism. Light relief came from the mad cow debate, the mad cow war, mad media cows in the British tabloids, and the ongoing adventures of Michael Lowry. Dark relief came from Israel, which conducted its elections by bombing southern Lebanon, and the struggle for peace in Bosnia and the North continued to display all the tell-tale signs of mad people disease.

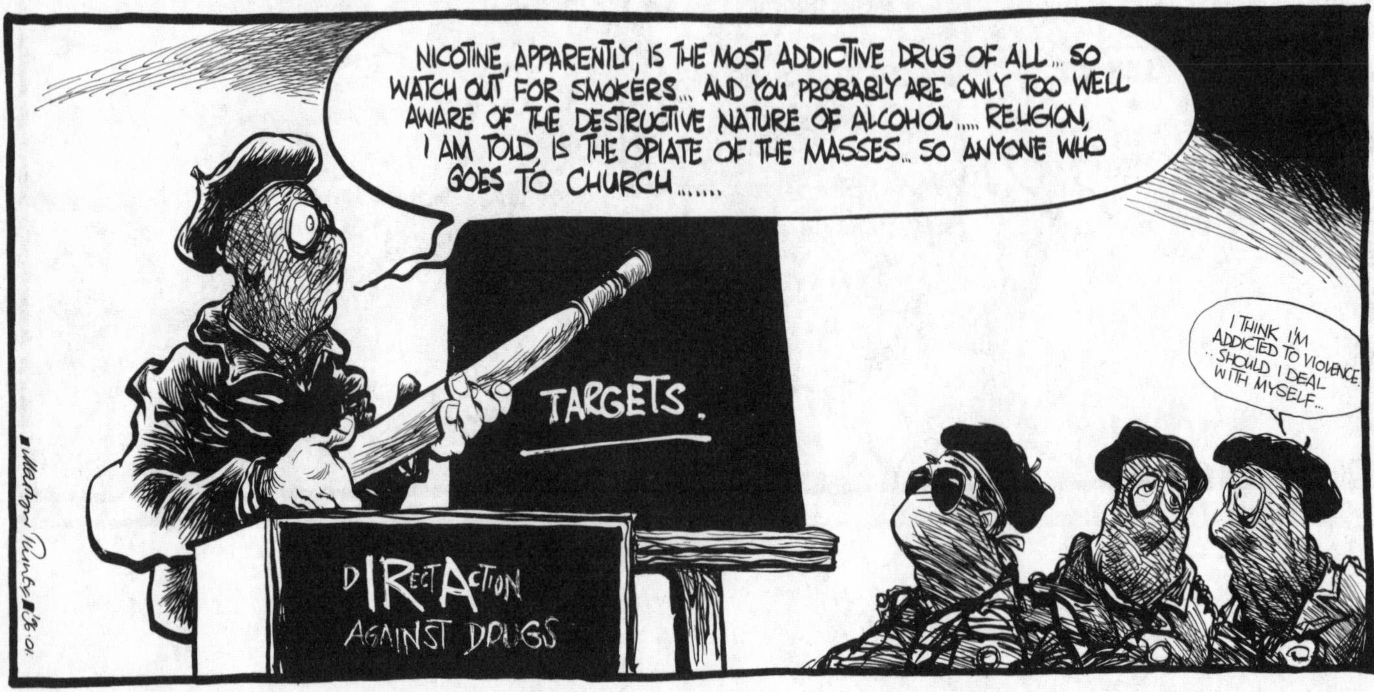
NICOTINE, APPARENTLY, IS THE MOST ADDICTIVE DRUG OF ALL... SO WATCH OUT FOR SMOKERS... AND YOU PROBABLY ARE ONLY TOO WELL AWARE OF THE DESTRUCTIVE NATURE OF ALCOHOL..... RELIGION, I AM TOLD, IS THE OPIATE OF THE MASSES... SO ANYONE WHO GOES TO CHURCH......
TARGETS.
DIRECT ACTION AGAINST DRUGS
I THINK I'M ADDICTED TO VIOLENCE.. SHOULD I DEAL WITH MYSELF...

At the Olympics those few medals that weren't won by Michelle Smith were gained by Americans of Colour . . . Americans of No Colour were occupied elsewhere marketing and selling arms and worrying about terrorism. Tony Blair smiled a lot and said a little; John Major said a lot and smiled little. In the South we had drugs, crime bosses, law and order and lots and lots of strange court cases – which is what we do best.

Martyn Turner '96·02·
WHAT SINN FEIN MUST REALISE IS THAT PEOPLE CONNECTED WITH SUMMARY JUSTICE, CRUEL AND VIOLENT PUNISHMENTS....
..AND LACK OF FULL DEMOCRATIC PROCEDURES CANNOT EXPECT TO ENGAGE FULLY WITH THE BRITISH GOVERNMENT.....
....UNLESS IT'S GOOD FOR BUSINESS, OF COURSE.....
SAUDI ARABIA
CHINA
CHINA

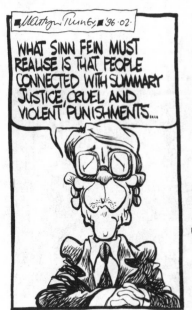

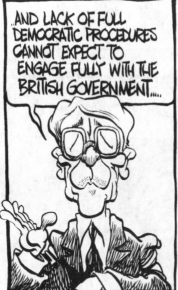

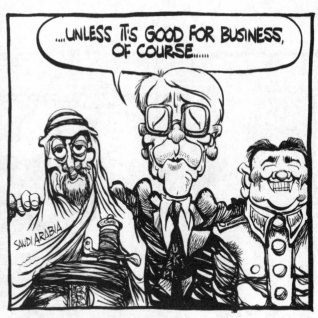

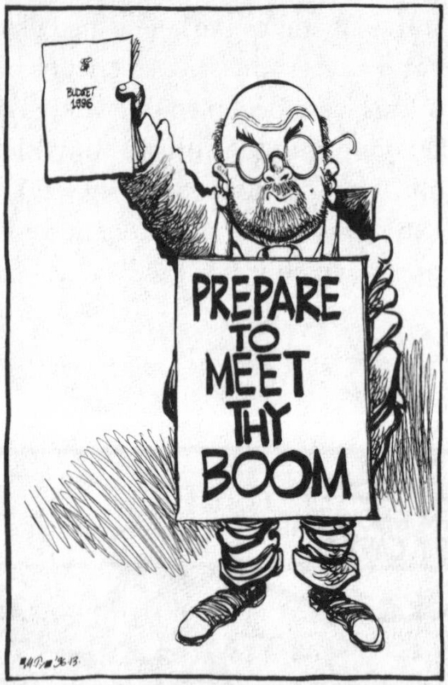
BUDGET
1996
PREPARE
TO
MEET
THY
BOOM

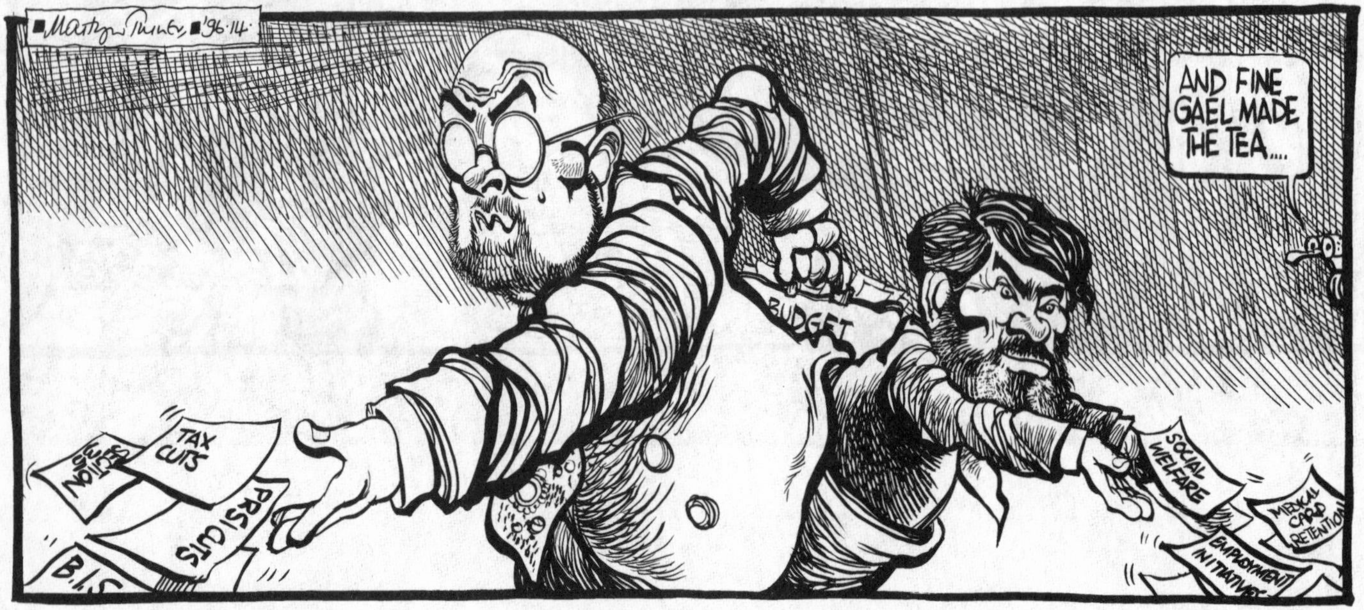
Martyn Turner '96·14·
AND FINE GAEL MADE THE TEA....
BUDGET
TAX CUTS
PRSI CUTS
SOCIAL WELFARE
MEDICAL CARD RETENTION
EMPLOYMENT INITIATIVES

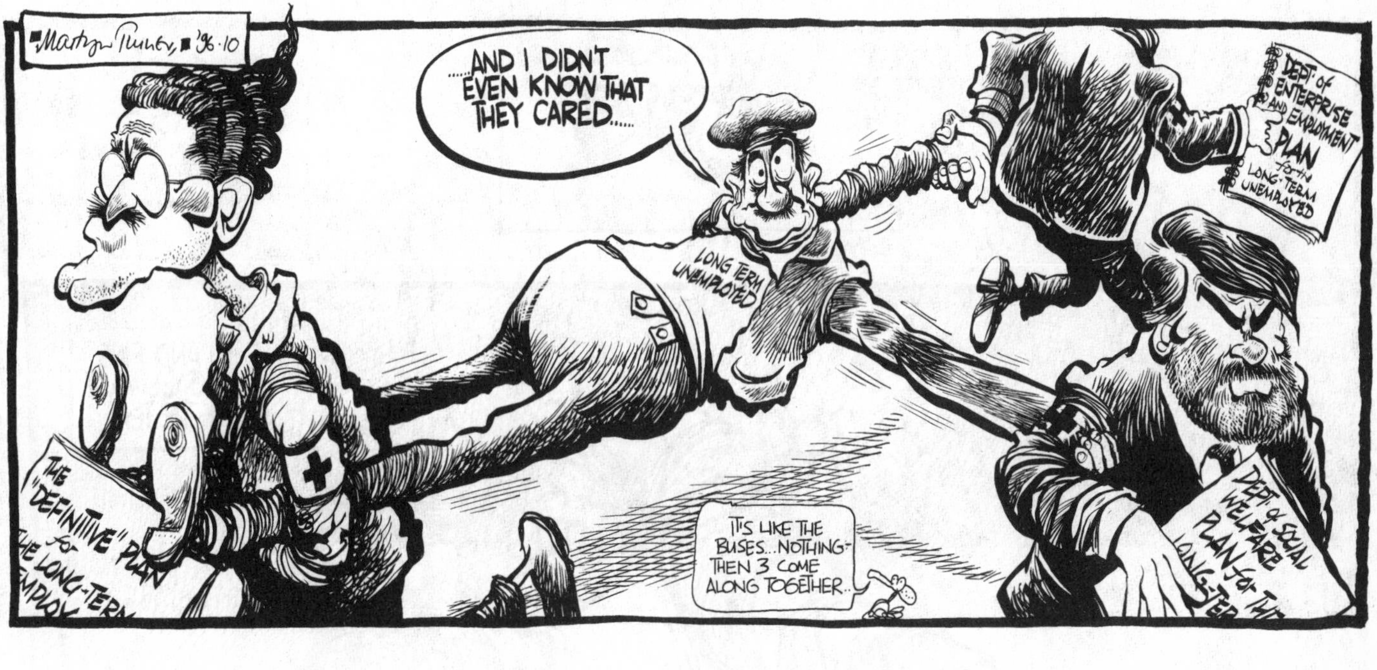
Martyn Turner '98.10
THE "DEFINITIVE" PLAN for THE LONG-TERM
...AND I DIDN'T EVEN KNOW THAT THEY CARED.....
LONG TERM UNEMPLOYED
DEPT. of ENTERPRISE AND EMPLOYMENT PLAN for the LONG-TERM UNEMPLOYED
DEPT. of SOCIAL WELFARE PLAN for THE
IT'S LIKE THE BUSES...NOTHING- THEN 3 COME ALONG TOGETHER..

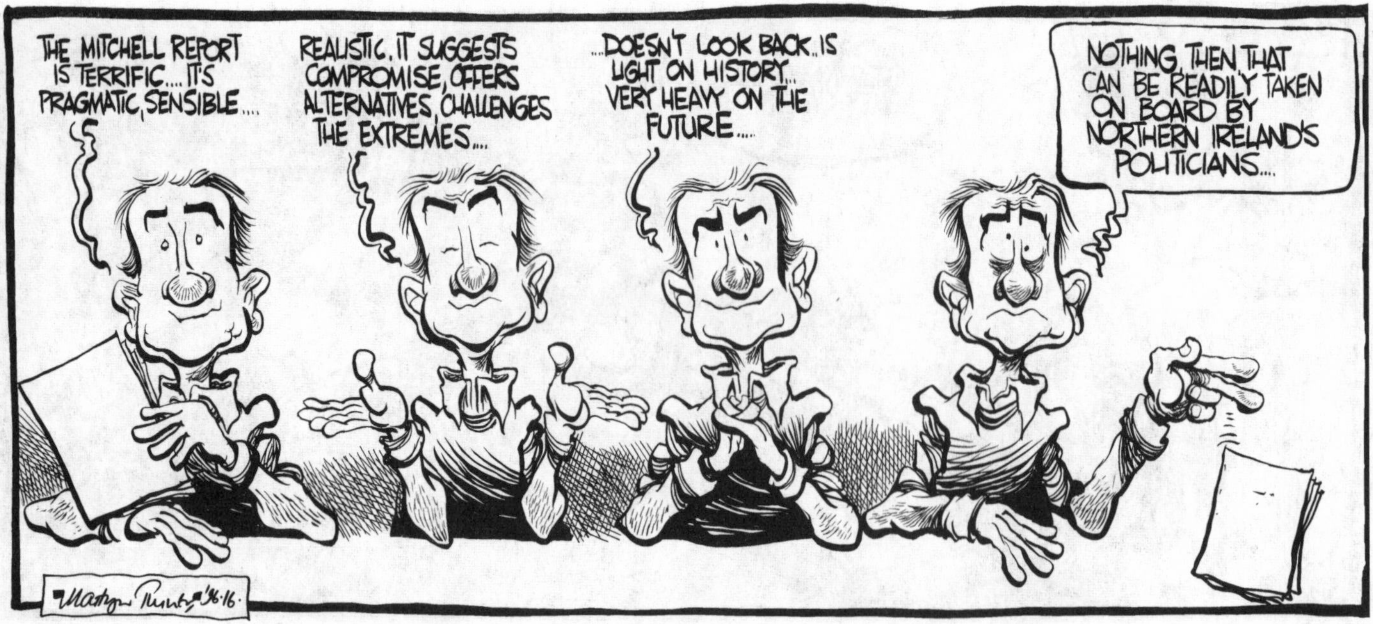
THE MITCHELL REPORT IS TERRIFIC.... IT'S PRAGMATIC, SENSIBLE....
REALISTIC. IT SUGGESTS COMPROMISE, OFFERS ALTERNATIVES, CHALLENGES THE EXTREMES....
....DOESN'T LOOK BACK.. IS LIGHT ON HISTORY... VERY HEAVY ON THE FUTURE.....
NOTHING, THEN, THAT CAN BE READILY TAKEN ON BOARD BY NORTHERN IRELAND'S POLITICIANS....
'96·16·

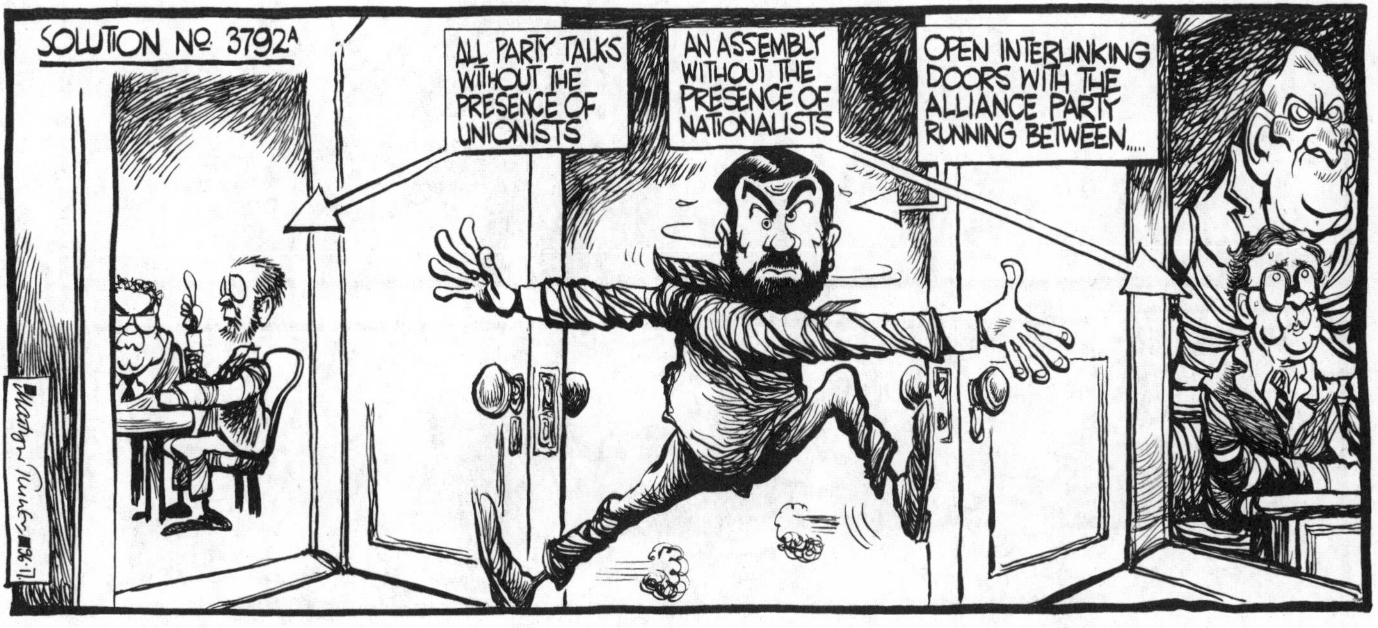
SOLUTION No. 3792A
ALL PARTY TALKS WITHOUT THE PRESENCE OF UNIONISTS
AN ASSEMBLY WITHOUT THE PRESENCE OF NATIONALISTS
OPEN INTERLINKING DOORS WITH THE ALLIANCE PARTY RUNNING BETWEEN.....

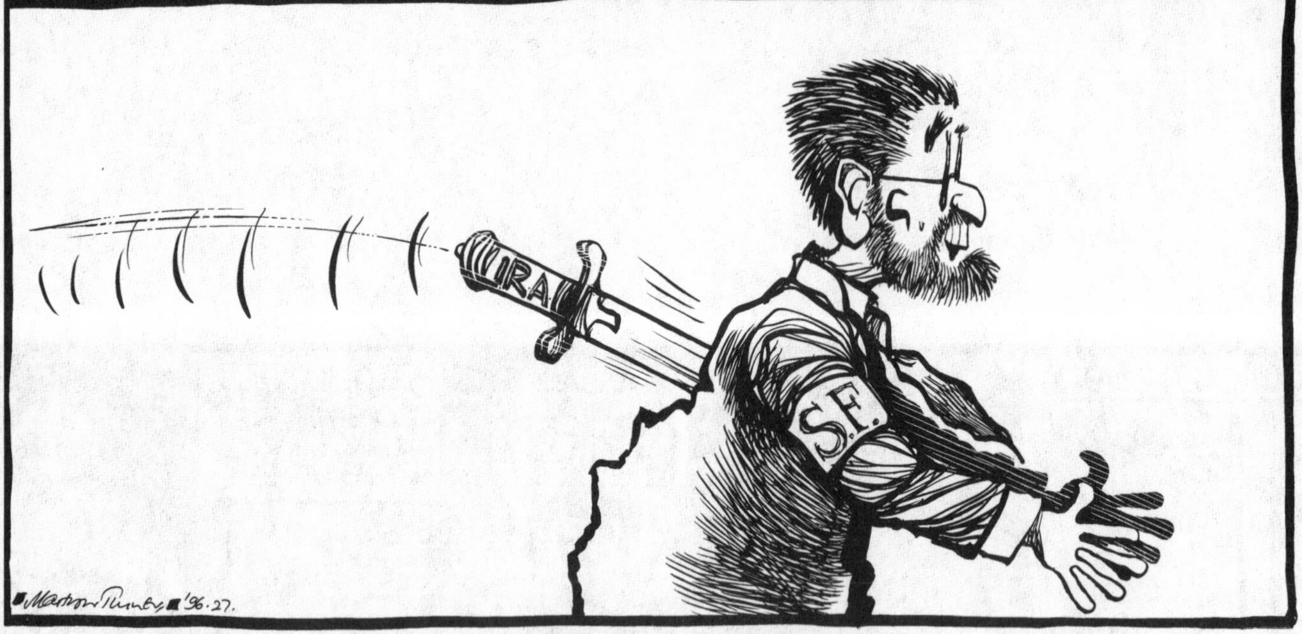
I.R.A.
S.F.

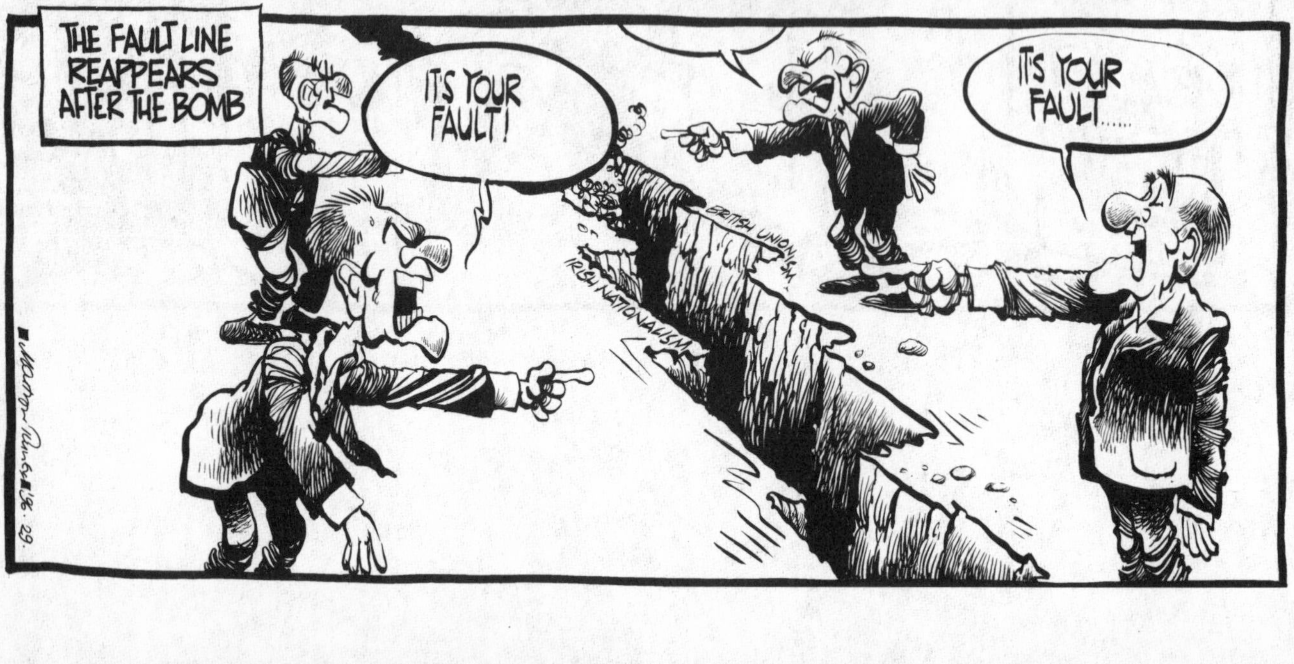
THE FAULT LINE REAPPEARS AFTER THE BOMB
IT'S YOUR FAULT!
IT'S YOUR FAULT......
BRITISH UNIONISM
IRISH NATIONALISM

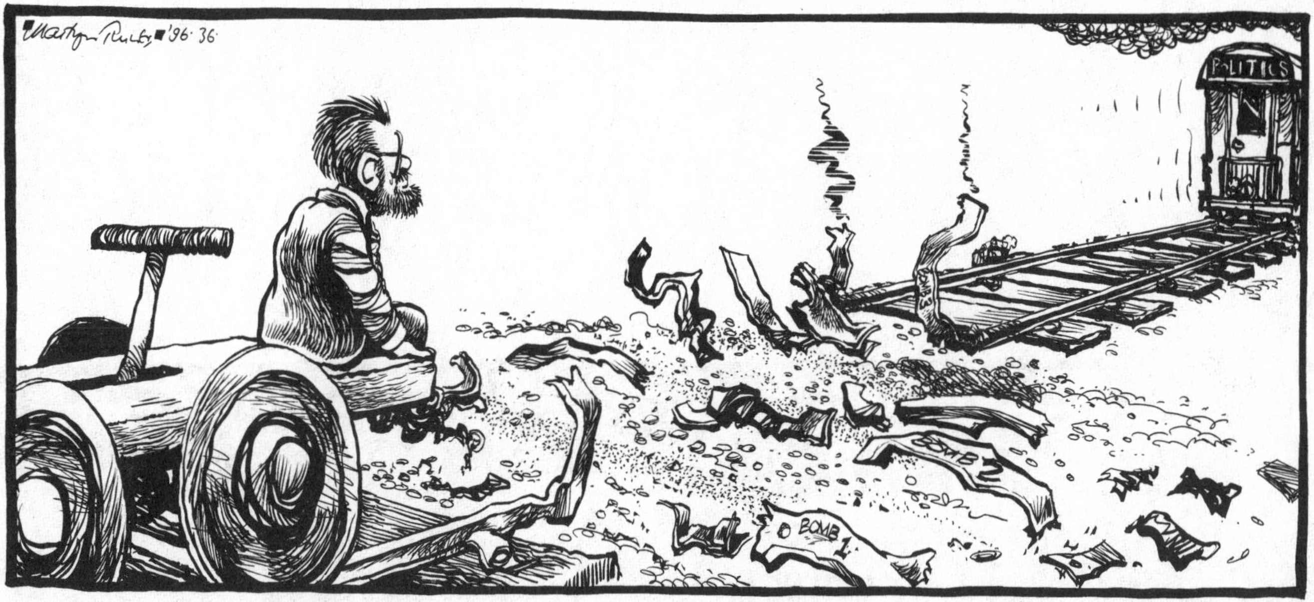
Martyn Turner '96 36
POLITICS
BOMB 2
BOMB 1

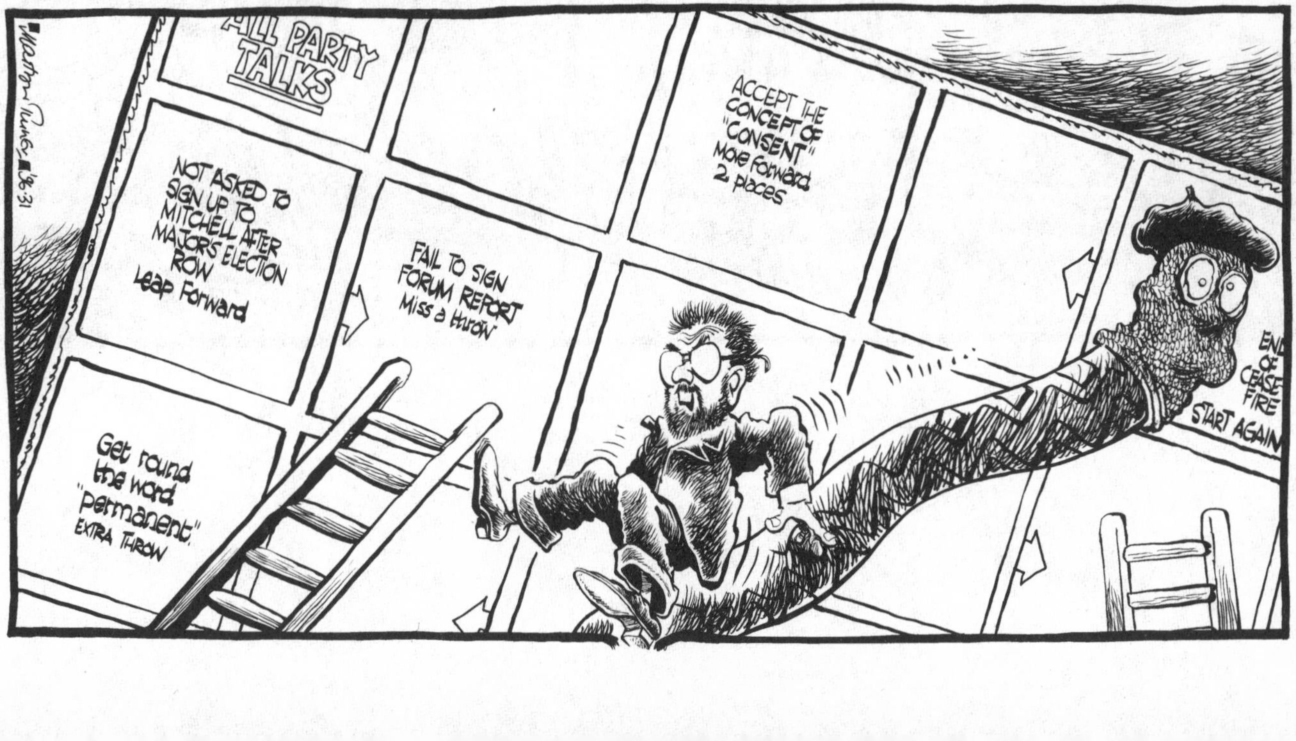
Martyn Turner '96 31
ALL PARTY TALKS
NOT ASKED TO SIGN UP TO MITCHELL AFTER MAJORS ELECTION ROW
Leap Forward
FAIL TO SIGN FORUM REPORT
Miss a throw
ACCEPT THE CONCEPT OF "CONSENT"
Move forward 2 places
Get round the word "permanent"
EXTRA THROW
END OF CEASE FIRE
START AGAIN

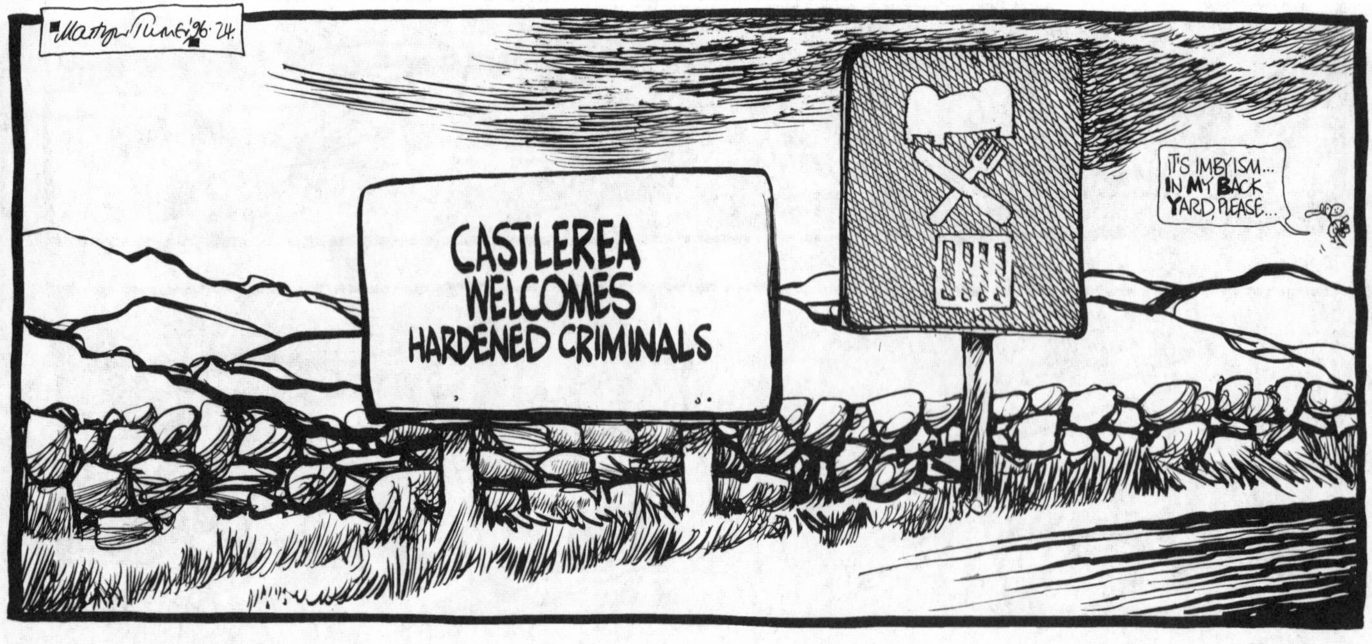
CASTLEREA
WELCOMES
HARDENED CRIMINALS
IT'S IMBYISM...
IN MY BACK
YARD, PLEASE...

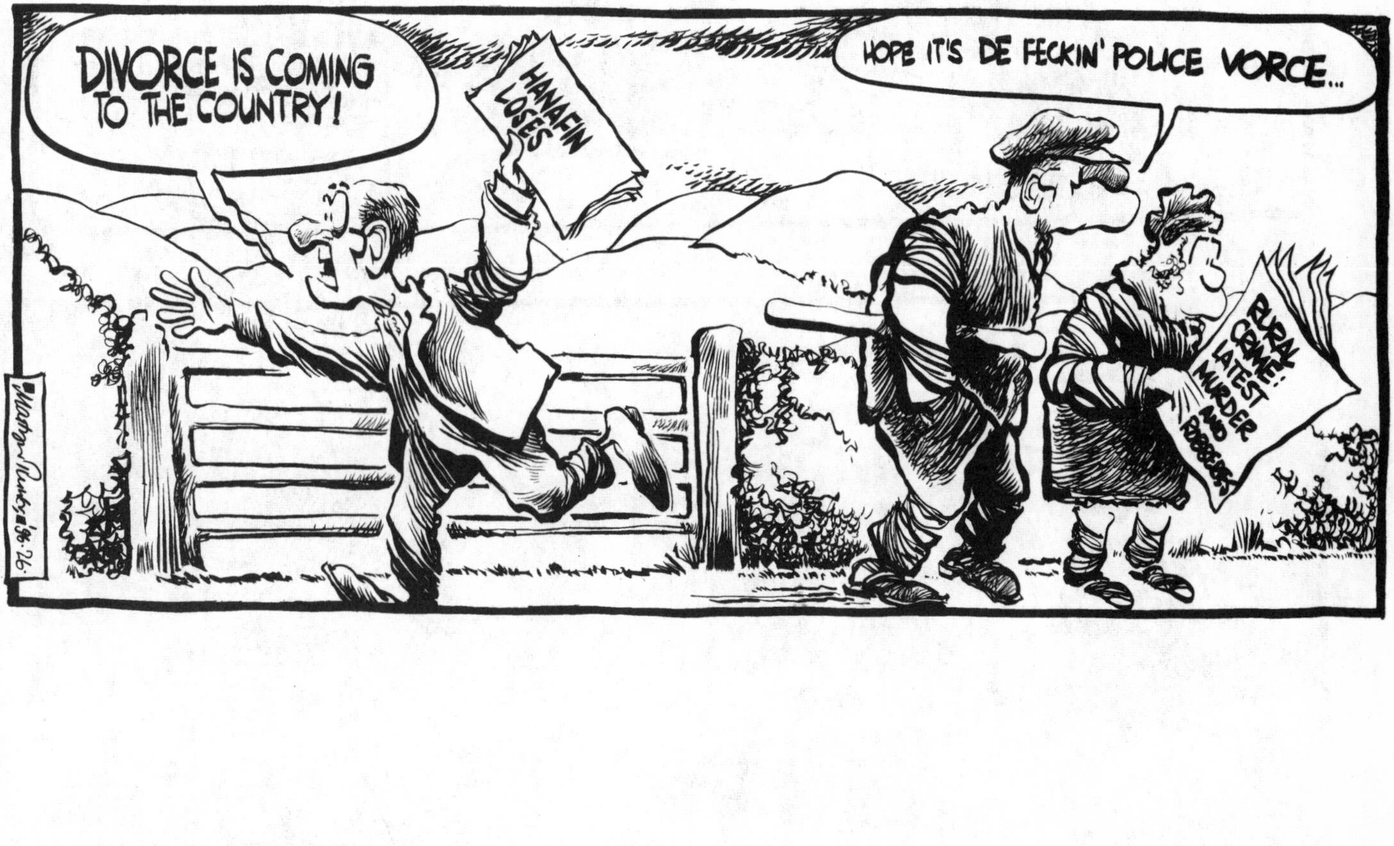
DIVORCE IS COMING TO THE COUNTRY!
HANAFIN LOSES
HOPE IT'S DE FECKIN' POLICE VORCE...
RURAL CRIME! LATEST MURDER AND ROBBERIES

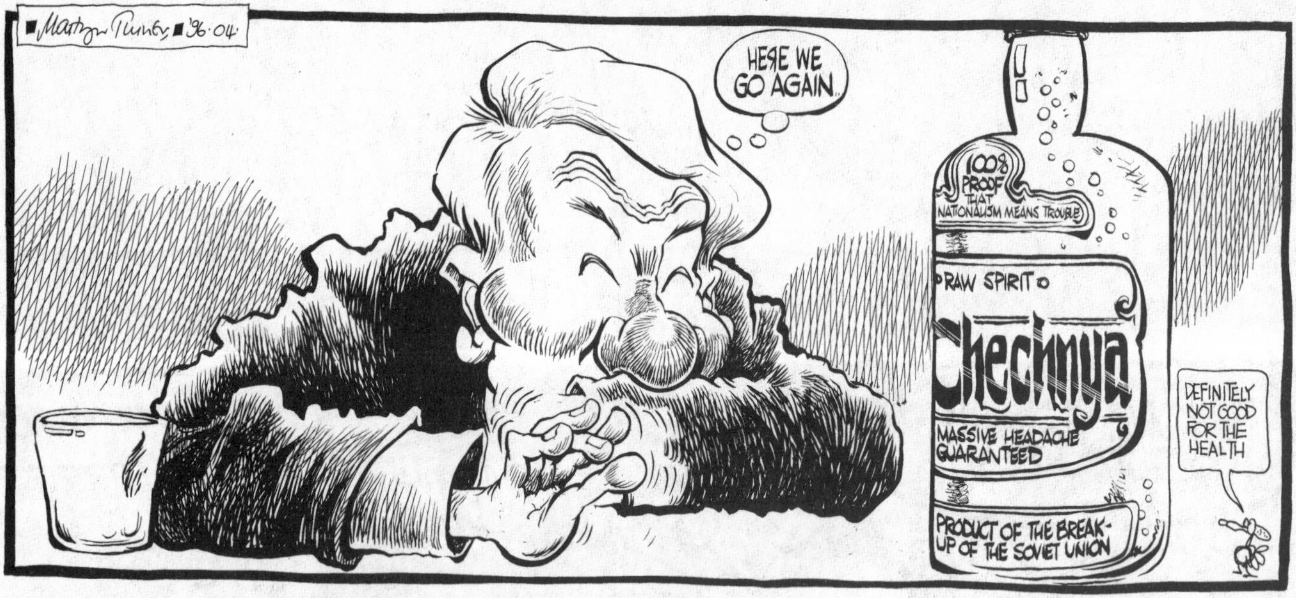
Martyn Turner '96·04
HERE WE GO AGAIN...
100% PROOF THAT NATIONALISM MEANS TROUBLE
RAW SPIRIT
Chechnya
MASSIVE HEADACHE GUARANTEED
PRODUCT OF THE BREAK-UP OF THE SOVIET UNION
DEFINITELY NOT GOOD FOR THE HEALTH

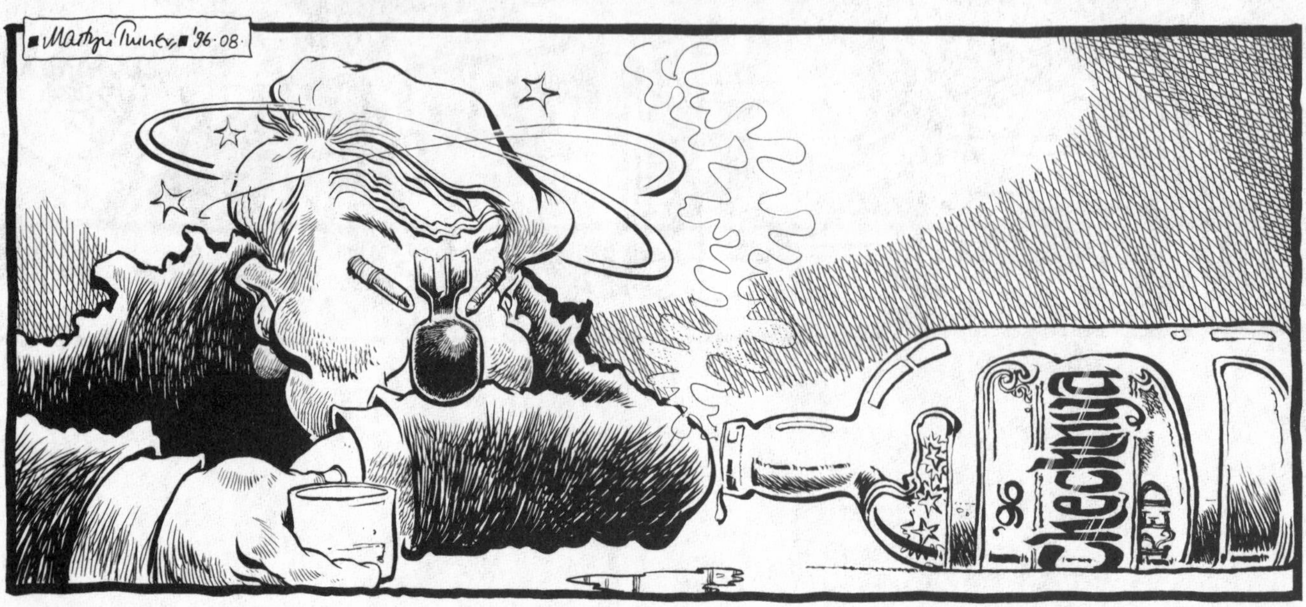
Martyn Turner '96·08
'96
Chechnya
RED

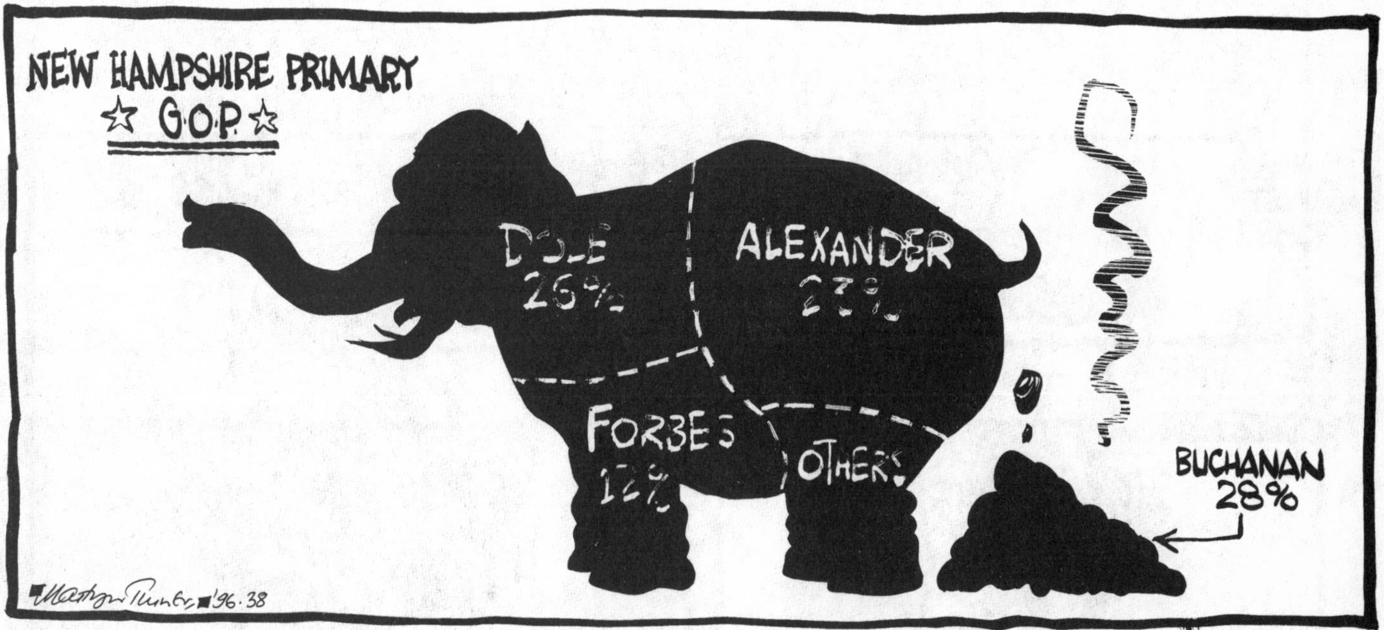
NEW HAMPSHIRE PRIMARY
G.O.P.
DOLE
26%
ALEXANDER
23%
FORBES
12%
OTHERS
BUCHANAN
28%

THE WAR AGAINST DRUGS
LET'S GET THE GUYS THAT PRODUCE THEM!
LET'S GET THE PEOPLE THAT SELL THEM
GOVERN-MENTS
BUSINESS
THE WAR AGAINST GUNS
LET'S GET THE CRAZIES THAT USE THEM....
WANNA BUY SOME?

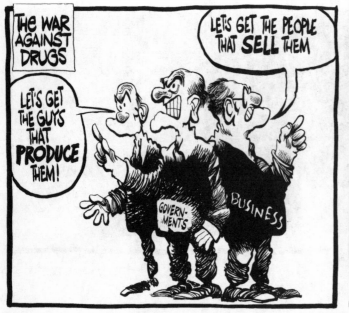

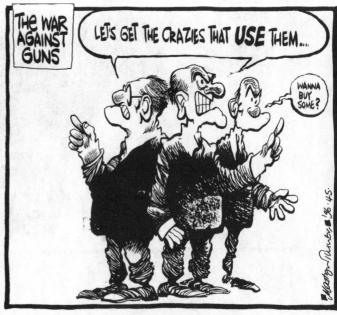

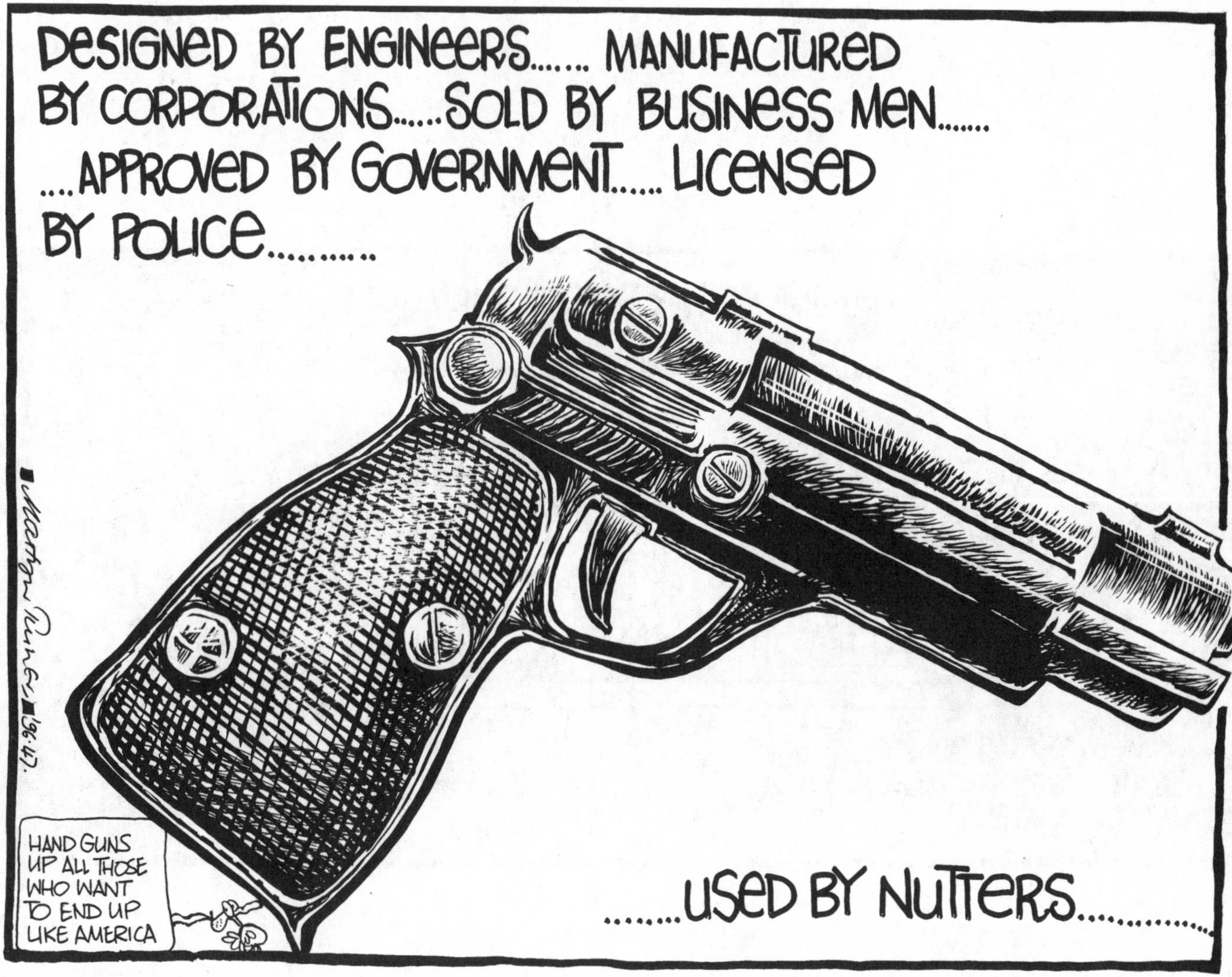
DESIGNED BY ENGINEERS...... MANUFACTURED BY CORPORATIONS..... SOLD BY BUSINESS MEN...... ....APPROVED BY GOVERNMENT...... LICENSED BY POLICE..........
HAND GUNS UP ALL THOSE WHO WANT TO END UP LIKE AMERICA
.......USED BY NUTTERS..............

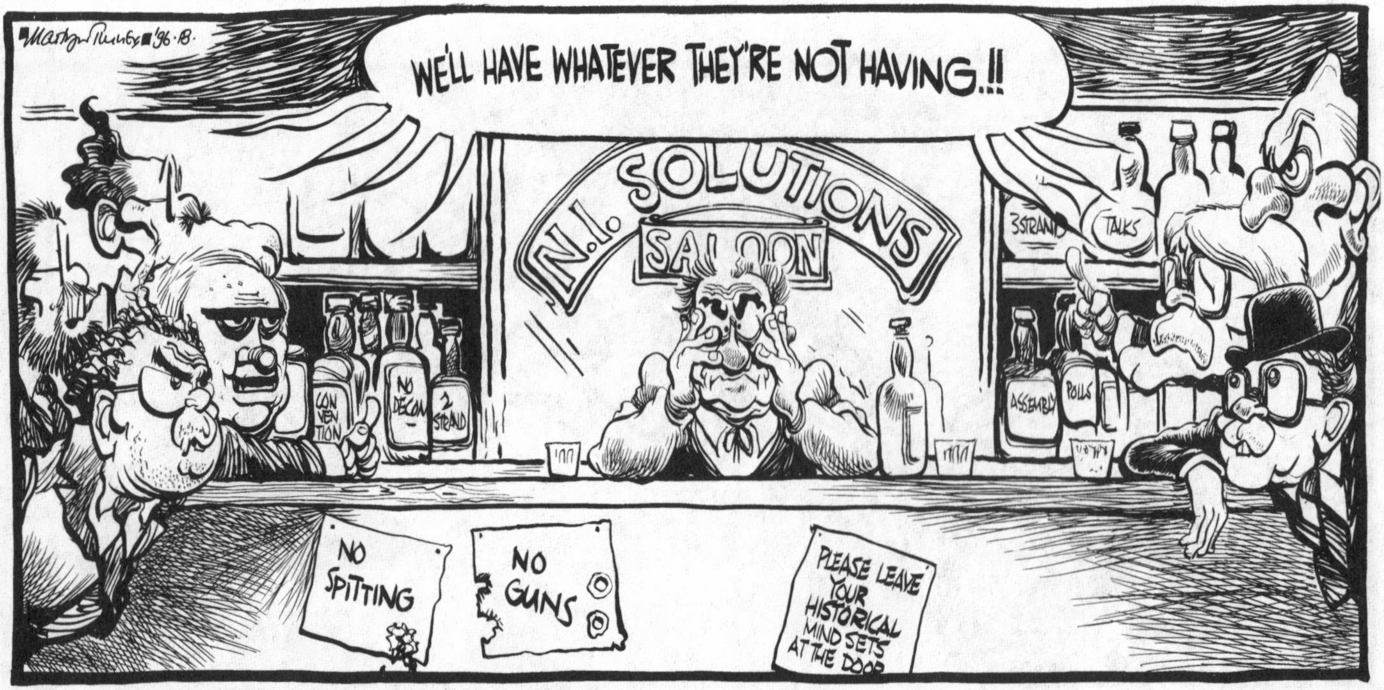
WE'LL HAVE WHATEVER THEY'RE NOT HAVING.!!
N.I. SOLUTIONS
SALOON
CONVENTION
NO DECON
2 STRAND
3 STRAND
TALKS
ASSEMBLY
POLLS
NO SPITTING
NO GUNS
PLEASE LEAVE YOUR HISTORICAL MIND SETS AT THE DOOR

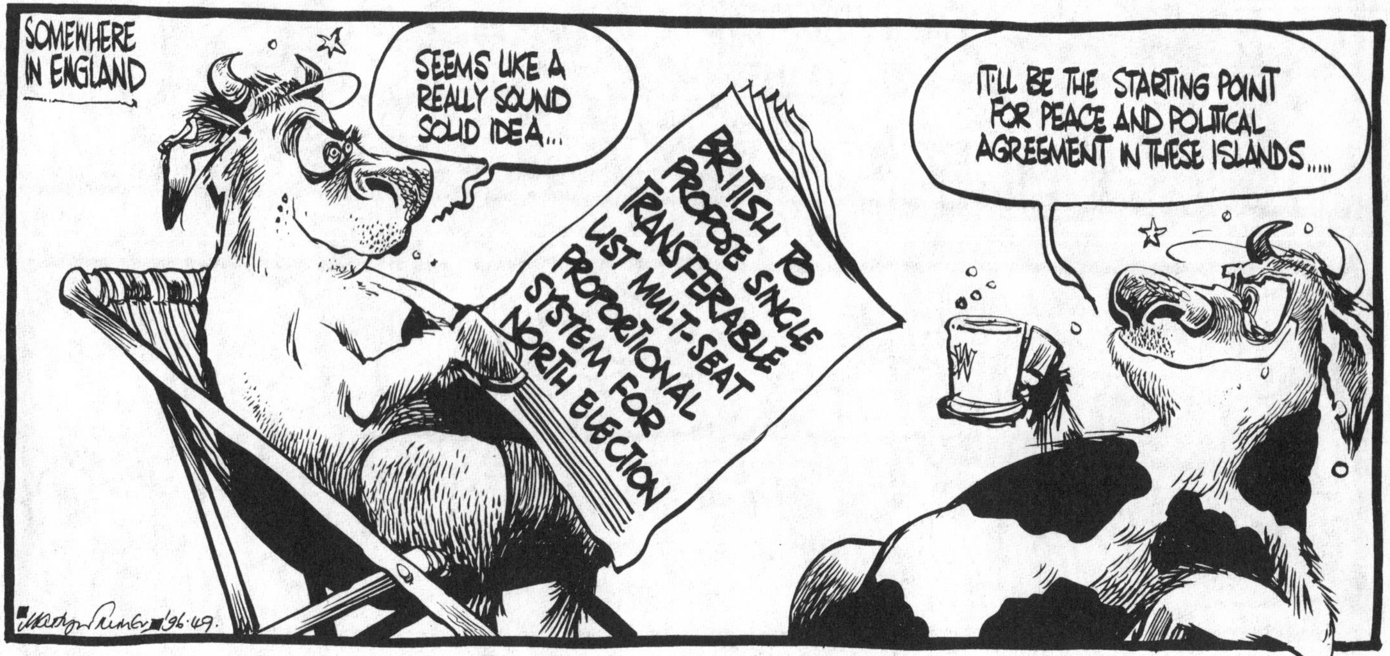
SOMEWHERE IN ENGLAND
SEEMS LIKE A REALLY SOUND SOLID IDEA...
BRITISH TO PROPOSE SINGLE TRANSFERABLE LIST MULTI-SEAT PROPORTIONAL SYSTEM FOR NORTH ELECTION
IT'LL BE THE STARTING POINT FOR PEACE AND POLITICAL AGREEMENT IN THESE ISLANDS.....

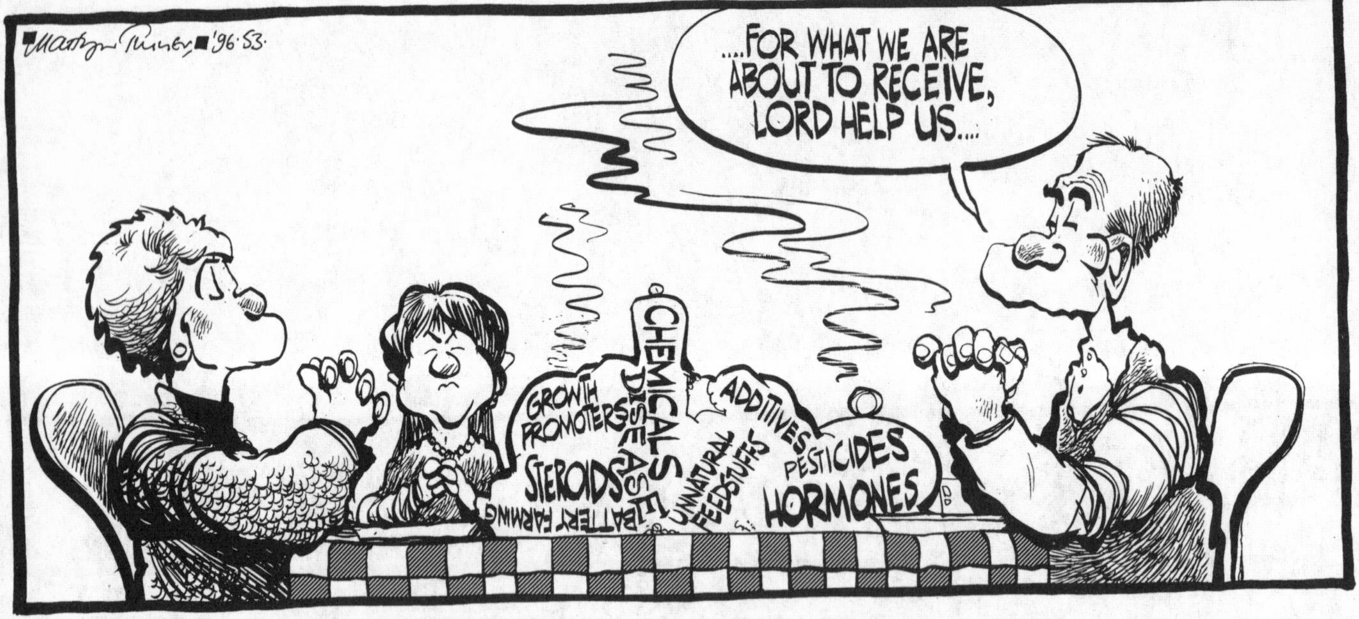
....FOR WHAT WE ARE ABOUT TO RECEIVE, LORD HELP US....
CHEMICALS
DISEASE
GROWTH PROMOTERS
STEROIDS
BATTERY FARMING
UNNATURAL FEEDSTUFFS
ADDITIVES
PESTICIDES
HORMONES

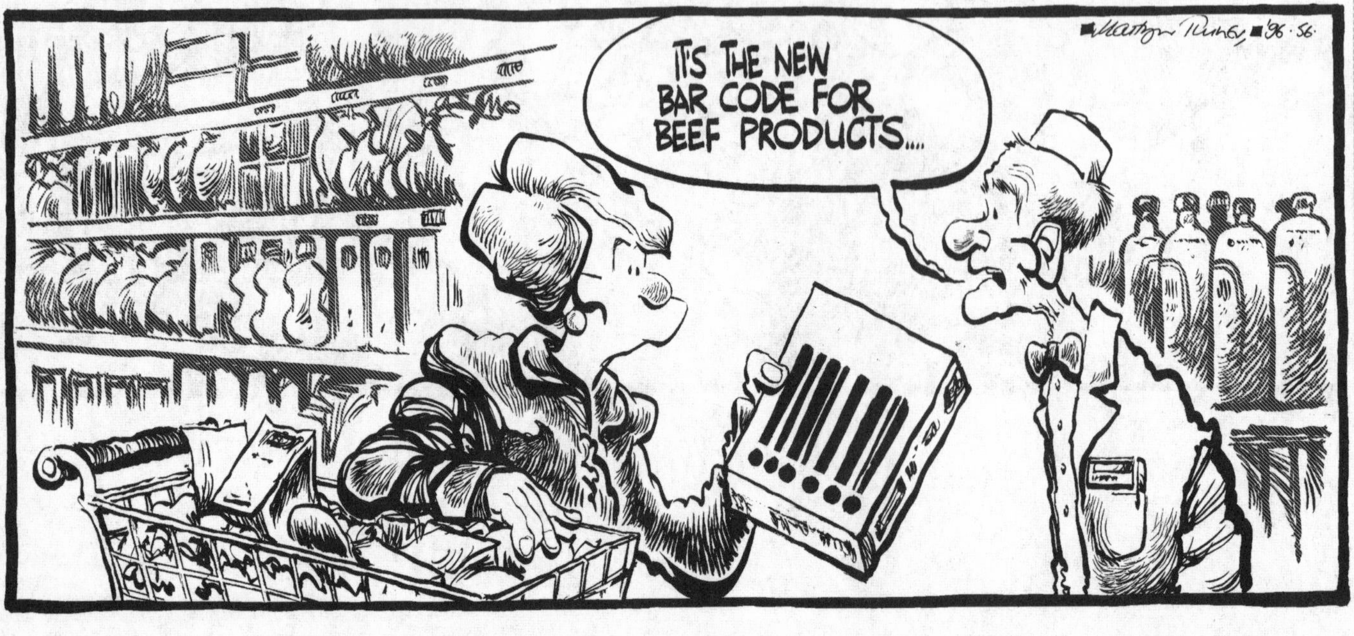
IT'S THE NEW BAR CODE FOR BEEF PRODUCTS....

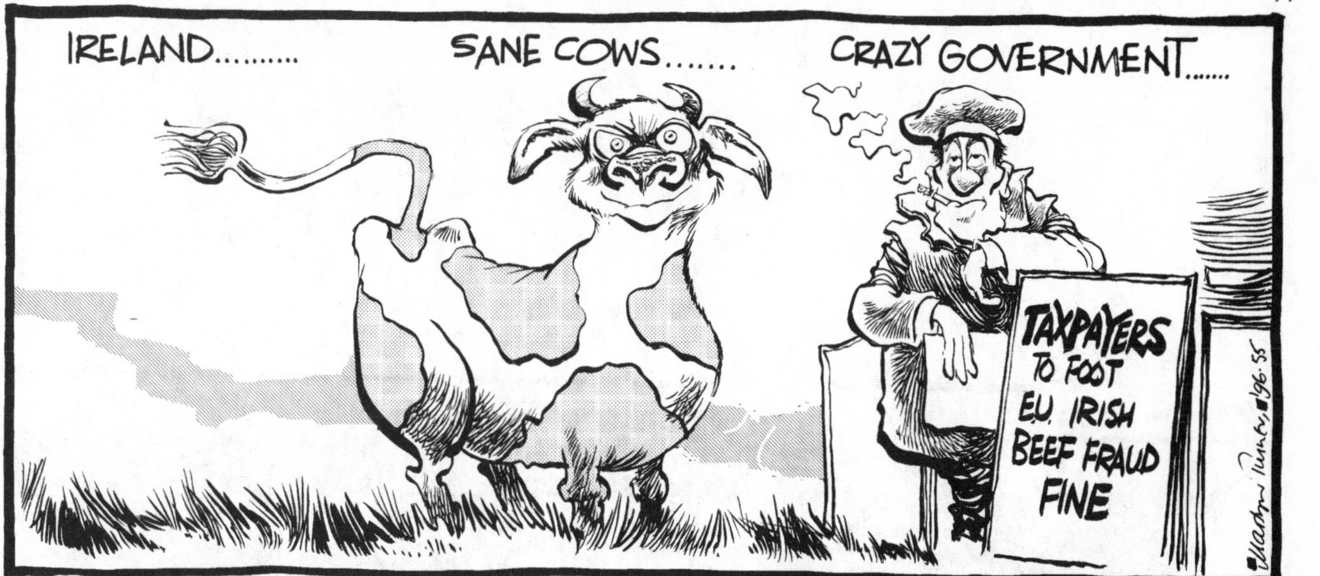
IRELAND..........
SANE COWS.......
CRAZY GOVERNMENT.......
TAXPAYERS TO FOOT E.U. IRISH BEEF FRAUD FINE

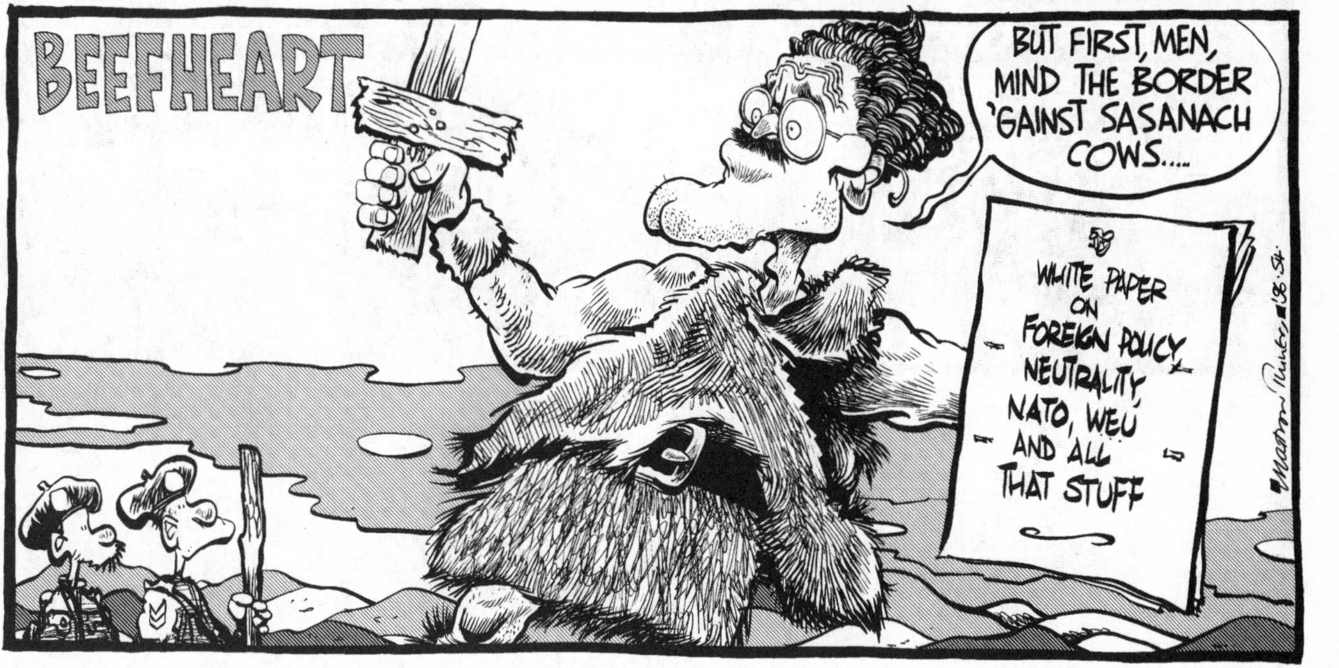
BEEFHEART
BUT FIRST, MEN, MIND THE BORDER 'GAINST SASANACH COWS.....
WHITE PAPER ON FOREIGN POLICY, NEUTRALITY, NATO, WEU AND ALL THAT STUFF

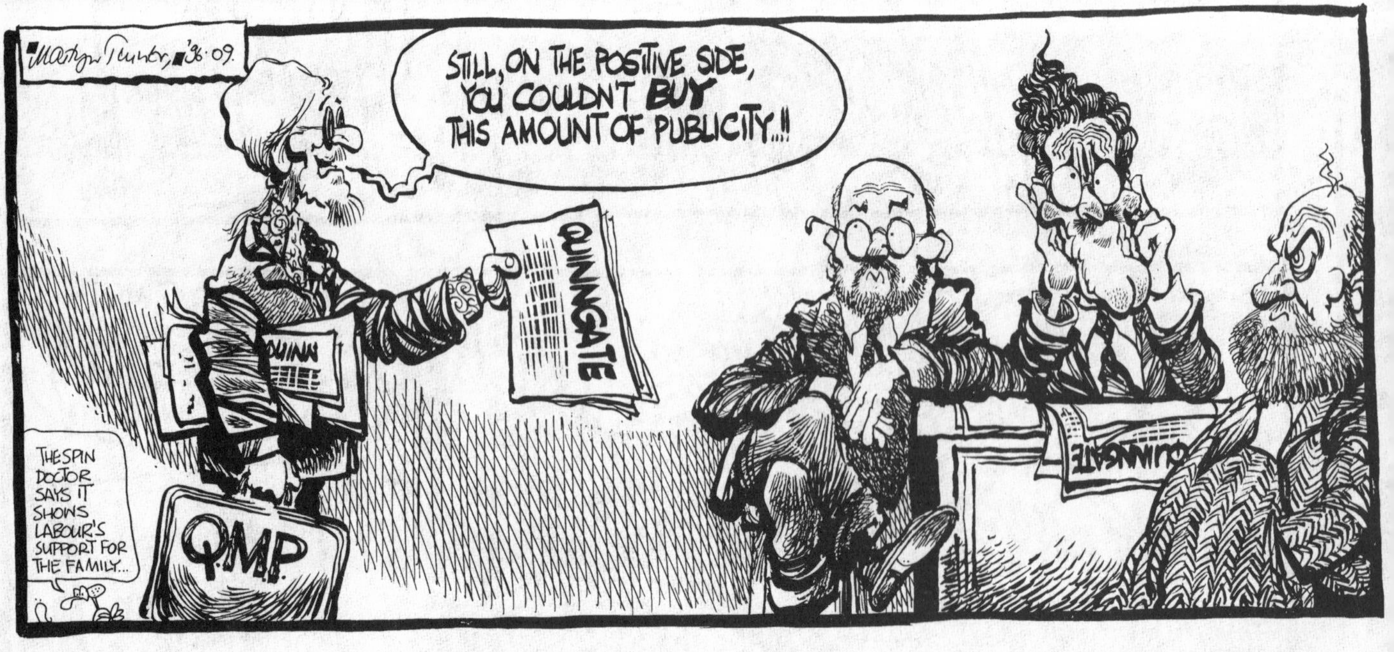
Martyn Turner 30.09.
STILL, ON THE POSITIVE SIDE, YOU COULDN'T BUY THIS AMOUNT OF PUBLICITY..!!
QUINNGATE
QUINN
QUINNGATE
Q.M.P.
THE SPIN DOCTOR SAYS IT SHOWS LABOUR'S SUPPORT FOR THE FAMILY...

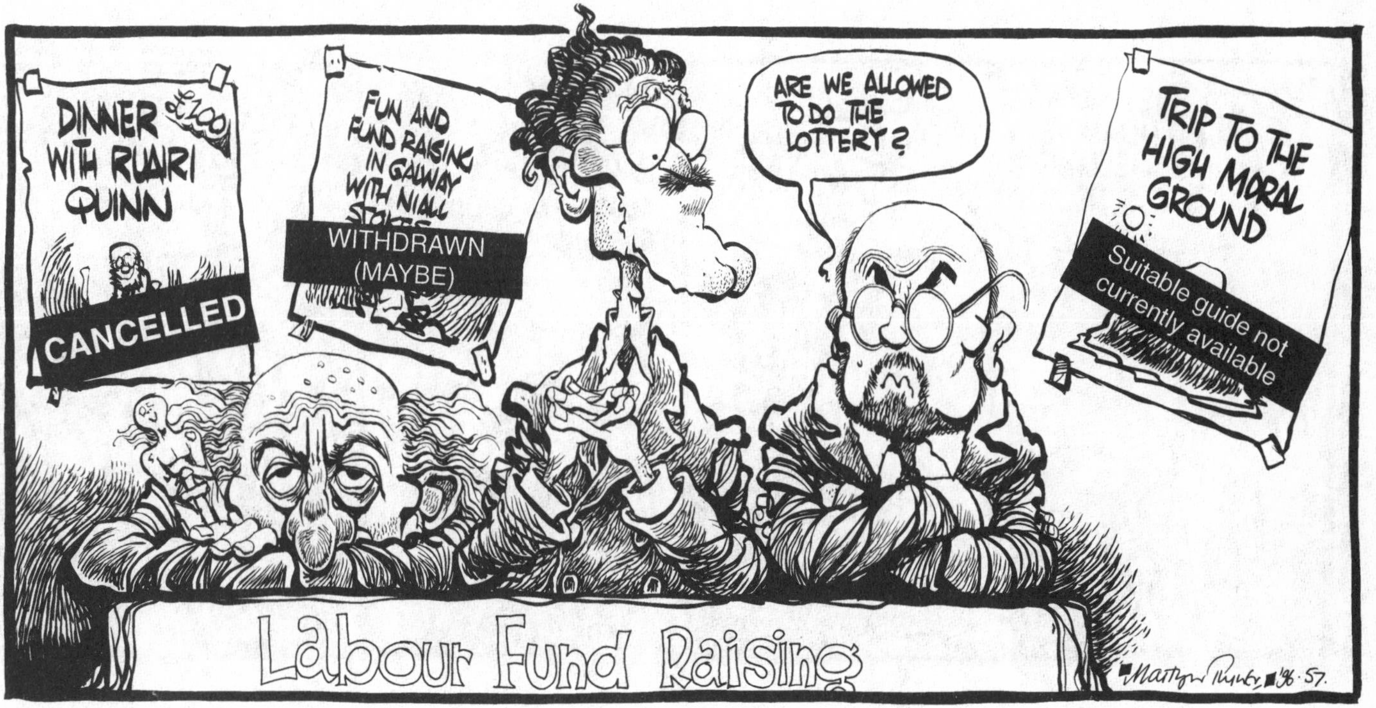
DINNER WITH RUAIRI QUINN
at £200
CANCELLED
FUN AND FUND RAISING IN GALWAY WITH NIALL
WITHDRAWN (MAYBE)
ARE WE ALLOWED TO DO THE LOTTERY?
TRIP TO THE HIGH MORAL GROUND
Suitable guide not currently available
Labour Fund Raising

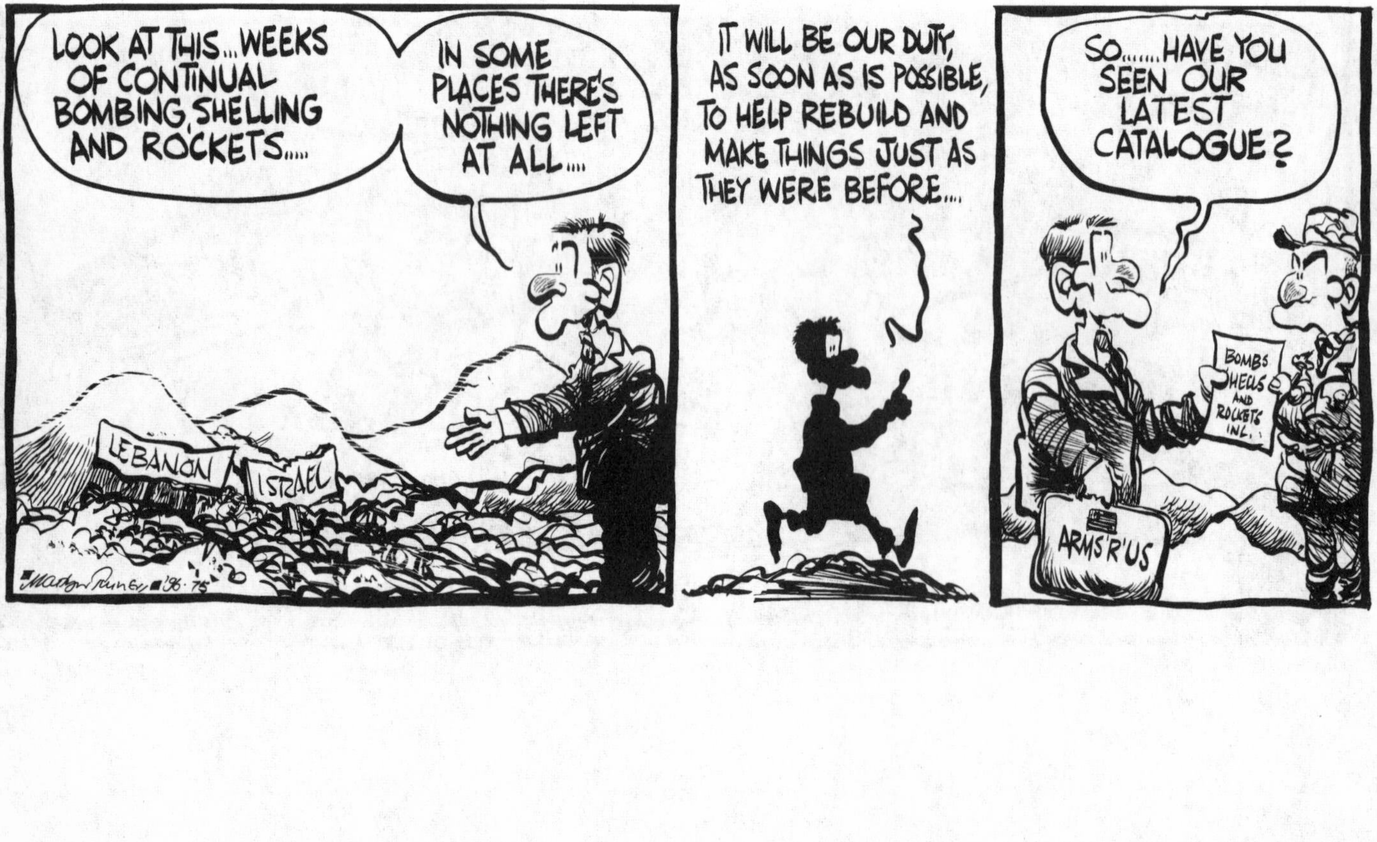
LOOK AT THIS... WEEKS OF CONTINUAL BOMBING, SHELLING AND ROCKETS.....
IN SOME PLACES THERE'S NOTHING LEFT AT ALL....
LEBANON
ISRAEL
IT WILL BE OUR DUTY, AS SOON AS IS POSSIBLE, TO HELP REBUILD AND MAKE THINGS JUST AS THEY WERE BEFORE....
SO....... HAVE YOU SEEN OUR LATEST CATALOGUE ?
BOMBS SHELLS AND ROCKETS INC.
ARMS'R'US

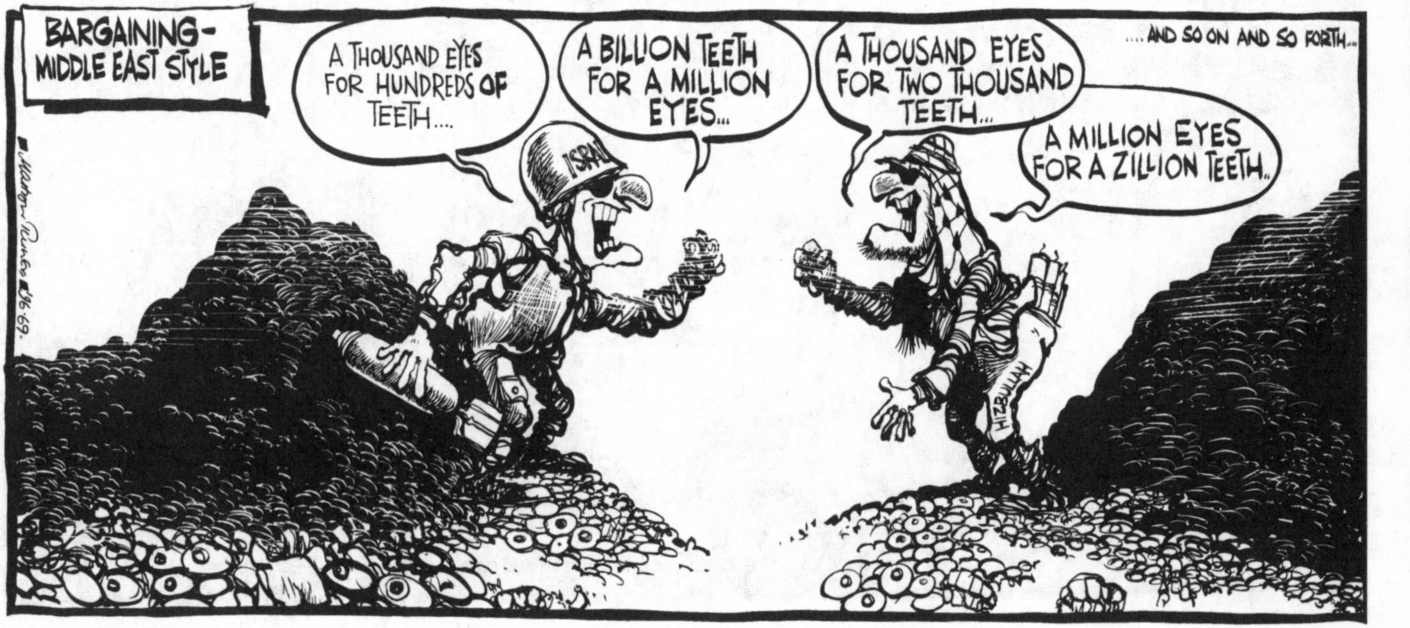
BARGAINING-
MIDDLE EAST STYLE
A THOUSAND EYES FOR HUNDREDS OF TEETH....
A BILLION TEETH FOR A MILLION EYES...
A THOUSAND EYES FOR TWO THOUSAND TEETH...
A MILLION EYES FOR A ZILLION TEETH..
....AND SO ON AND SO FORTH....
ISRAEL
HIZBULLAH

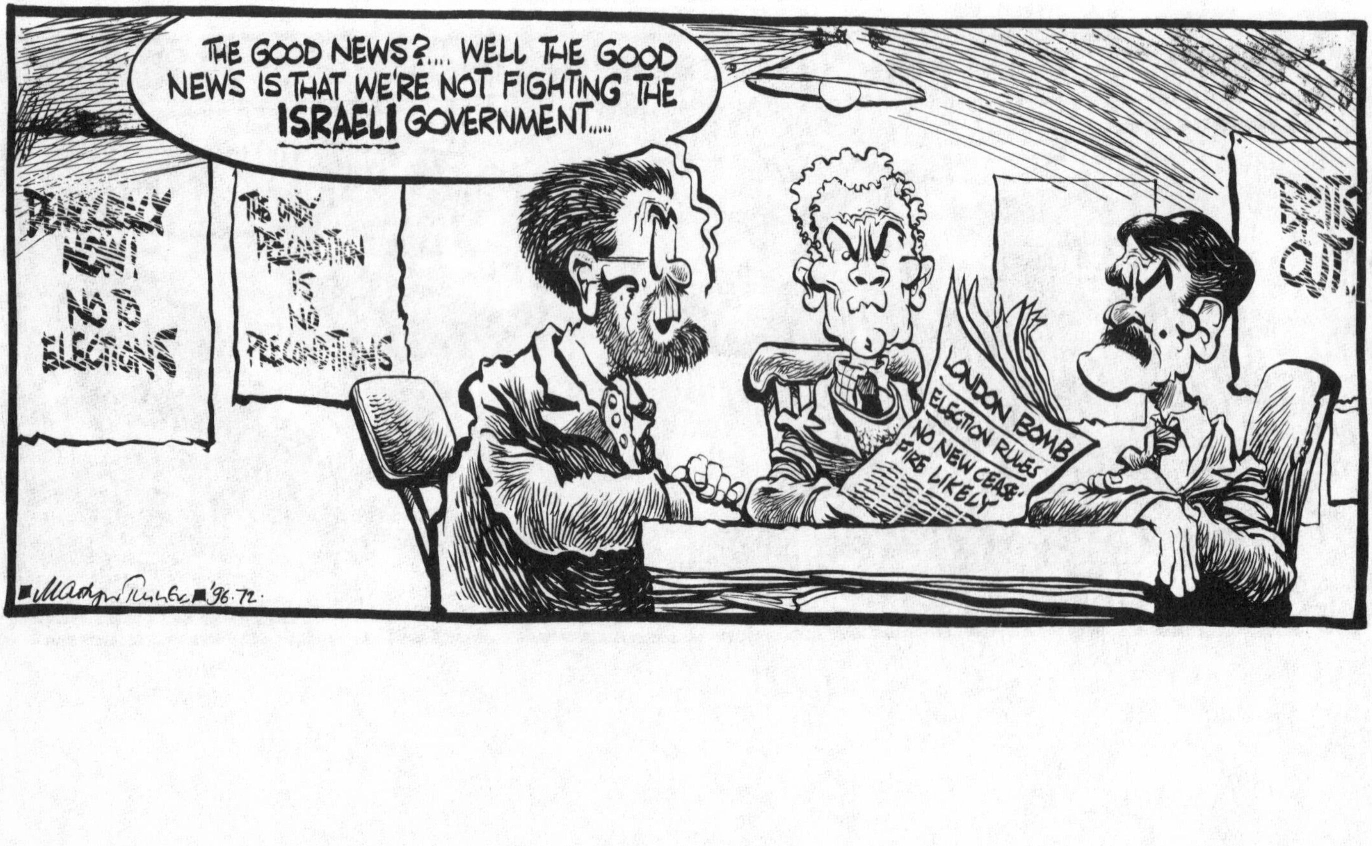
THE GOOD NEWS?.... WELL THE GOOD NEWS IS THAT WE'RE NOT FIGHTING THE ISRAELI GOVERNMENT.....
DEMOCRACY NOW! NO TO ELECTIONS
THE ONLY PRECONDITION IS NO PRECONDITIONS
BRITS OUT..
LONDON BOMB
ELECTION RULES
NO NEW CEASE-FIRE LIKELY

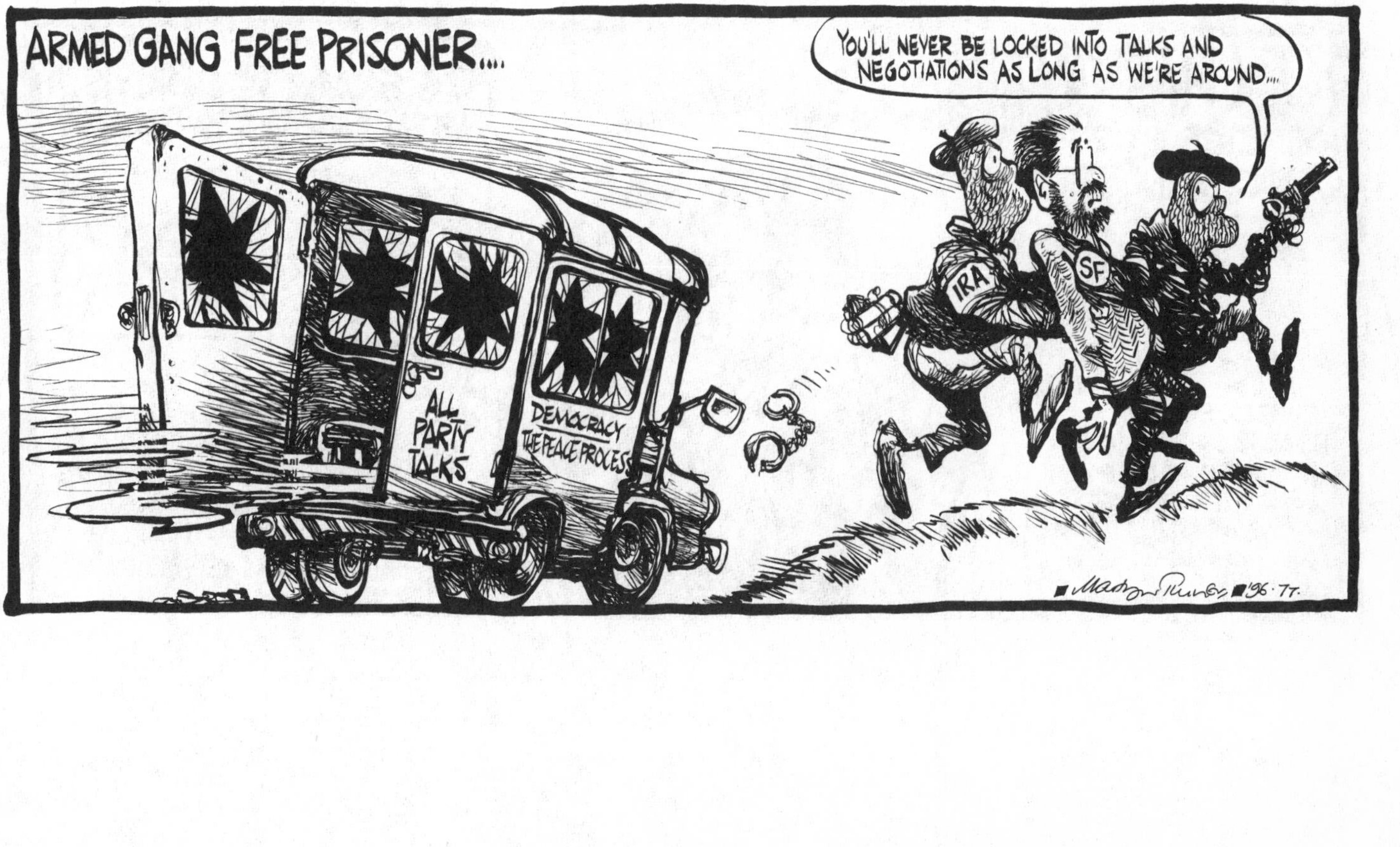
ARMED GANG FREE PRISONER....
YOU'LL NEVER BE LOCKED INTO TALKS AND NEGOTIATIONS AS LONG AS WE'RE AROUND....
ALL PARTY TALKS
DEMOCRACY
THE PEACE PROCESS
IRA
SF

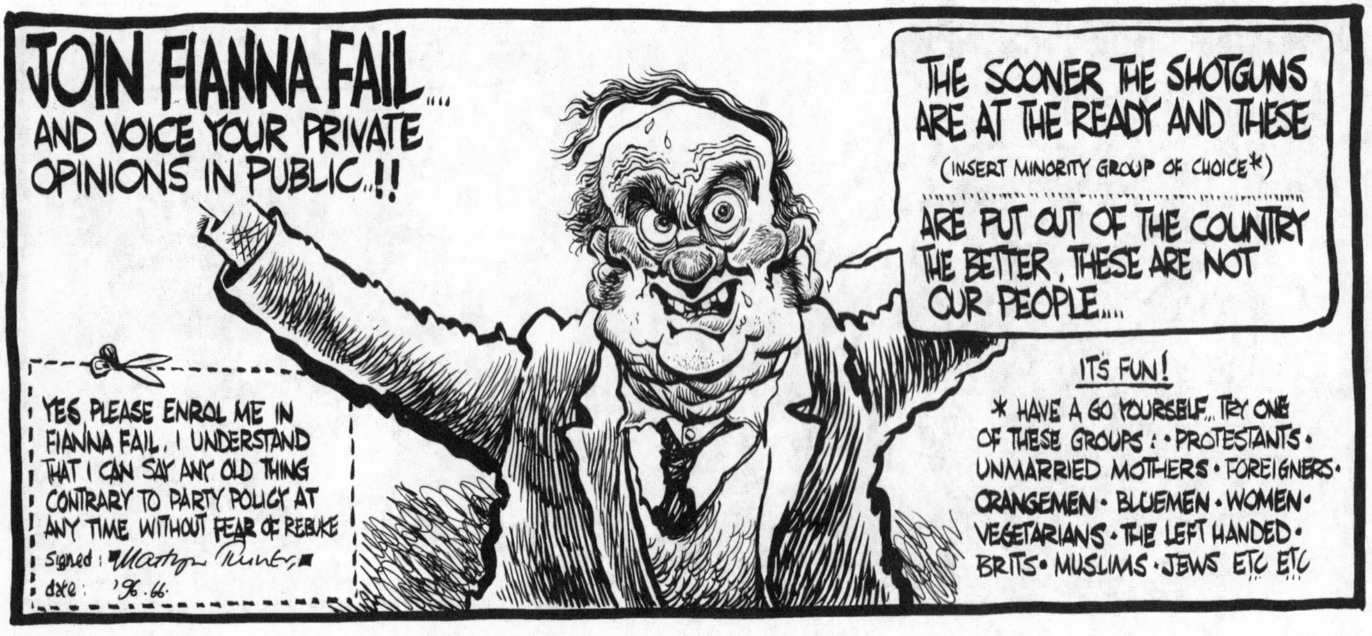
JOIN FIANNA FAIL....
AND VOICE YOUR PRIVATE OPINIONS IN PUBLIC..!!
THE SOONER THE SHOTGUNS ARE AT THE READY AND THESE
(INSERT MINORITY GROUP OF CHOICE*)
ARE PUT OUT OF THE COUNTRY THE BETTER. THESE ARE NOT OUR PEOPLE....
YES PLEASE ENROL ME IN FIANNA FAIL. I UNDERSTAND THAT I CAN SAY ANY OLD THING CONTRARY TO PARTY POLICY AT ANY TIME WITHOUT FEAR OF REBUKE
Signed:
date:
IT'S FUN!
* HAVE A GO YOURSELF... TRY ONE OF THESE GROUPS: • PROTESTANTS • UNMARRIED MOTHERS • FOREIGNERS • ORANGEMEN • BLUEMEN • WOMEN • VEGETARIANS • THE LEFT HANDED • BRITS • MUSLIMS • JEWS ETC ETC

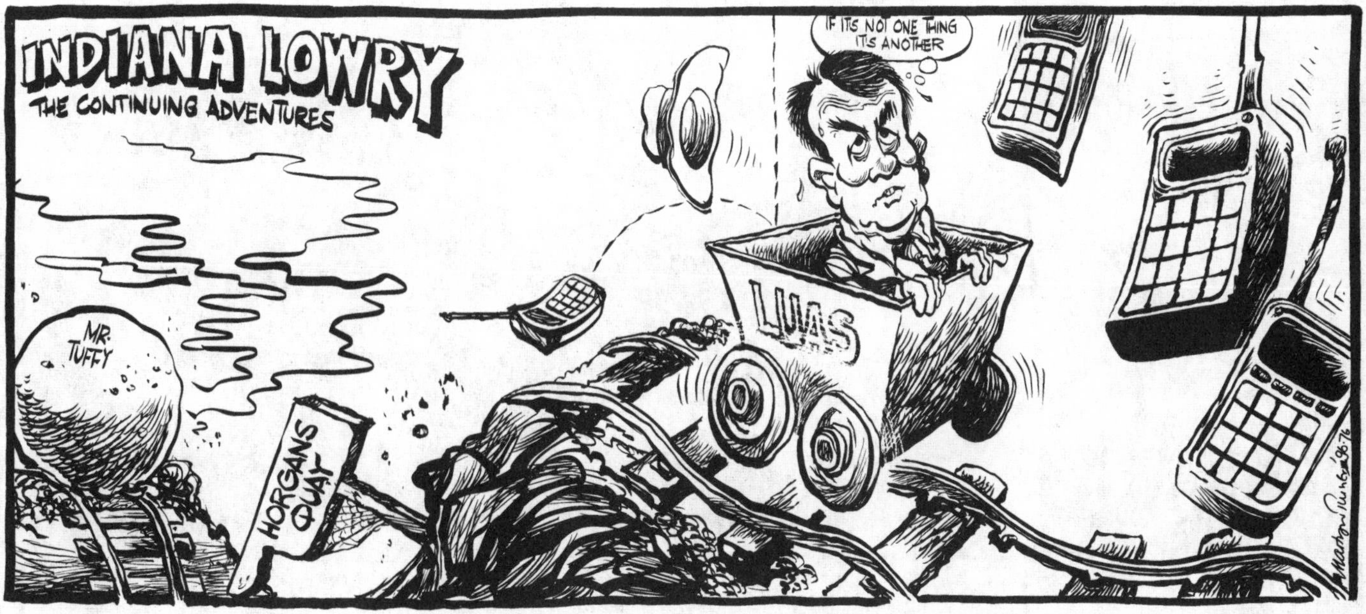
INDIANA LOWRY
THE CONTINUING ADVENTURES
IF ITS NOT ONE THING IT'S ANOTHER
MR. TUFFY
LUAS
HORGANS QUAY

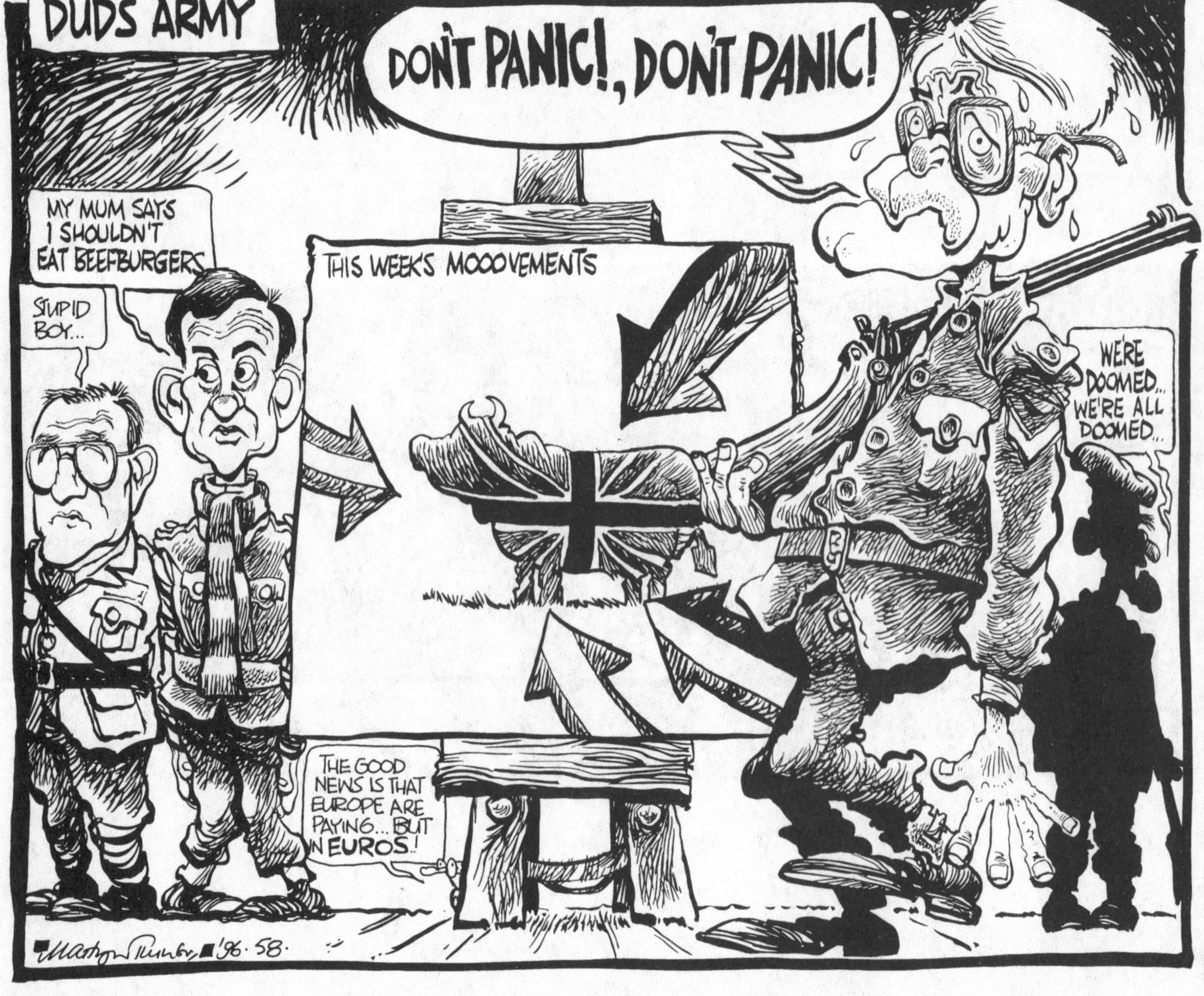
DUDS ARMY
DON'T PANIC!, DON'T PANIC!
MY MUM SAYS I SHOULDN'T EAT BEEFBURGERS
STUPID BOY...
THIS WEEK'S MOOOVEMENTS
WE'RE DOOMED.. WE'RE ALL DOOMED...
THE GOOD NEWS IS THAT EUROPE ARE PAYING... BUT IN EUROS!
'96 · 58 ·

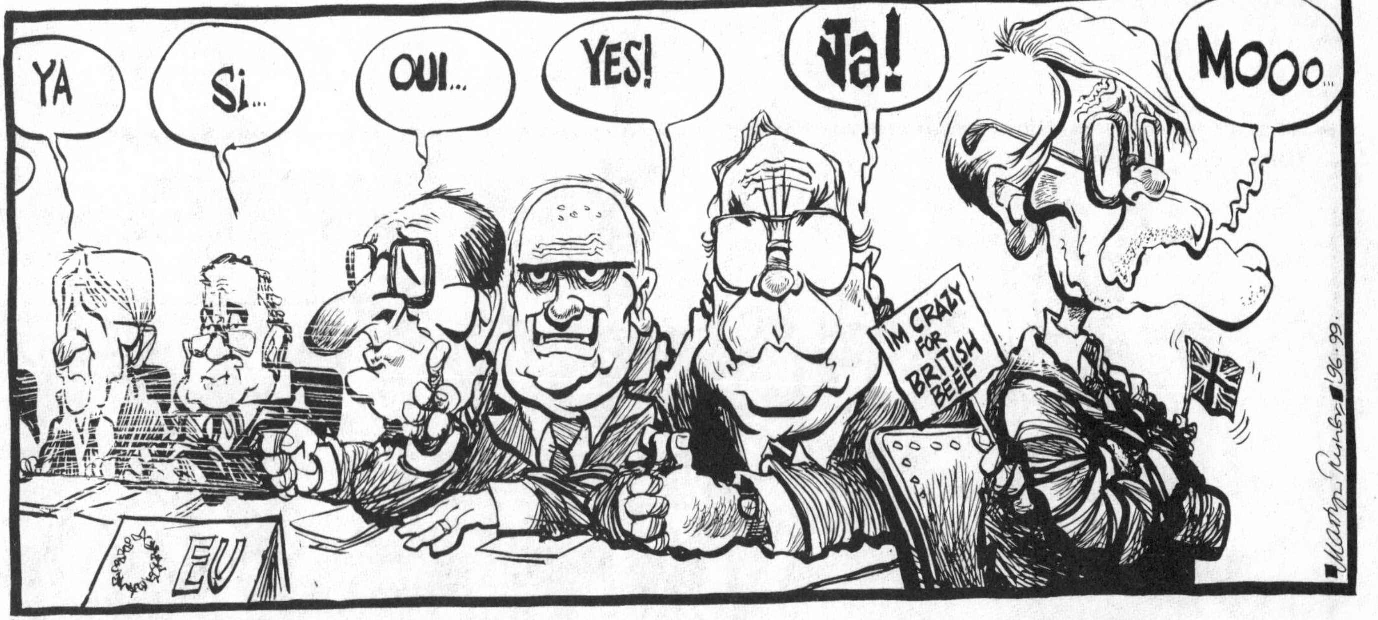
YA
Si...
OUI...
YES!
Ja!
MOOo...
IM CRAZY FOR BRITISH BEEF
EU
'96.99.

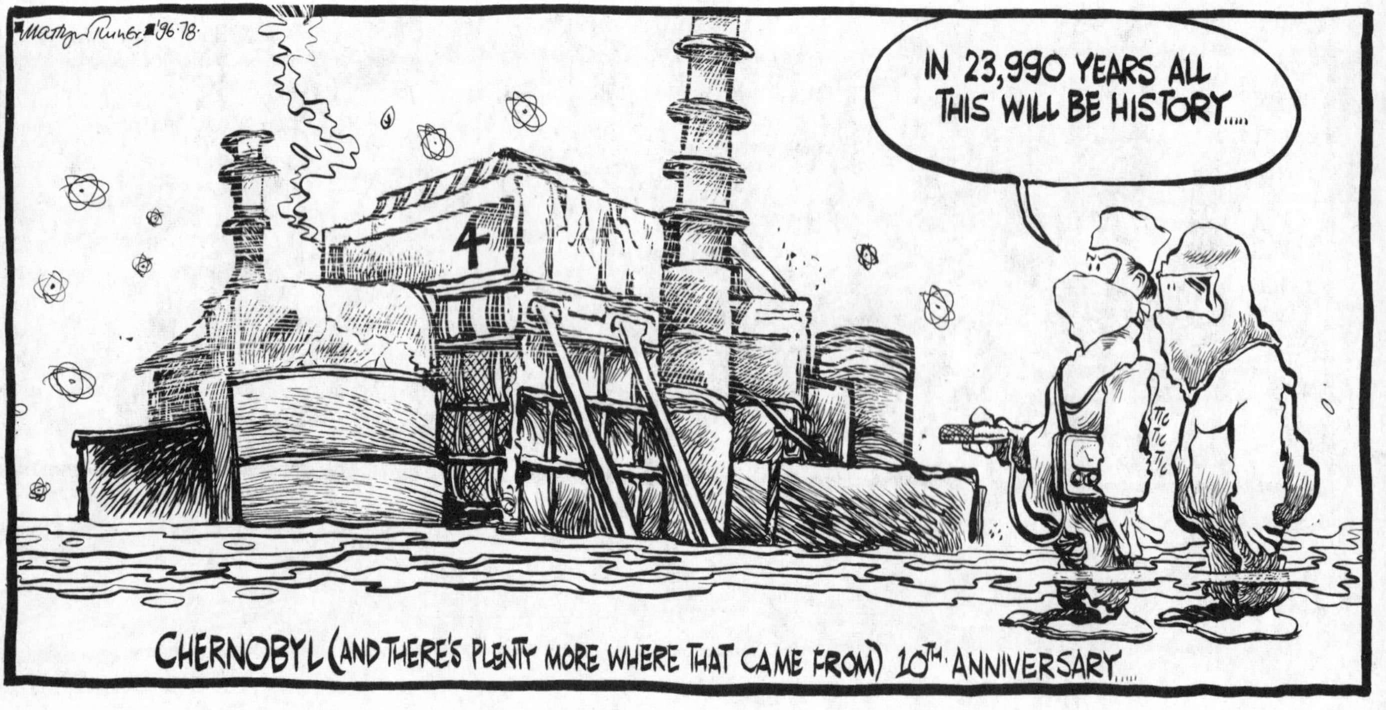
IN 23,990 YEARS ALL THIS WILL BE HISTORY.....

CHERNOBYL (AND THERE'S PLENTY MORE WHERE THAT CAME FROM) 10TH. ANNIVERSARY.....

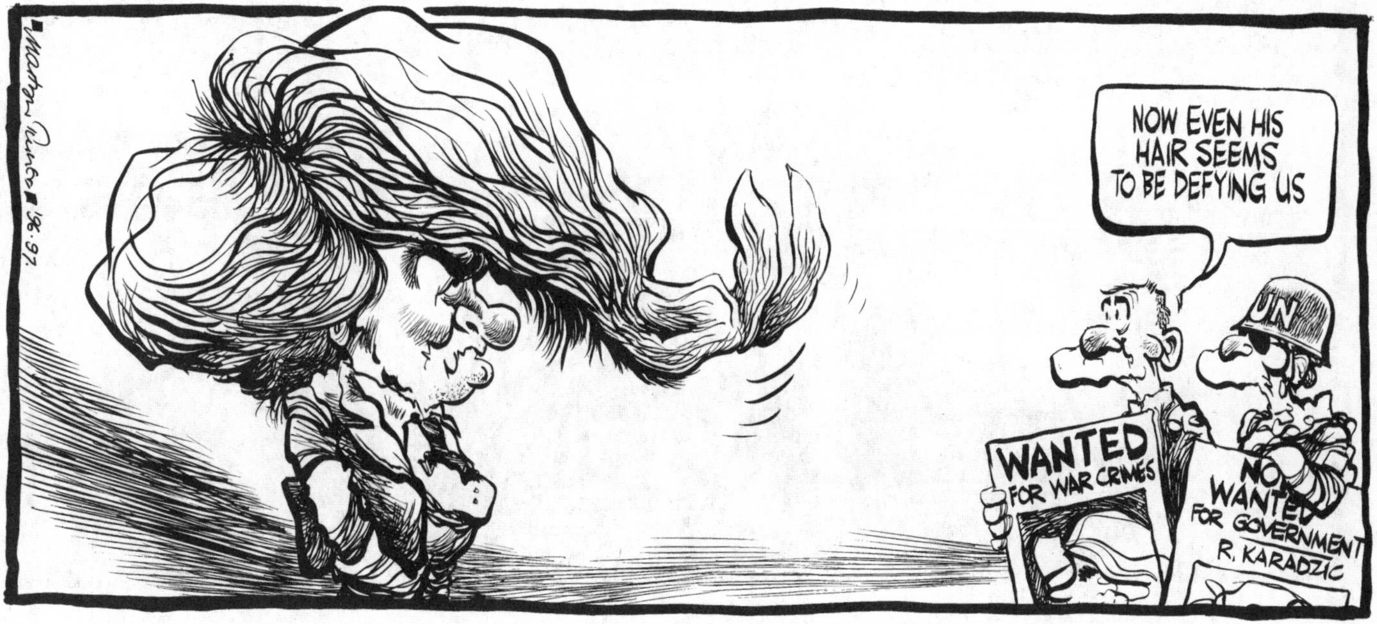
NOW EVEN HIS HAIR SEEMS TO BE DEFYING US
WANTED FOR WAR CRIMES
NOT WANTED FOR GOVERNMENT
R. KARADZIC
UN

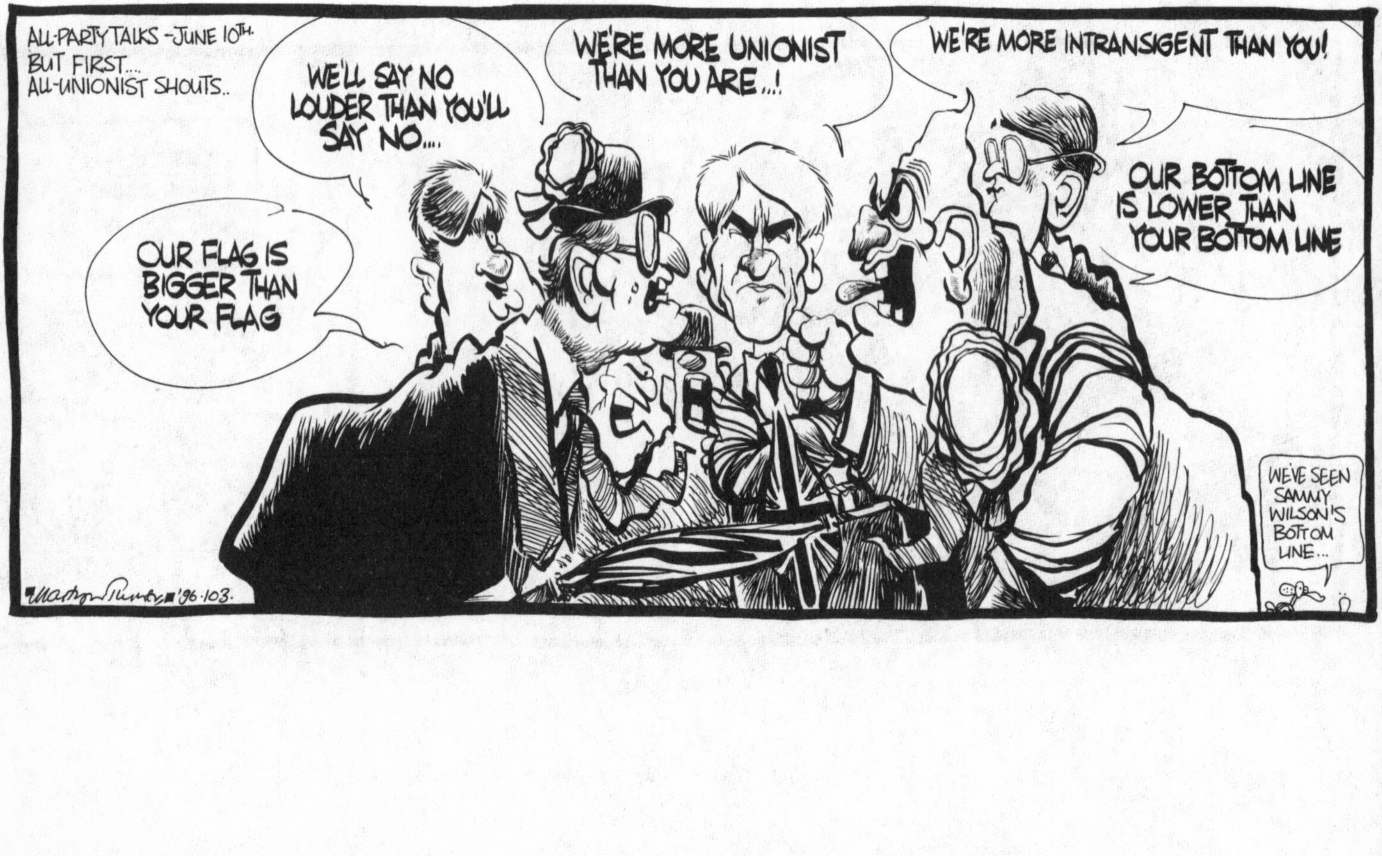
ALL-PARTY TALKS -JUNE 10TH.
BUT FIRST....
ALL-UNIONIST SHOUTS..
OUR FLAG IS BIGGER THAN YOUR FLAG
WE'LL SAY NO LOUDER THAN YOU'LL SAY NO....
WE'RE MORE UNIONIST THAN YOU ARE..!
WE'RE MORE INTRANSIGENT THAN YOU!
OUR BOTTOM LINE IS LOWER THAN YOUR BOTTOM LINE
WE'VE SEEN SAMMY WILSON'S BOTTOM LINE...
'96·103.

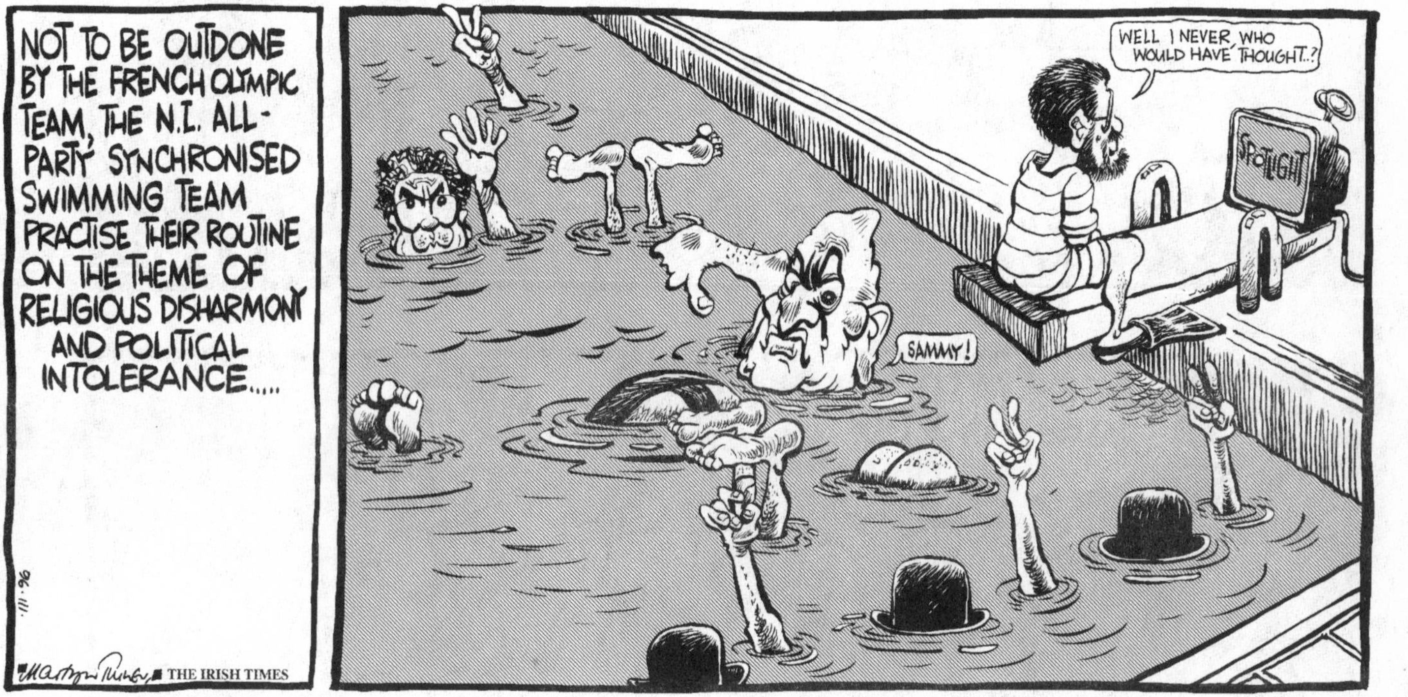
NOT TO BE OUTDONE BY THE FRENCH OLYMPIC TEAM, THE N.I. ALL-PARTY SYNCHRONISED SWIMMING TEAM PRACTISE THEIR ROUTINE ON THE THEME OF RELIGIOUS DISHARMONY AND POLITICAL INTOLERANCE.....
·1·11·96
THE IRISH TIMES
WELL I NEVER, WHO WOULD HAVE THOUGHT..?
SPOTLIGHT
SAMMY!

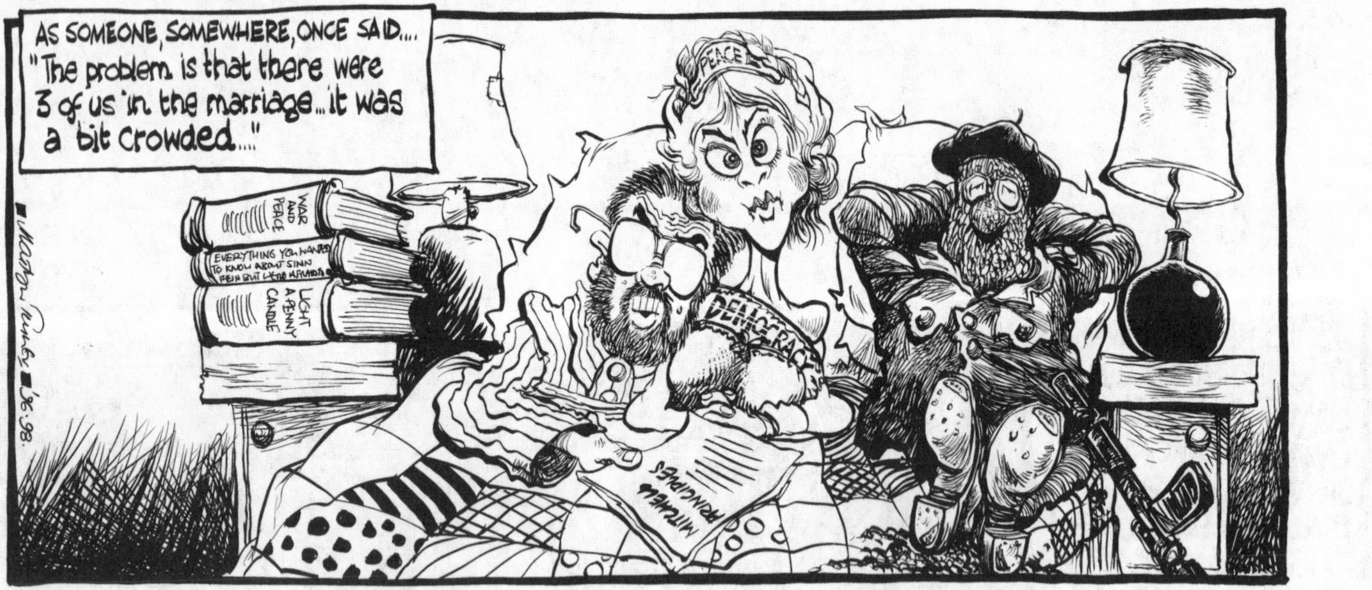
AS SOMEONE, SOMEWHERE, ONCE SAID...
"The problem is that there were 3 of us in the marriage... it was a bit crowded..."
PEACE
WAR AND PEACE
EVERYTHING YOU WANTED TO KNOW ABOUT SINN FEIN
LIGHT A PENNY CANDLE
DEMOCRACY
MITCHELL PRINCIPLES

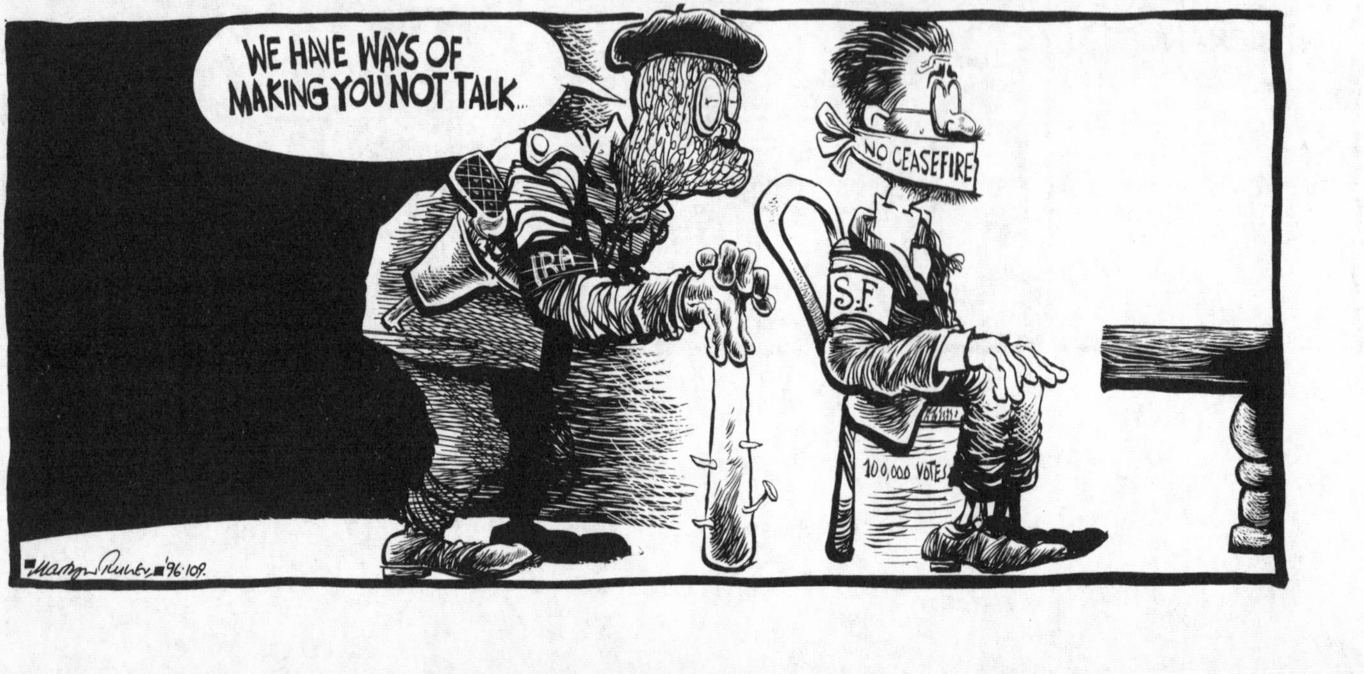
WE HAVE WAYS OF MAKING YOU NOT TALK...
NO CEASEFIRE
IRA
S.F.
100,000 VOTES

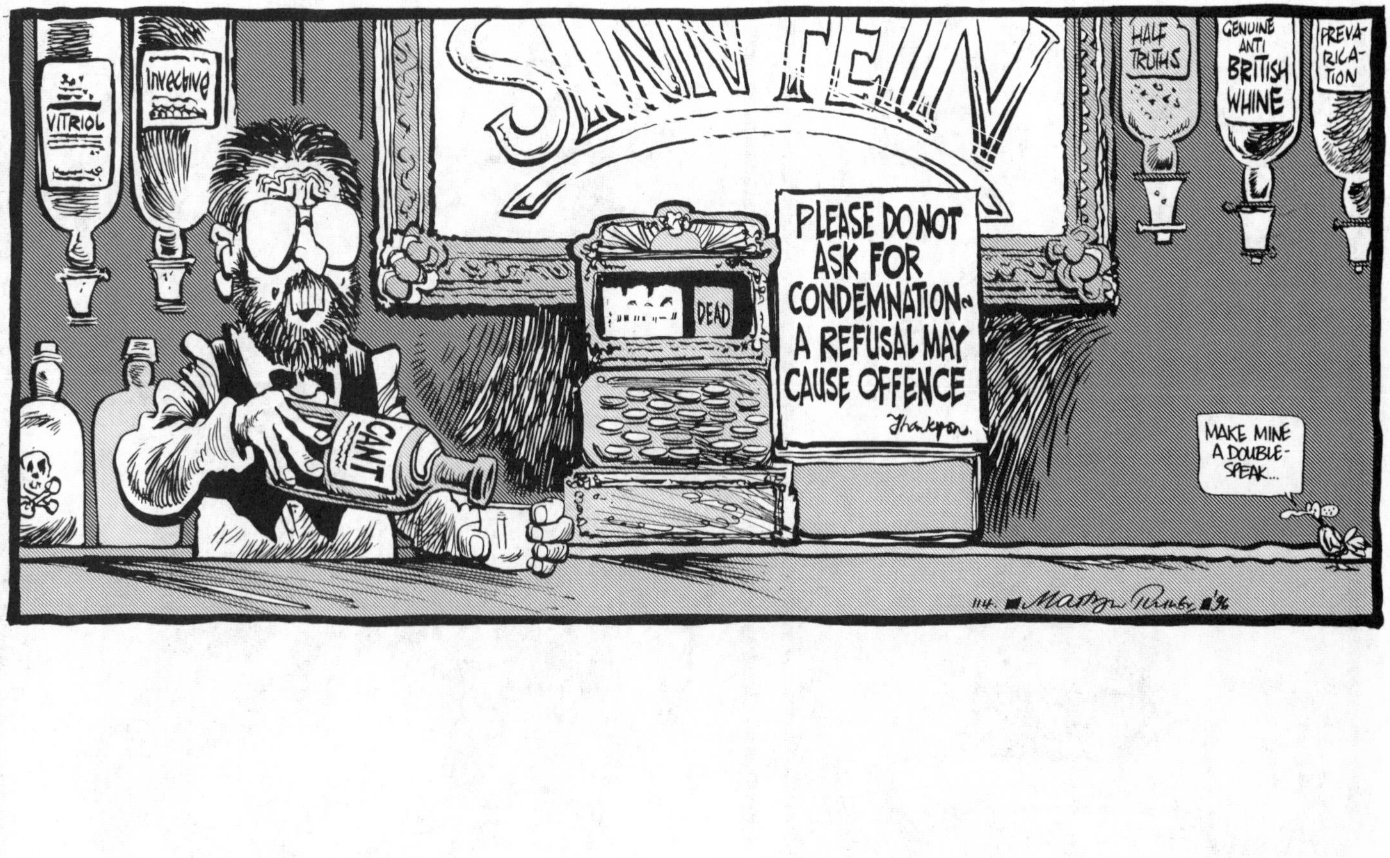
VITRIOL
Invective
SINN FEIN
HALF TRUTHS
GENUINE ANTI BRITISH WHINE
PREVA-RICA-TION
DEAD
PLEASE DO NOT ASK FOR CONDEMNATION~ A REFUSAL MAY CAUSE OFFENCE
CANT
MAKE MINE A DOUBLE-SPEAK...

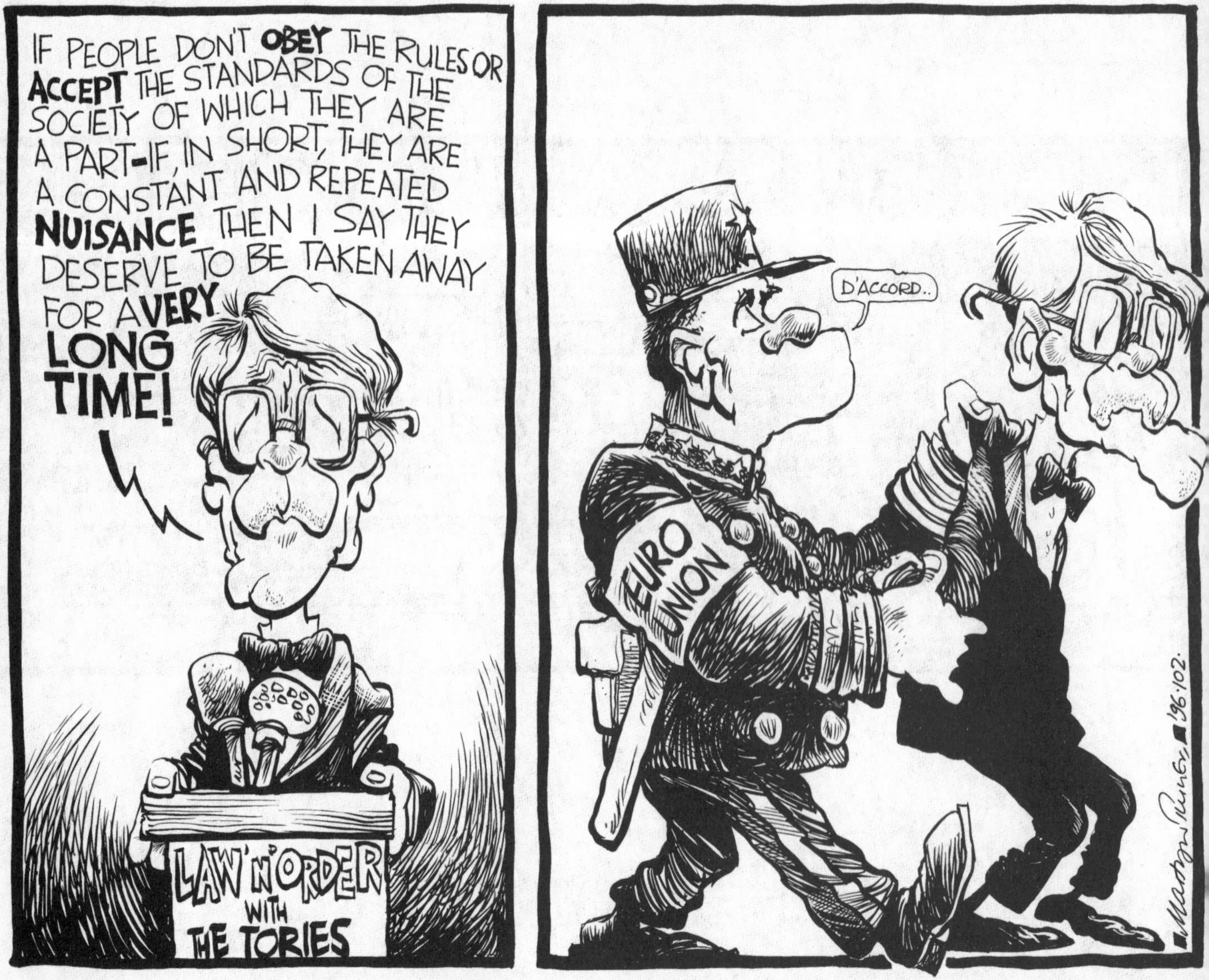
IF PEOPLE DON'T OBEY THE RULES OR ACCEPT THE STANDARDS OF THE SOCIETY OF WHICH THEY ARE A PART-IF, IN SHORT, THEY ARE A CONSTANT AND REPEATED NUISANCE THEN I SAY THEY DESERVE TO BE TAKEN AWAY FOR A VERY LONG TIME!
LAW 'N' ORDER WITH THE TORIES
D'ACCORD..
EURO UNION

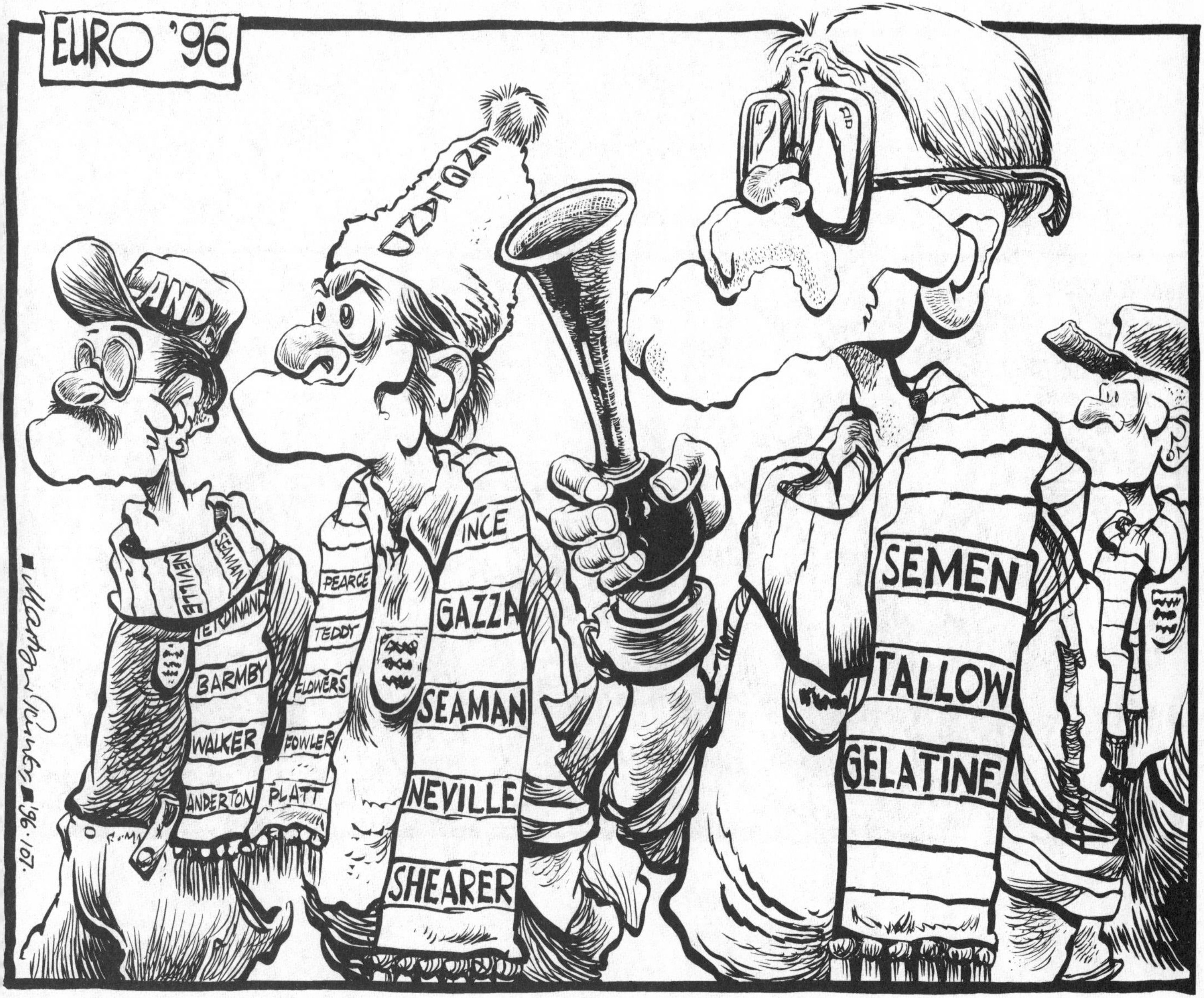
EURO '96
AND
ENGLAND
NEVILLE
SEAMAN
FERDINAND
BARMBY
WALKER
ANDERTON
PEARCE
TEDDY
FLOWERS
FOWLER
PLATT
INCE
GAZZA
SEAMAN
NEVILLE
SHEARER
SEMEN
TALLOW
GELATINE
'96.107.

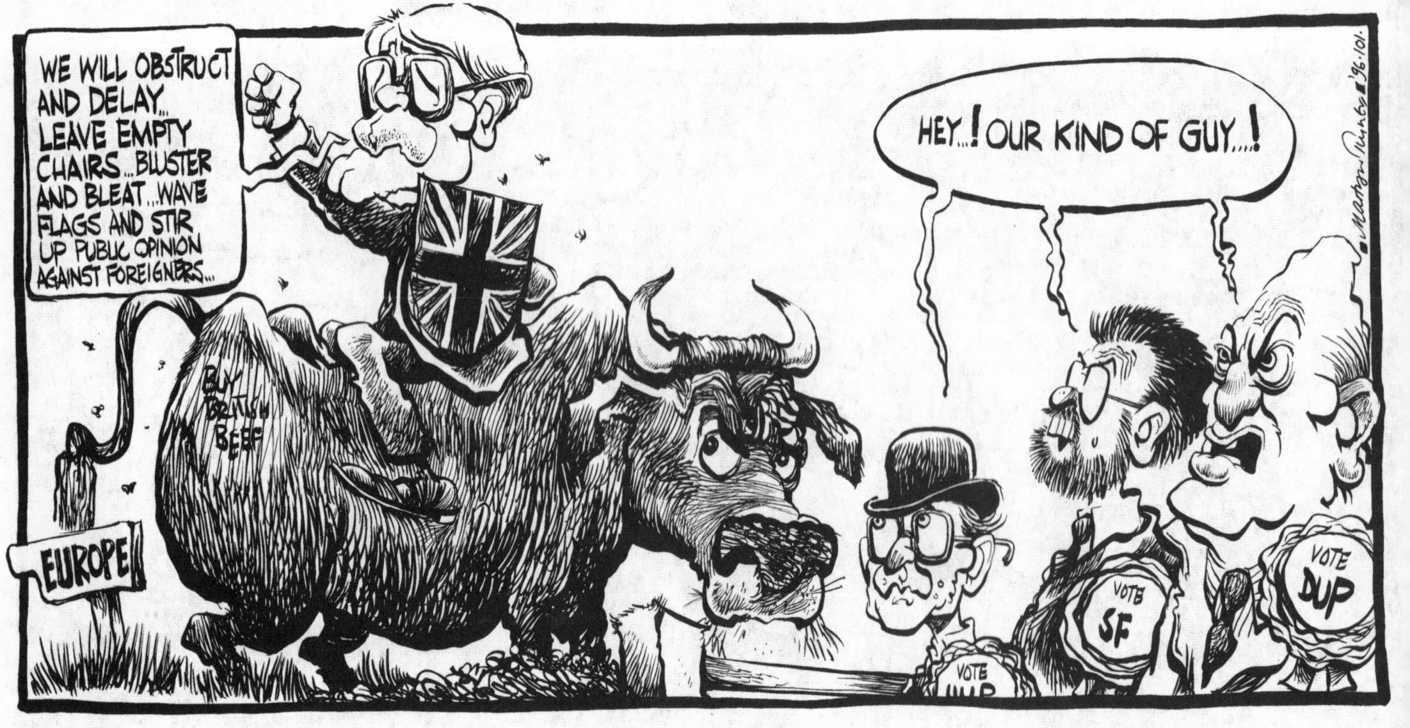
WE WILL OBSTRUCT AND DELAY... LEAVE EMPTY CHAIRS...BLUSTER AND BLEAT...WAVE FLAGS AND STIR UP PUBLIC OPINION AGAINST FOREIGNERS...
BUY BRITISH BEEF
EUROPE
HEY...! OUR KIND OF GUY...!
VOTE
VOTE SF
VOTE DUP

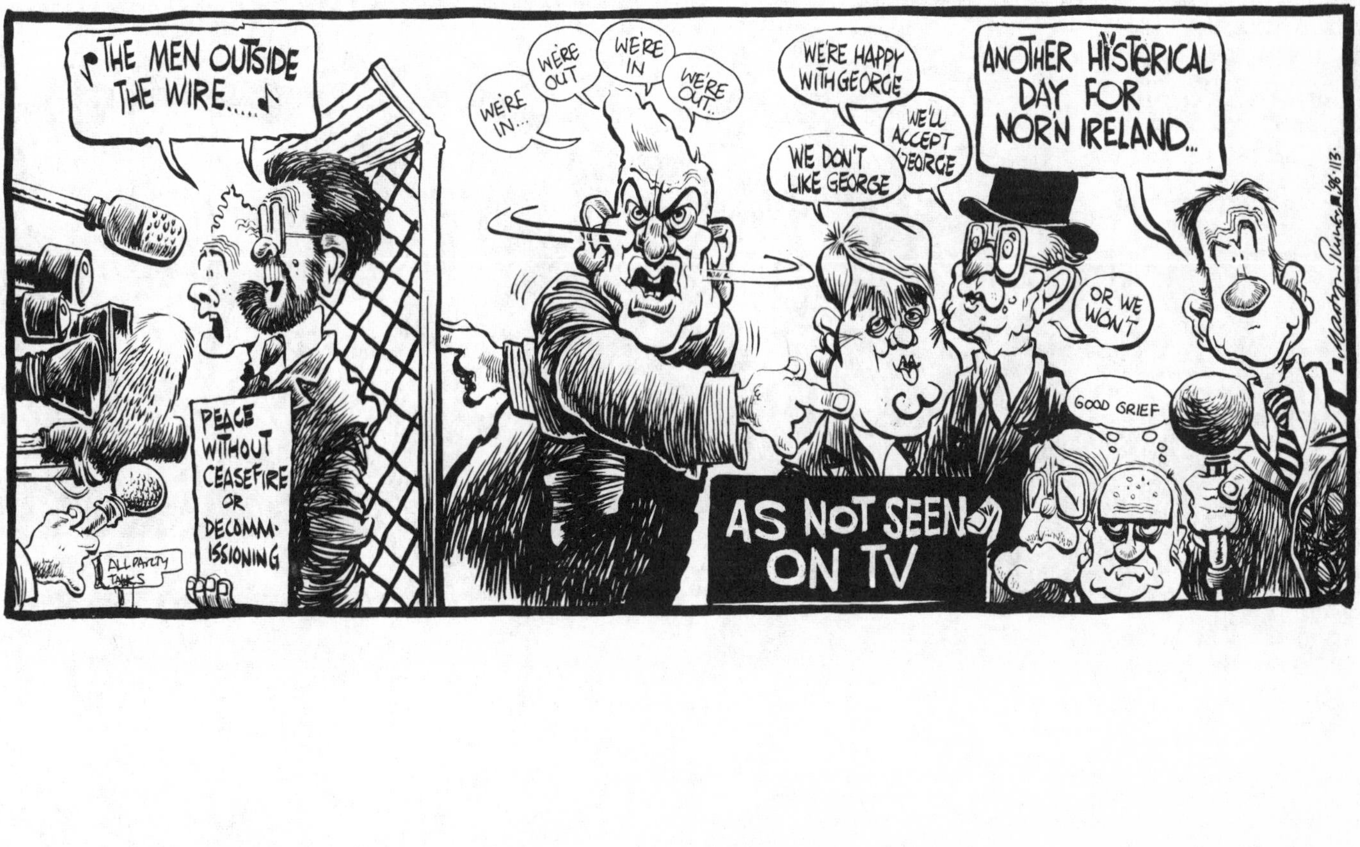
THE MEN OUTSIDE THE WIRE.....
PEACE WITHOUT CEASEFIRE OR DECOMMISSIONING
ALL PARTY TALKS
WE'RE IN...
WE'RE OUT
WE'RE IN
WE'RE OUT...
WE'RE HAPPY WITH GEORGE
WE DON'T LIKE GEORGE
WE'LL ACCEPT GEORGE
OR WE WON'T
ANOTHER HISTERICAL DAY FOR NOR'N IRELAND...
GOOD GRIEF
AS NOT SEEN ON TV

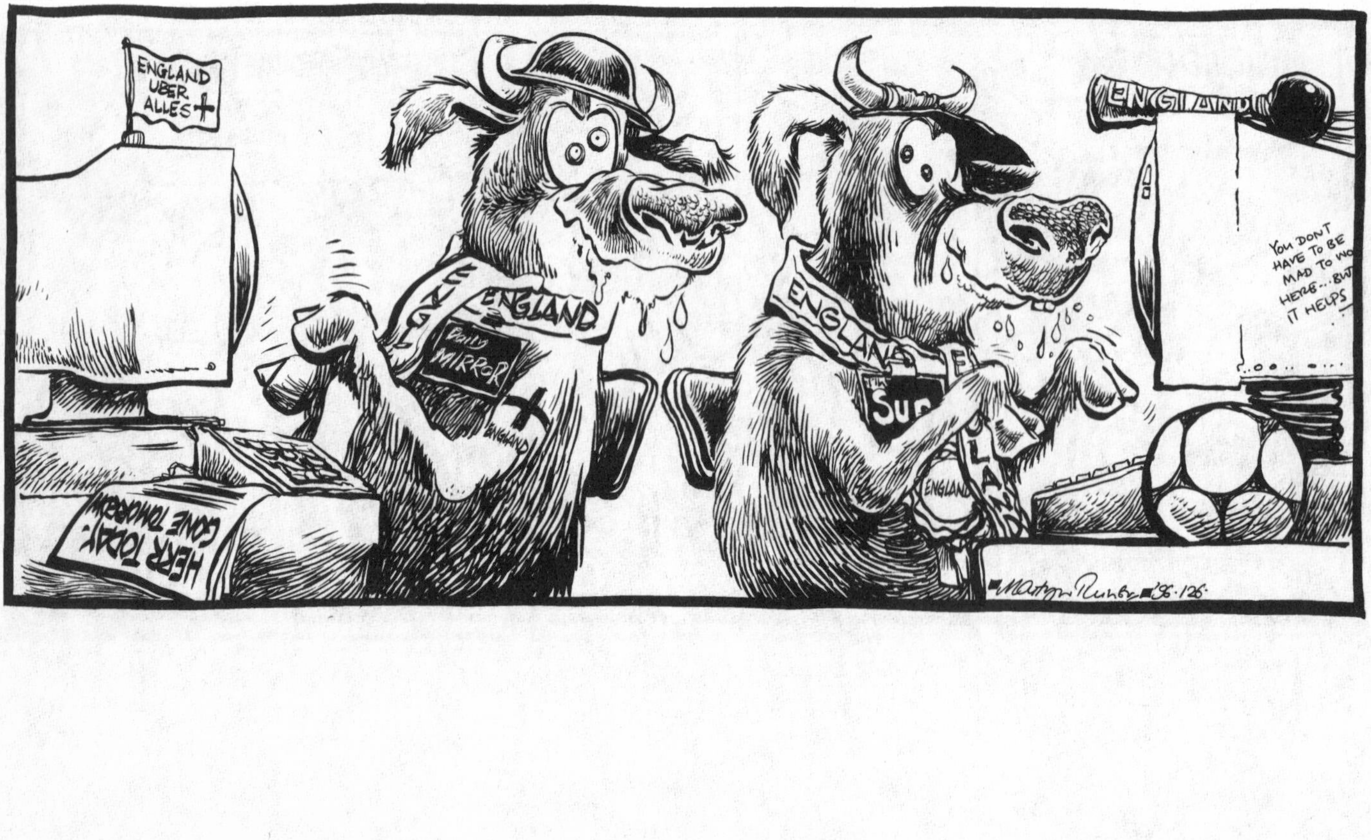
ENGLAND UBER ALLES
ENGLAND
Daily MIRROR
ENGLAND
HERR TODAY. GONE TOMORROW
ENGLAND
ENGLAND
SUN
ENGLAND
YOU DONT HAVE TO BE MAD TO WO HERE... BUT IT HELPS

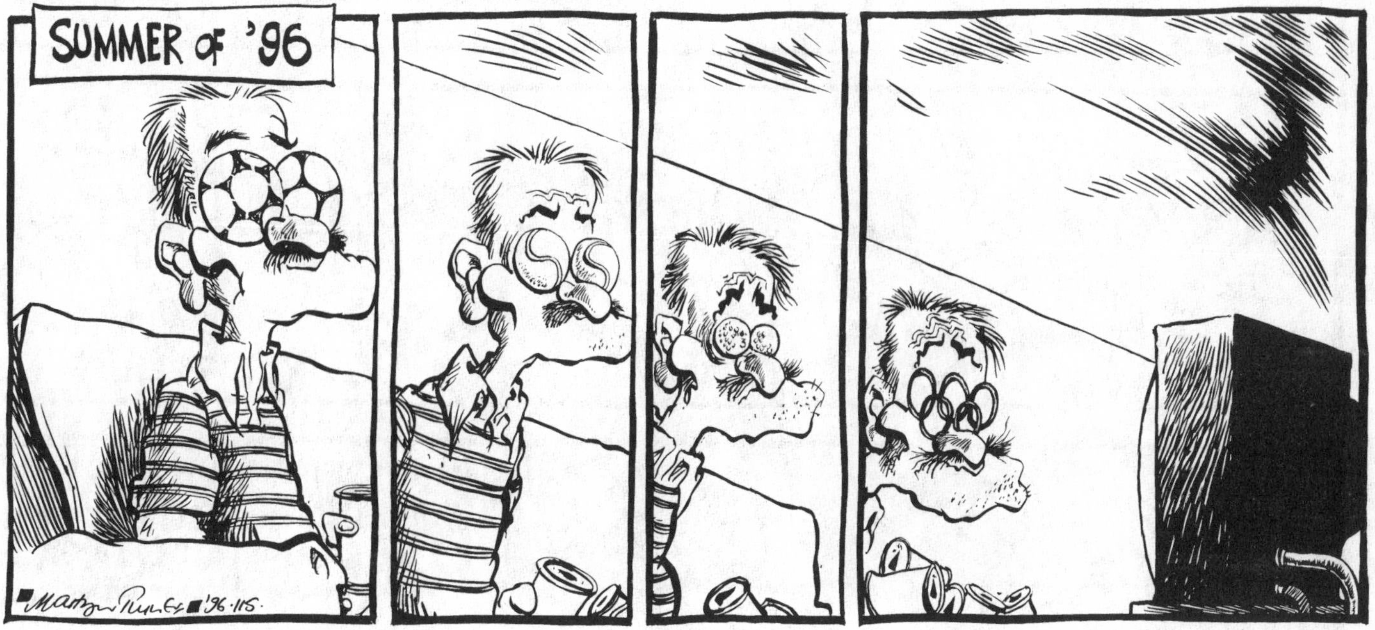
SUMMER OF '96

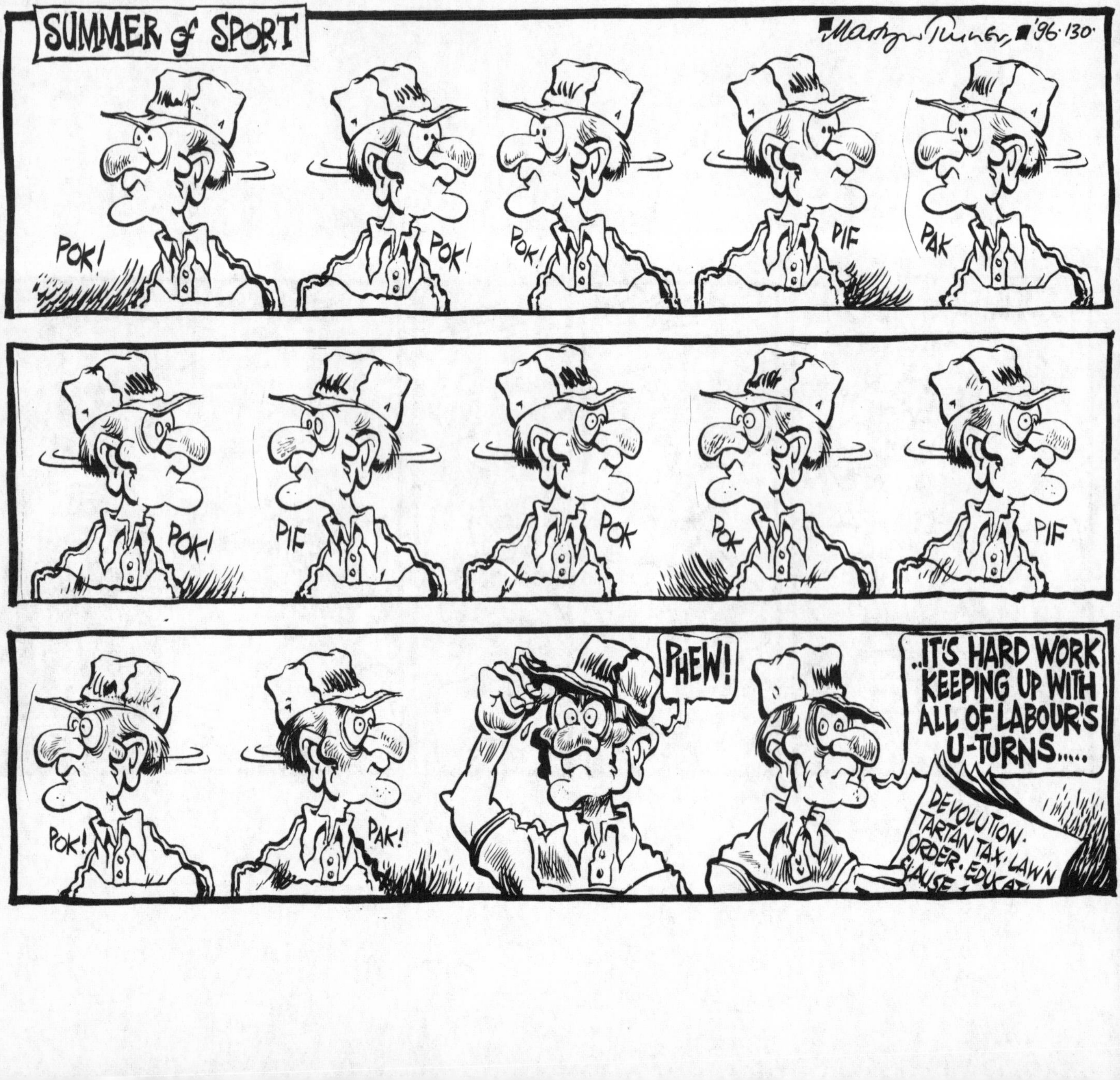
SUMMER of SPORT
'96·130
POK!
POK!
POK!
PIF
PAK
POK!
PIF
POK
POK
PIF
POK!
PAK!
PHEW!
..IT'S HARD WORK KEEPING UP WITH ALL OF LABOUR'S U-TURNS.....
DEVOLUTION·
TARTAN TAX·LAW'N
ORDER·EDUCAT

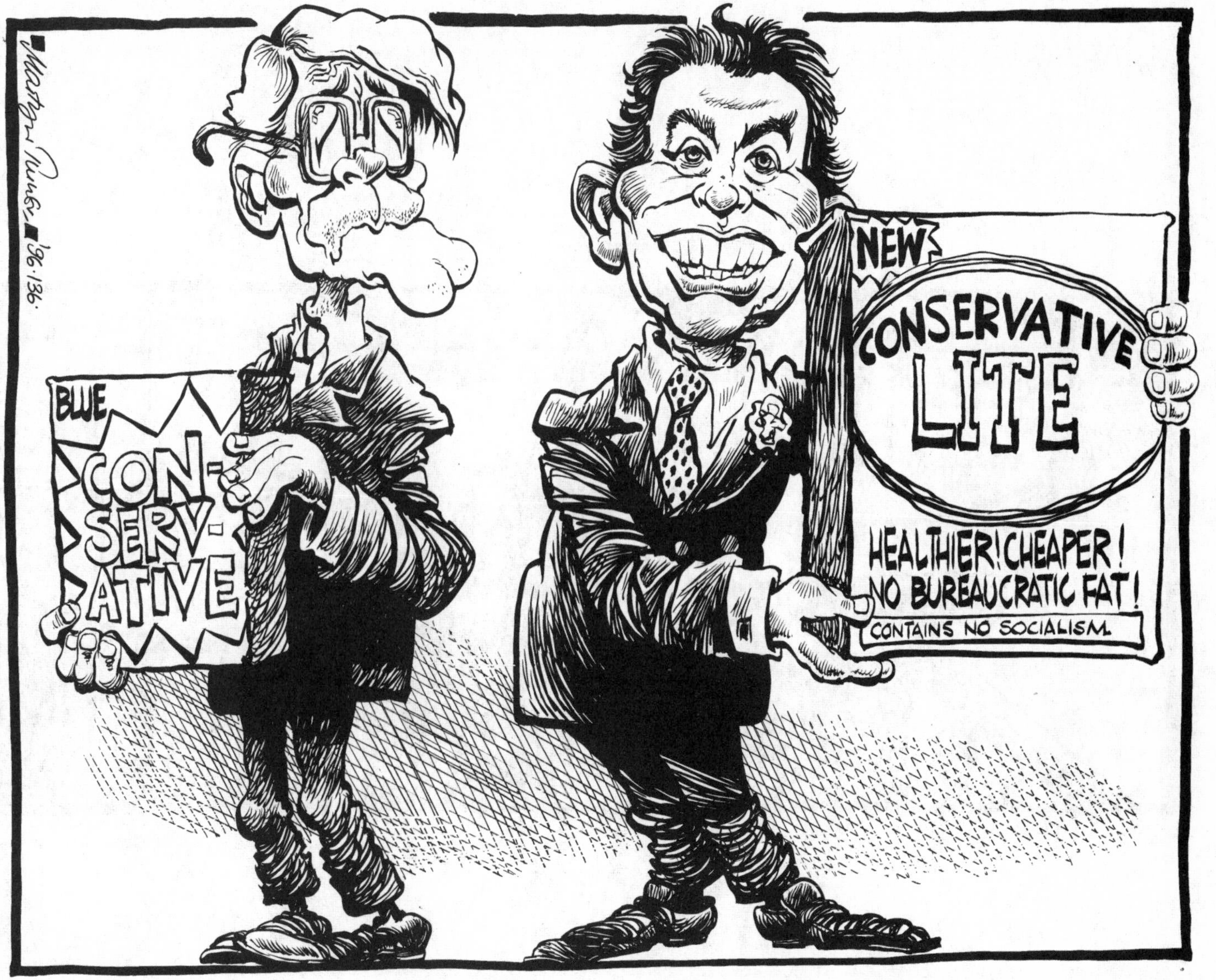

BLUE
CON-SERV-ATIVE
NEW
CONSERVATIVE LITE
HEALTHIER! CHEAPER!
NO BUREAUCRATIC FAT!
CONTAINS NO SOCIALISM

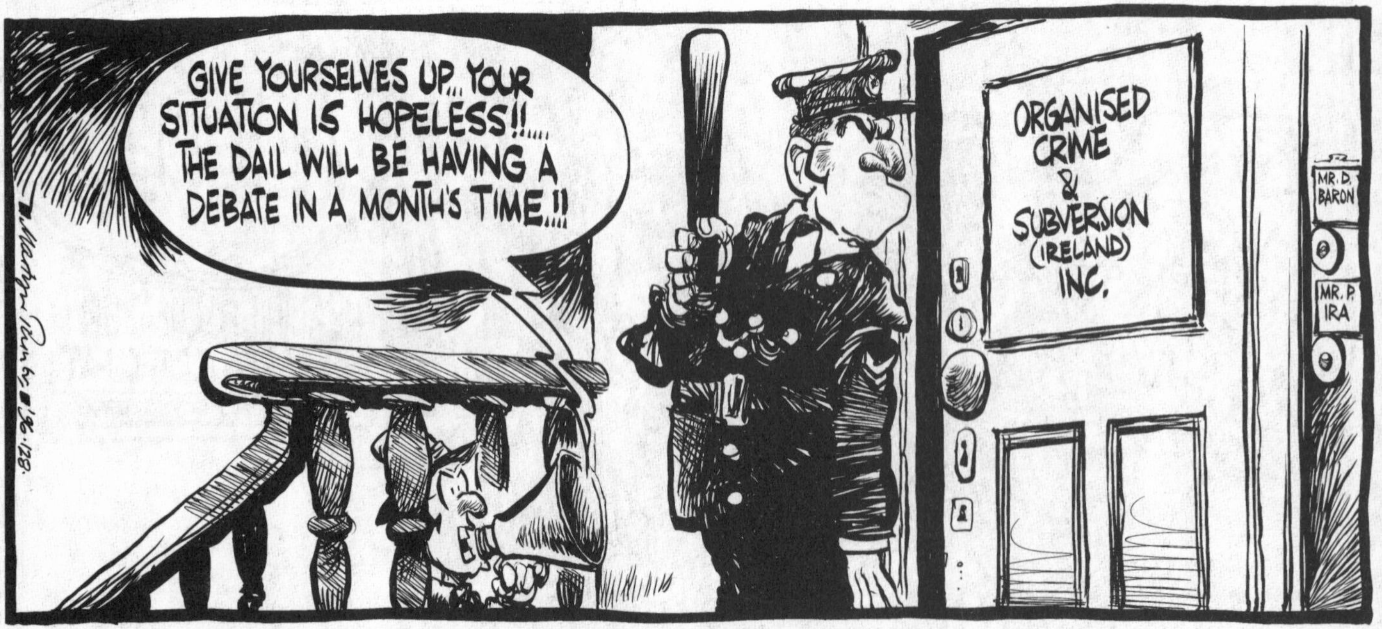
GIVE YOURSELVES UP... YOUR SITUATION IS HOPELESS!!..... THE DAIL WILL BE HAVING A DEBATE IN A MONTH'S TIME.!!
ORGANISED CRIME & SUBVERSION (IRELAND) INC.
MR. D. BARON
MR. P. IRA

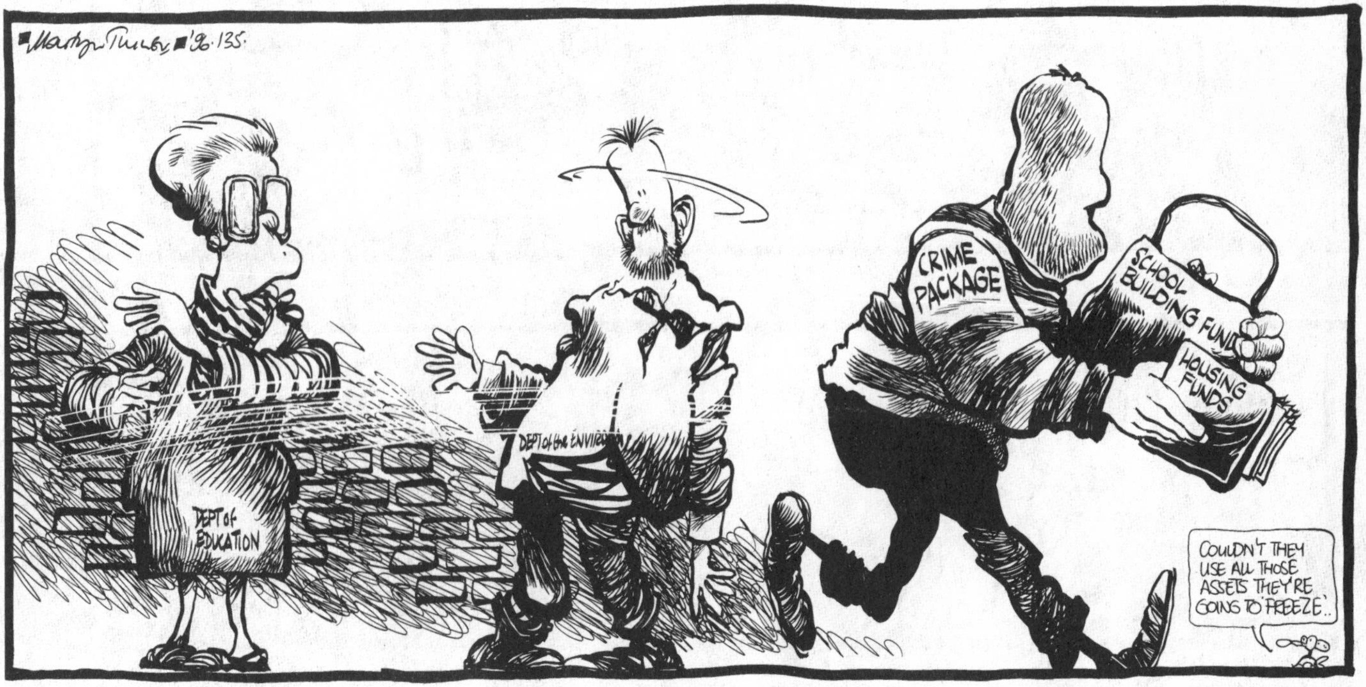
Martyn Turner '96·135·
CRIME PACKAGE
SCHOOL BUILDING FUND
HOUSING FUNDS
DEPT of the ENVIRO
DEPT of EDUCATION
COULDN'T THEY USE ALL THOSE ASSETS THEY'RE GOING TO 'FREEZE'..

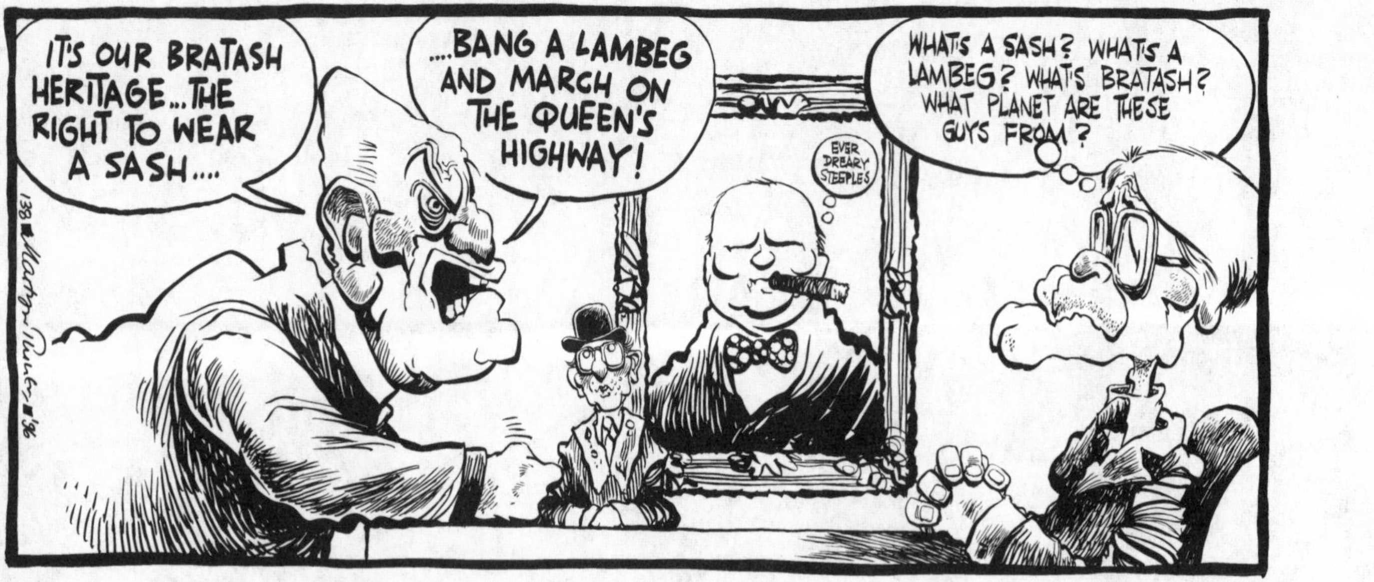
IT'S OUR BRATASH HERITAGE...THE RIGHT TO WEAR A SASH....
....BANG A LAMBEG AND MARCH ON THE QUEEN'S HIGHWAY!
EVER DREARY STEEPLES
WHAT'S A SASH? WHAT'S A LAMBEG? WHAT'S BRATASH? WHAT PLANET ARE THESE GUYS FROM?

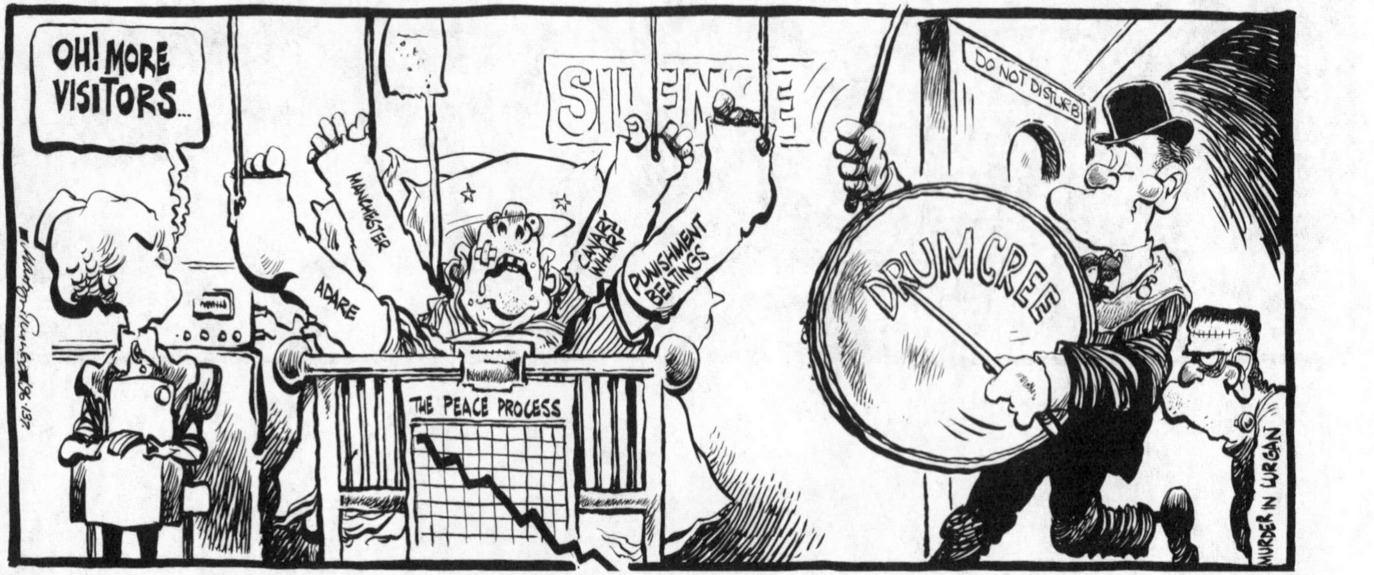
OH! MORE VISITORS...
DO NOT DISTURB
MANCHESTER
ADARE
CANARY WHARF
PUNISHMENT BEATINGS
THE PEACE PROCESS
DRUMCREE
MURDER IN LURGAN

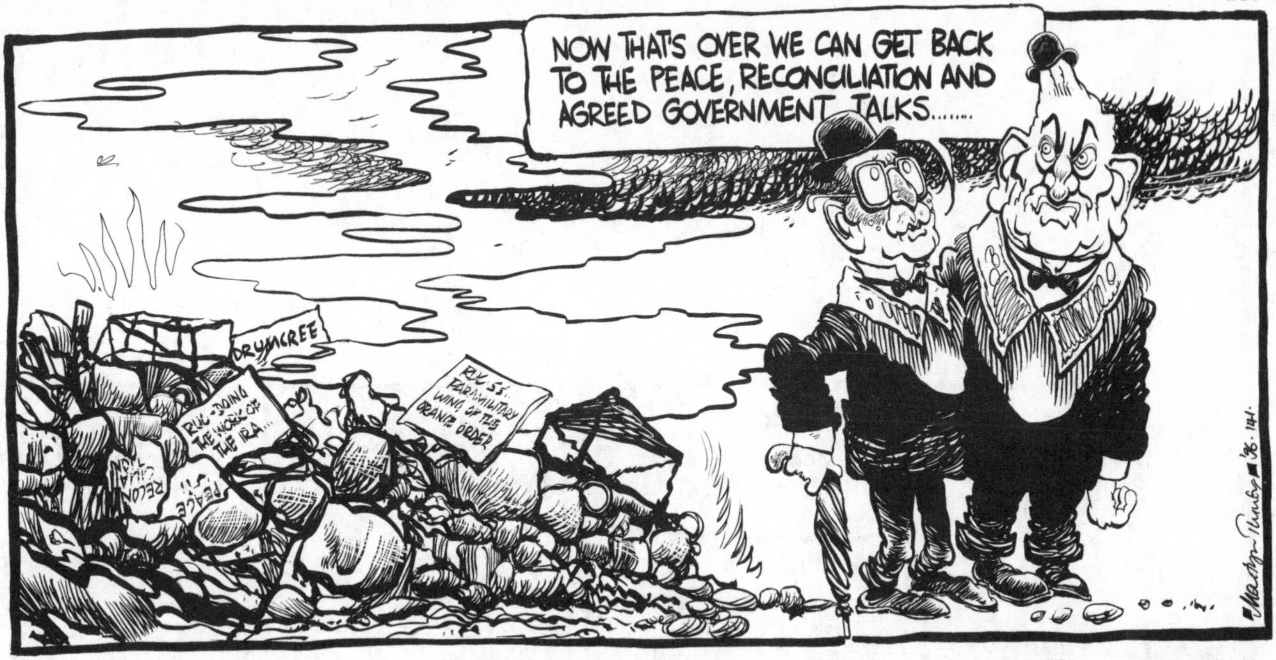
NOW THAT'S OVER WE CAN GET BACK TO THE PEACE, RECONCILIATION AND AGREED GOVERNMENT TALKS.......
DRUMCREE
RUC - DOING THE WORK OF THE IRA...
RUC SS. PARAMILITARY WING OF THE ORANGE ORDER
RECON CILIATION
PEACE

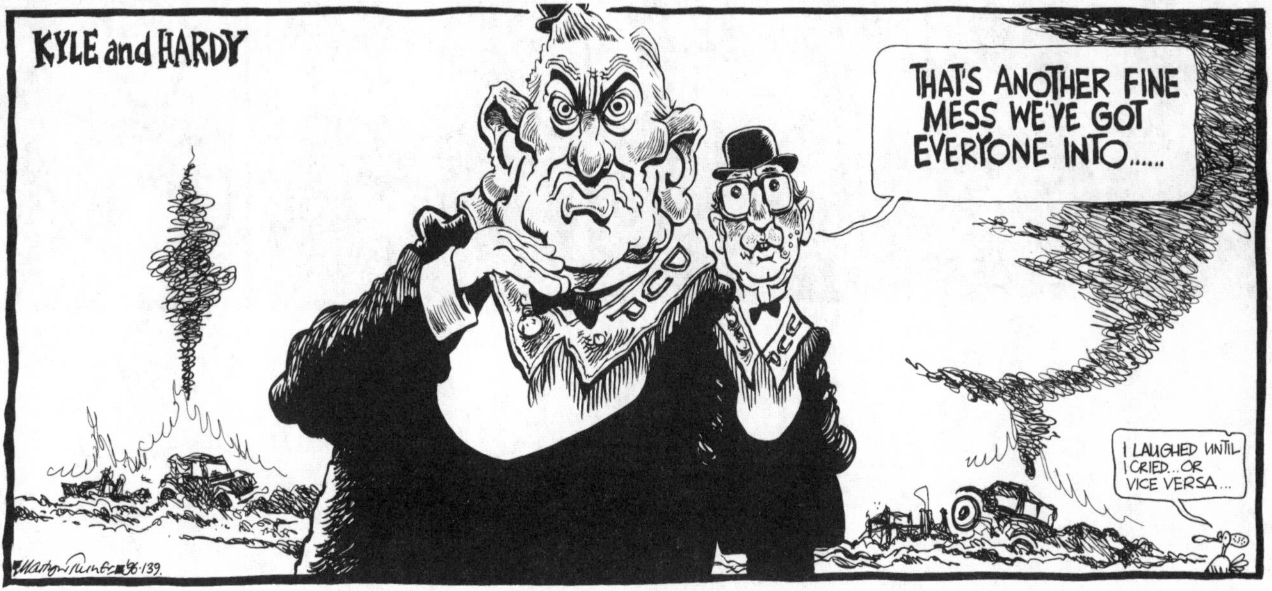
KYLE and HARDY
THAT'S ANOTHER FINE MESS WE'VE GOT EVERYONE INTO......
I LAUGHED UNTIL I CRIED...OR VICE VERSA...

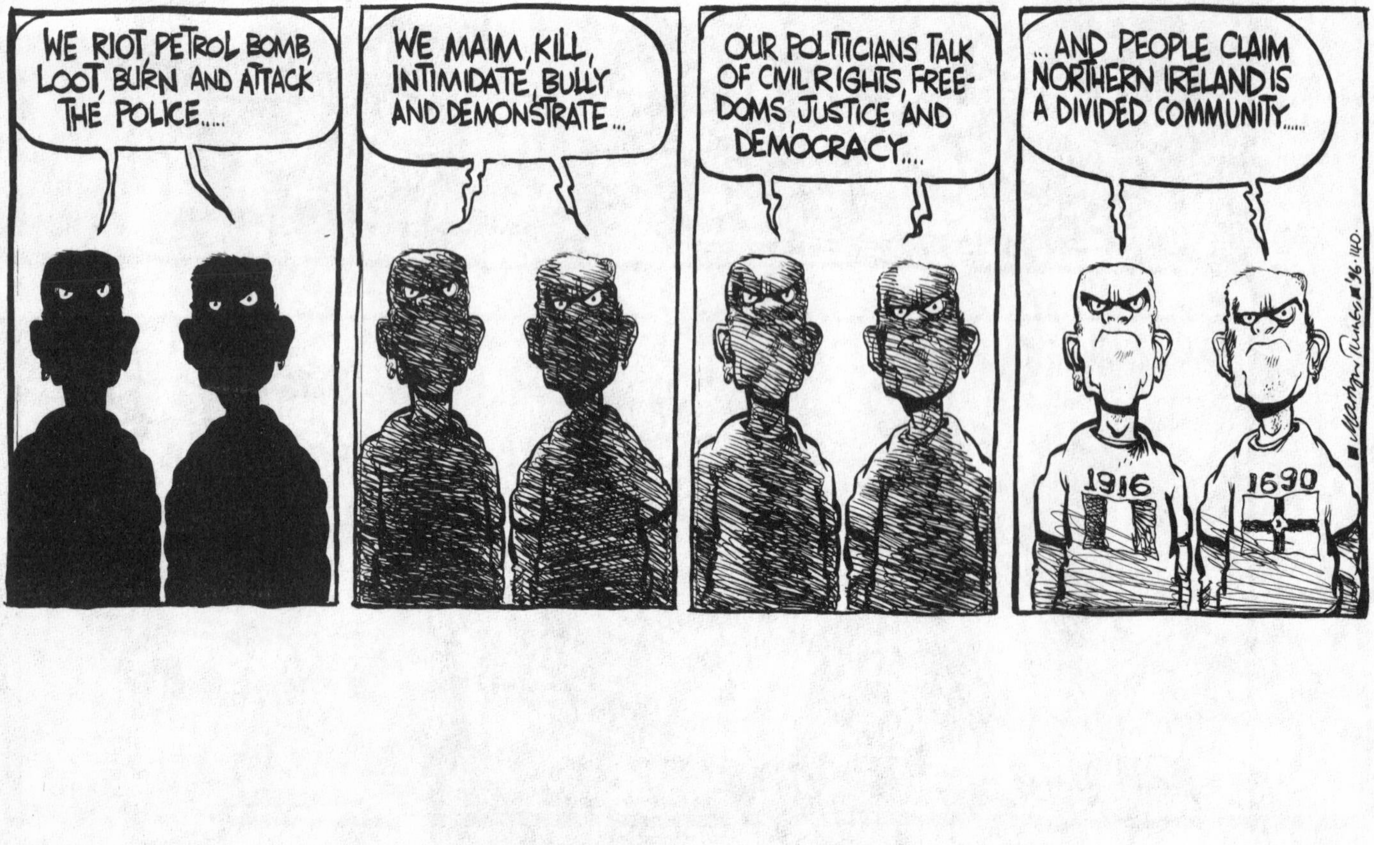
WE RIOT, PETROL BOMB, LOOT, BURN AND ATTACK THE POLICE.....
WE MAIM, KILL, INTIMIDATE, BULLY AND DEMONSTRATE...
OUR POLITICIANS TALK OF CIVIL RIGHTS, FREE-DOMS, JUSTICE AND DEMOCRACY....
...AND PEOPLE CLAIM NORTHERN IRELAND IS A DIVIDED COMMUNITY.....
1916
1690

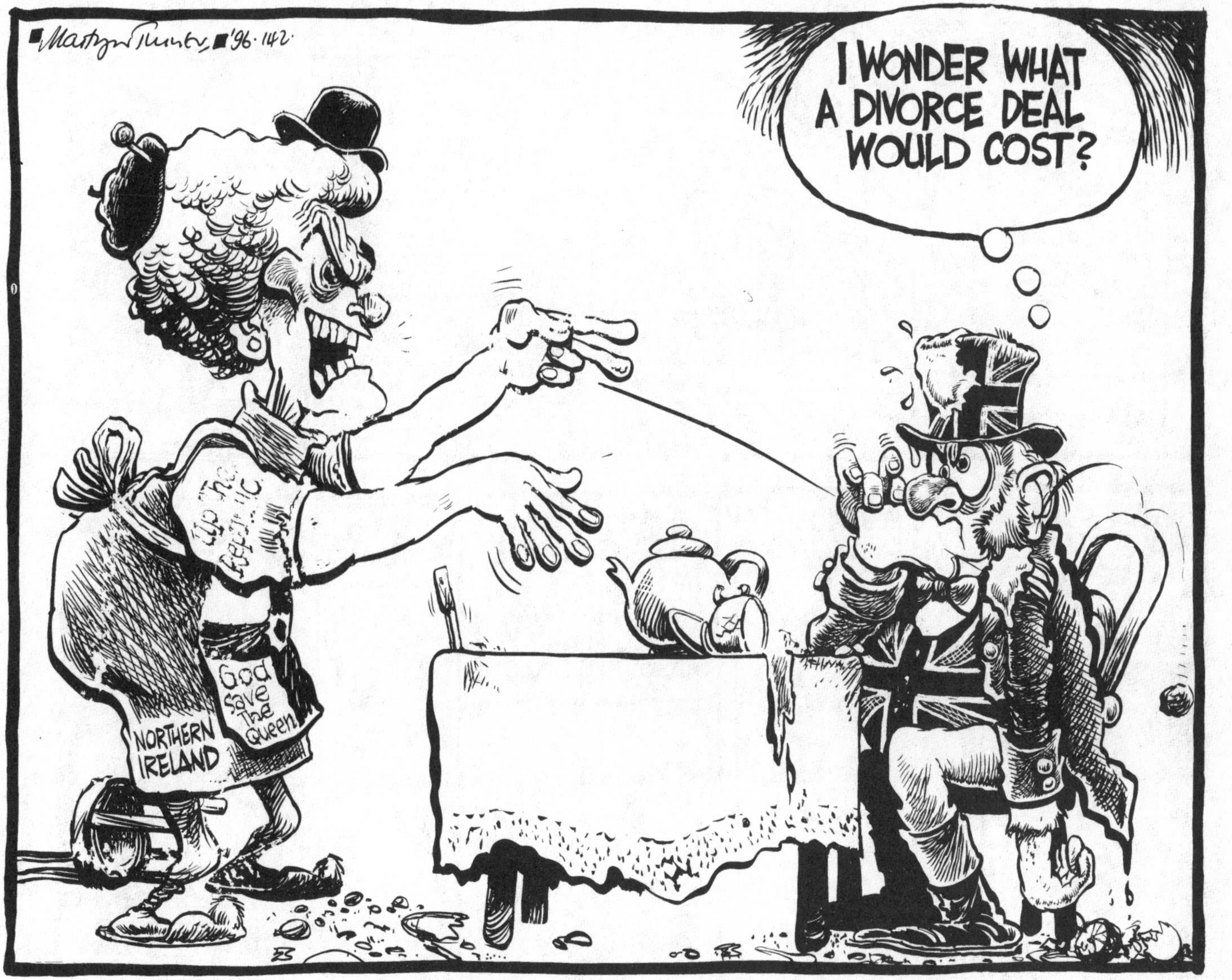
Martyn Turner '96·142
I WONDER WHAT A DIVORCE DEAL WOULD COST?
Up The Republic
God Save The Queen
NORTHERN IRELAND

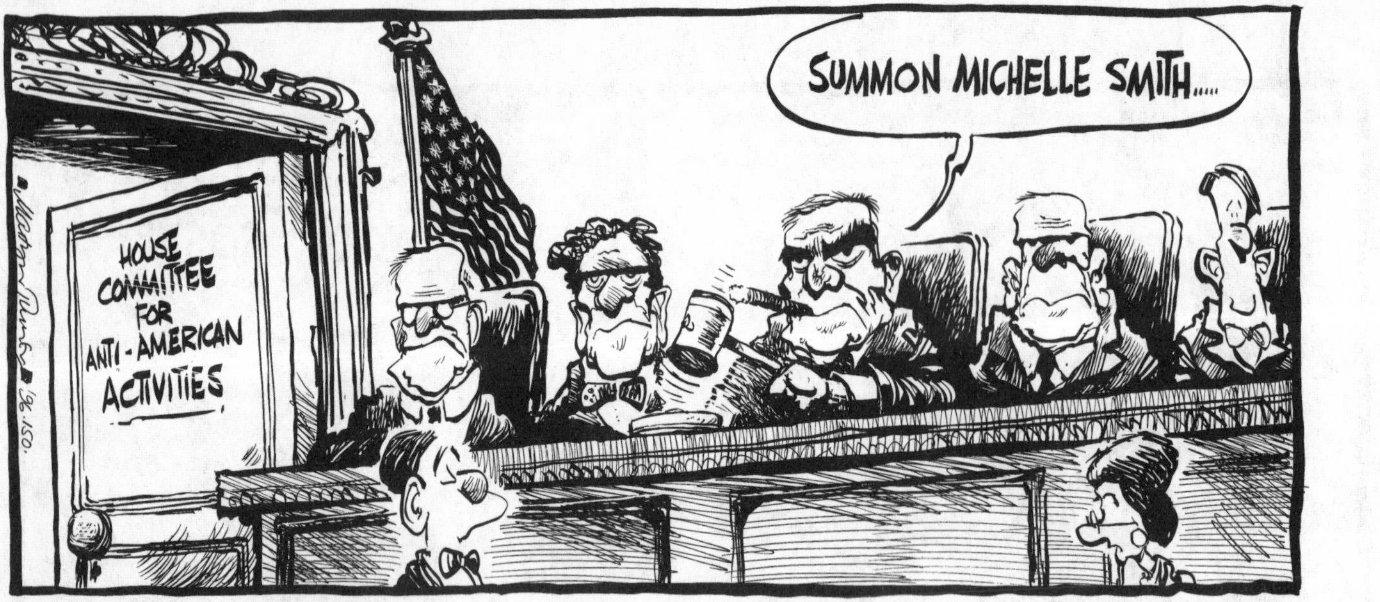
SUMMON MICHELLE SMITH.....
HOUSE COMMITTEE FOR ANTI-AMERICAN ACTIVITIES

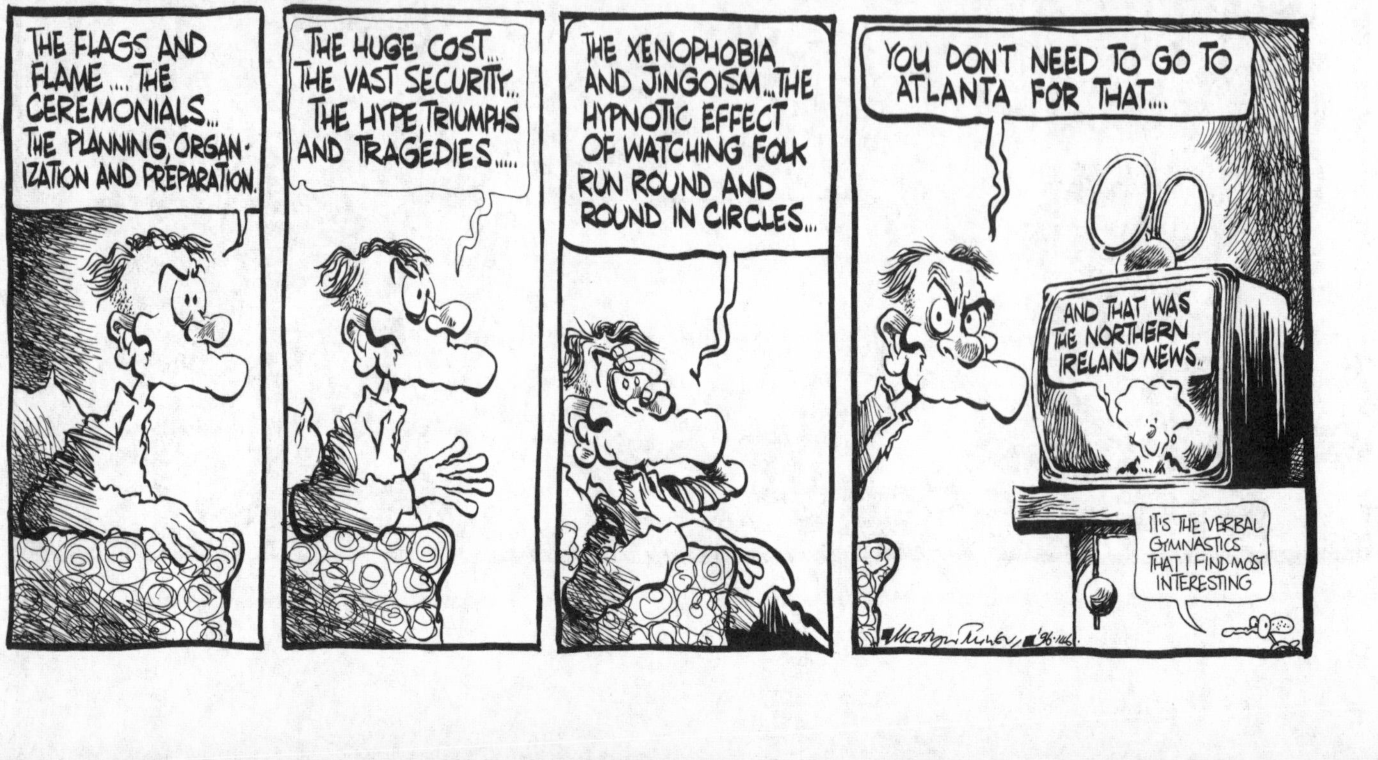
THE FLAGS AND FLAME .... THE CEREMONIALS... THE PLANNING, ORGANIZATION AND PREPARATION.
THE HUGE COST... THE VAST SECURITY... THE HYPE, TRIUMPHS AND TRAGEDIES.....
THE XENOPHOBIA AND JINGOISM...THE HYPNOTIC EFFECT OF WATCHING FOLK RUN ROUND AND ROUND IN CIRCLES...
YOU DON'T NEED TO GO TO ATLANTA FOR THAT....
AND THAT WAS THE NORTHERN IRELAND NEWS..
IT'S THE VERBAL GYMNASTICS THAT I FIND MOST INTERESTING

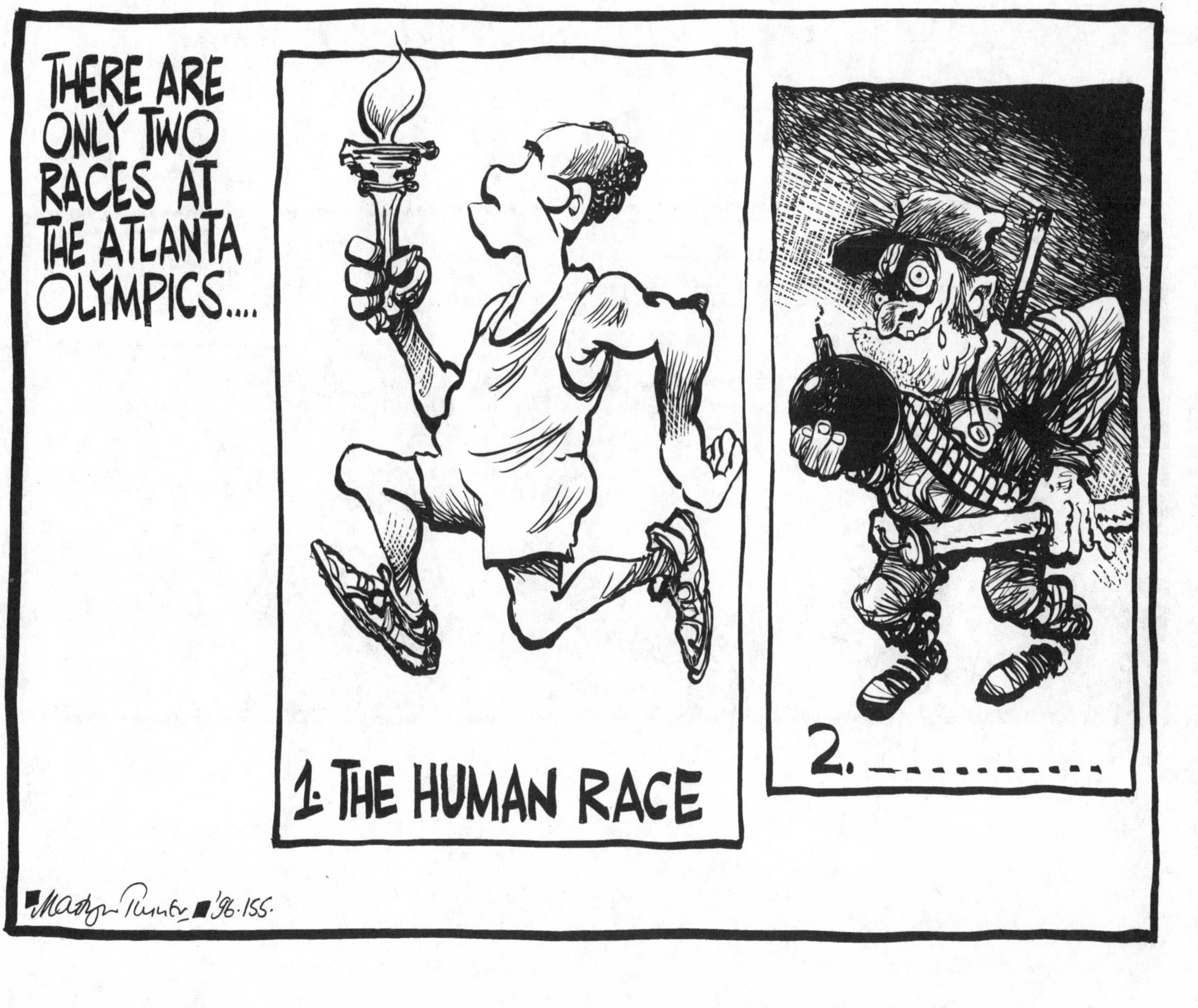
THERE ARE ONLY TWO RACES AT THE ATLANTA OLYMPICS....
1. THE HUMAN RACE
2. ....
Martyn Turner '96.155.

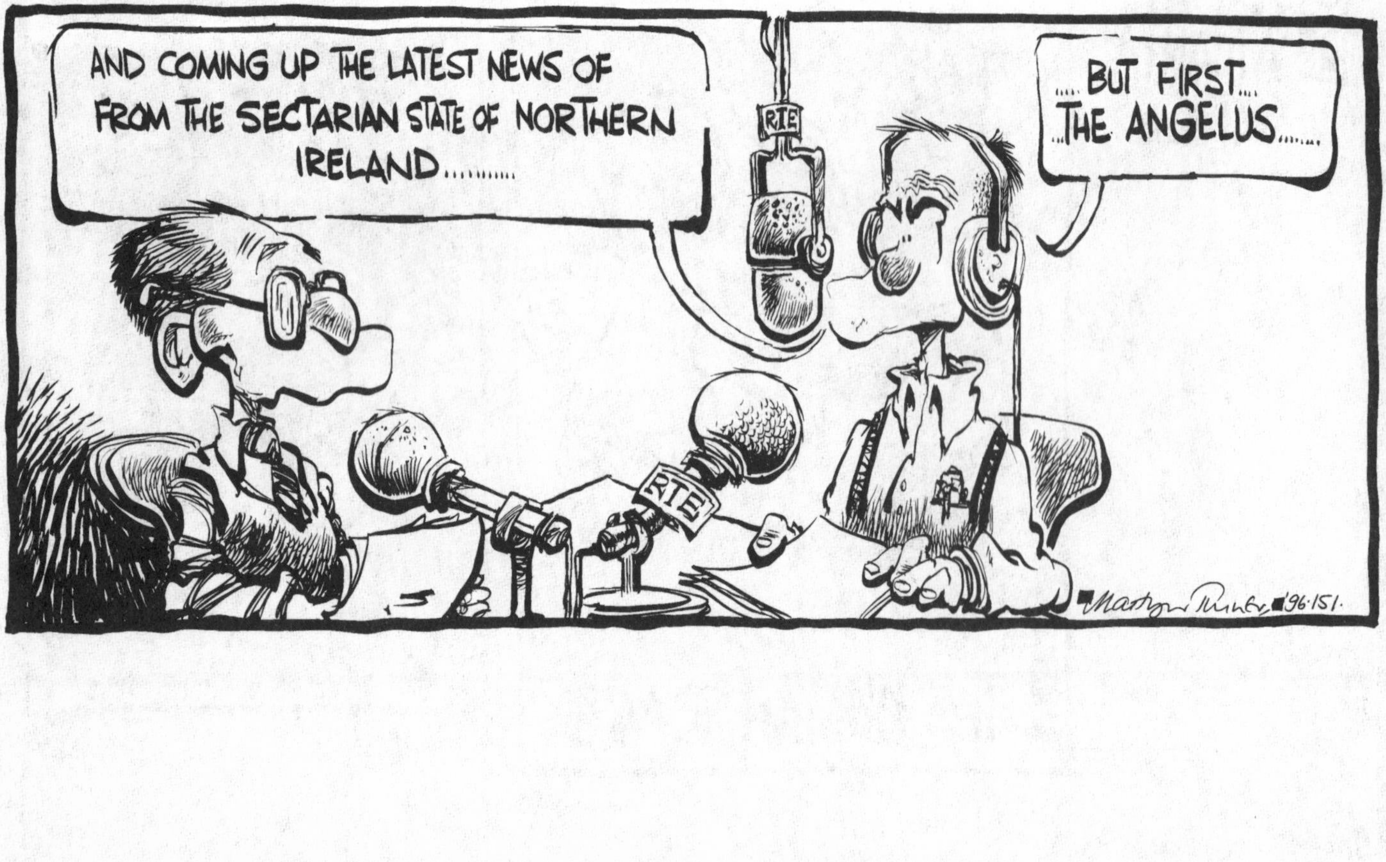
AND COMING UP THE LATEST NEWS OF FROM THE SECTARIAN STATE OF NORTHERN IRELAND..........
....BUT FIRST.... ..THE ANGELUS.......
RTE
RTE

MONA
LISA

BORD
na
MONA
LISA

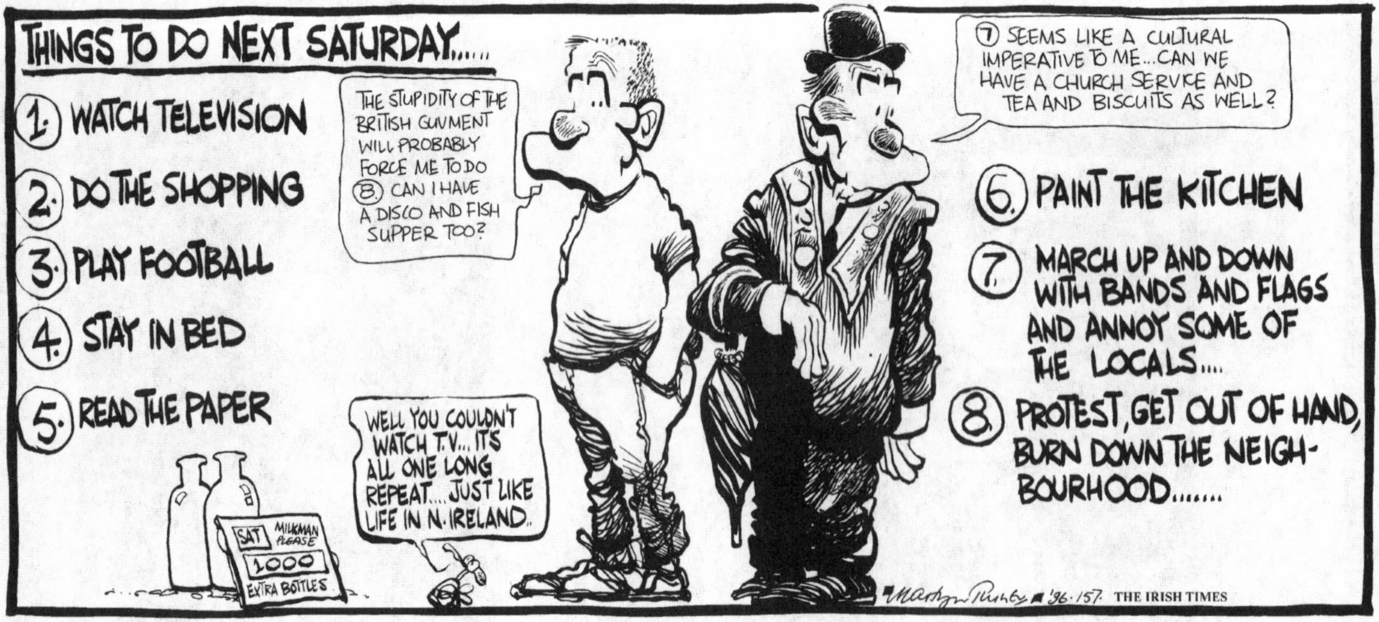
THINGS TO DO NEXT SATURDAY......
1. WATCH TELEVISION
2. DO THE SHOPPING
3. PLAY FOOTBALL
4. STAY IN BED
5. READ THE PAPER
THE STUPIDITY OF THE BRITISH GUVMENT WILL PROBABLY FORCE ME TO DO 8. CAN I HAVE A DISCO AND FISH SUPPER TOO?
7 SEEMS LIKE A CULTURAL IMPERATIVE TO ME...CAN WE HAVE A CHURCH SERVICE AND TEA AND BISCUITS AS WELL?
6. PAINT THE KITCHEN
7. MARCH UP AND DOWN WITH BANDS AND FLAGS AND ANNOY SOME OF THE LOCALS....
8. PROTEST, GET OUT OF HAND, BURN DOWN THE NEIGH-BOURHOOD.......
WELL YOU COULDN'T WATCH T.V... IT'S ALL ONE LONG REPEAT.... JUST LIKE LIFE IN N. IRELAND.
SAT MILKMAN PLEASE 1000 EXTRA BOTTLES
'96 · 157 · THE IRISH TIMES

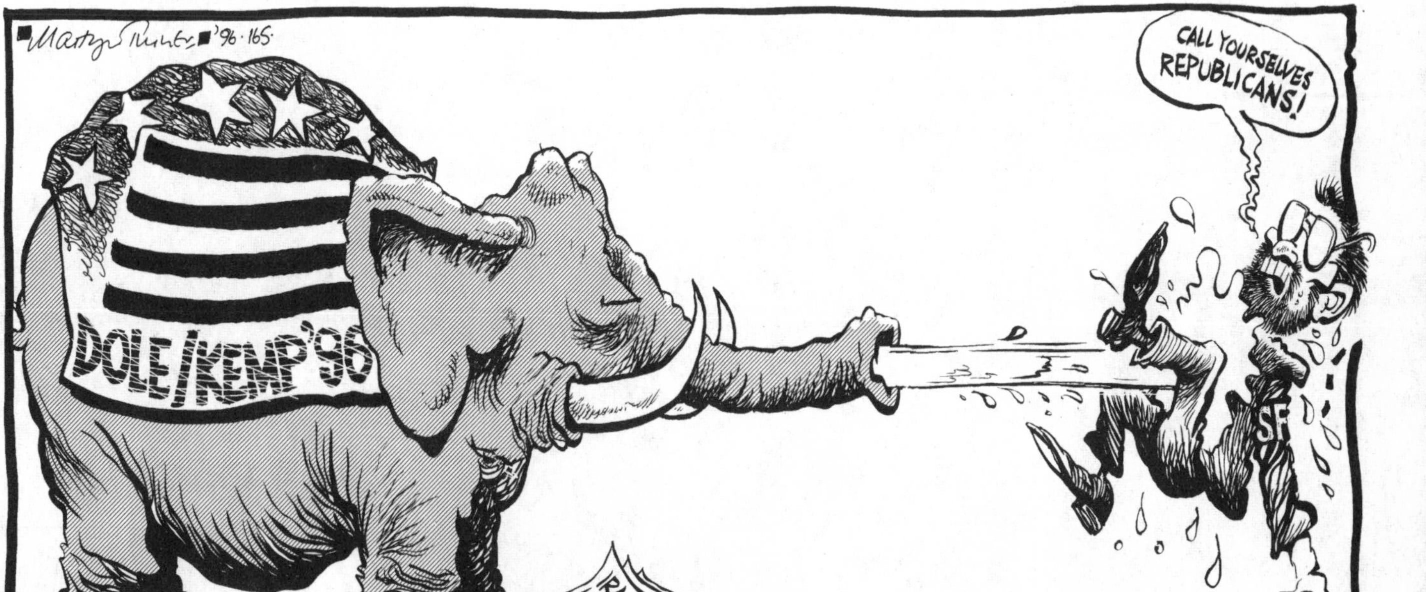
CALL YOURSELVES REPUBLICANS!
DOLE/KEMP '96
SF
IRA IN THE WHITE HOUSE
NEED TO BE STRONG ON TERRORISM

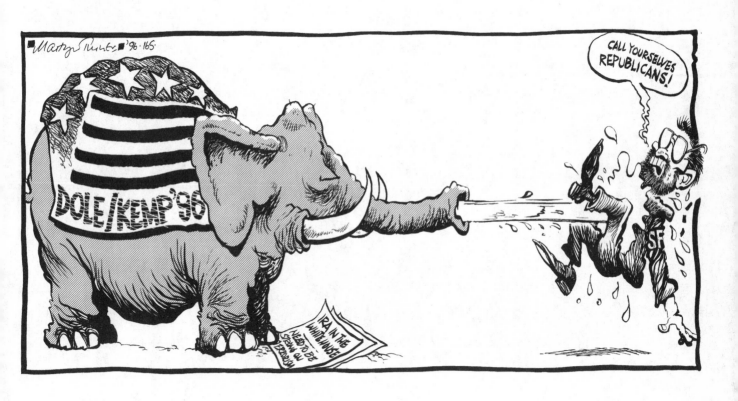